Christopher Berry-Dee

Talking
with
Psychopaths
and Savages

BEYOND EVIL

A deeper journey into the minds of
the most cold-blooded killers

JOHN BLAKE

Published by John Blake Publishing,
The Plaza,
535 Kings Road,
Chelsea Harbour,
London SW10 0SZ

www.johnblakebooks.com

www.facebook.com/johnblakebooks 🅕
twitter.com/jblakebooks 🅓

First published in paperback in 2019

Paperback ISBN: 978-1-78946-115-2
Ebook ISBN: 978-1-78946-116-9

British Library Cataloguing-in-Publication Data:

A catalogue record for this book is available from the British Library.

Design by www.envydesign.co.uk

Printed and bound in Great Britain by Clays Ltd, Elcograf S.p.A

3 5 7 9 10 8 6 4 2

John Blake Publishing is an imprint of Bonnier Books UK
www.bonnierbooks.co.uk

Talking
with
Psychopaths
and Savages
BEYOND EVIL

Born **Berry-Dee** is descended from Dr John Dee, ⟨...⟩ to Queen Elizabeth I, and is the founder and former Director of the Criminology Research Institute (CRI), and former publisher and Editor-in-Chief of *The Criminologist*, a highly respected journal on matters concerning all aspects of criminology from law enforcement to forensic psychology.

Christopher has interviewed and interrogated over thirty of the world's most notorious killers – serial, mass and one-off – including Peter Sutcliffe, Ted Bundy, Aileen Wuornos, Dennis Nilsen and Joanne Dennehy. He was co-producer/interviewer for the acclaimed 12-part TV documentary series *The Serial Killers*, and has appeared on television as a consultant on serial homicide, and, in the series *Born to Kill?*, on the cases of Fred and Rose West, the 'Moors Murderers' and Dr Harold Shipman. He has also assisted in criminal investigations as far afield as Russia and the United States.

Notable book successes include: *Monster* (basis for the movie of the same title, about Aileen Wuornos); *Dad Help Me Please*, about the tragic Derek Bentley, hanged for a murder he did not commit (subsequently subject of the film *Let Him Have It*) – and *Talking With Serial Killers I*, Christopher's international bestseller, now, with its sequel, *Talking With Serial Killers: World's Most Evil*, required reading at the FBI Behavioral Science Unit Academy at Quantico, Virginia. His *Talking With Psychopaths and Savages: A Journey Into the Evil Mind*, the forerunner to this volume, was the UK's bestselling true-crime title of 2017.

For
Toby Buchan

Contents

Acknowledgements

Very fortunately, the acknowledgements are the one part of any writer's book which the publisher's editor/s cannot tinker with. Nevertheless, to curry some favour with my editor-in-chief, Toby Buchan, this book is dedicated to him. Oh, my, what a super chap Toby is, so thank you, sir, for all of the hard work and dedication and support you have given me over so many books published over so many years. You have the patience of a saint.

Also to my publishers and the entire team at John Blake/ Bonnier. We go back to 2003 when the indefatigable John Blake first commissioned me to write *Talking with Serial Killers*. This was the first ever true-crime book where the author was permitted to include vast amounts of the killers' own words and it was based on many of the unique filmed then televised face-to-face interviews I had conducted with homicidal maniacs over previous years. A controversial move this was. I had pitched the idea both to Virgin and John Blake at the same time. Virgin – who had published me before – rejected it instantly telling me that the content might upset their elderly readers. Then

John snapped it up. The following afternoon Virgin came back to me with a change of heart. Oops! The book was effectively sold. I have been with John Blake ever since.

Here, I mention my mentor, true-crime historian and author, Robin Odell, who co-wrote several books with me as I started to learn penmanship. Graciously, he gave me lead author credit every time and I owe 'Bob' a great deal of gratitude. Then along the same lines, I thank my former TV documentary producer, Frazer Ashford, who made the twelve-part TV series *The Serial Killers*. This series was once again a first in TV broadcasting. I could easily write a book about the exciting adventures, trials and tribulations we suffered went through (author's subtle deletion there), but still we remain the closest buddies to this day.

To end the professional acknowledgements, let me thank the media – both press and television, including current affairs – for not only have you guys helped promote my books, you have invited me to appear on more international TV documentaries and contribute to even more articles than I can count. But, it's not just the promotional value I am referring to, for there have been many occasions when they have supported me when trying to help solve cold-case homicides or work on other issues of equal importance. I cannot list the names but you all know who you are. Thank you.

Turning to law enforcement. I have to say that US police are very forthcoming, and I include the FBI, US Marshals Service, Florida Department of Law Enforcement (FDLE) and numerous state, county and city agencies. They are a delight to work with. The same applies to the Russian police, and agencies in the Far East, but only with a few exceptions can I say for the same for our somewhat closed-minded UK law enforcement. Yes, they will work with one if there is something in it for them, and in those instances it has all proved beneficial on both sides, but they still fail to realise that the work some of us writers do can prove to be an invaluable tool in their investigative box.

For personal acknowledgements I refer to my Filipina partner, Maui. Researching and writing true crime can lead one into a dark world and she has brought real light into my life. God bless her. As you will note as you read this book, I love the Philippine people and their country. I also have a great fondness for Russia, come to that. It seems to me that us westerners have become far to materialistic these days so visiting the Philippines brings me back down to earth with a jolt. They are a happy people, ever-smiling despite the hardships the very poor suffer. Maui and I always try to help where we can and if it means rebuilding a couple of squatters' homes destroyed in a blaze, providing power, light and an electric fan to cool them down in the blistering summer heat, food, and making sure the kids have new school uniforms and stuff for their lessons – as was the case in the two recent fires in Lapu Lapu – then that's my small way of saying 'thank you'. So, you see, some of the royalties I earn from the books you read do go to a good cause.

Claire and my son Jack are always in the forefront of my mind. I also thank all of my Facebook pals: Clive, Jon; my co-author on a different subject, BitCoin Pete; Gary Roberts. Boris, Steve, Karl, Jay. The mega-fab Hollie. Wayne and his wife, Sherri;. Jennie aka 'The Admiral's Car Crash Magnet'. Paul 'Dinger' Bell. My sister Lizzie and husband, Jim, Laura-Dee and my nephews; also the amazing former 'Miss World'

Ann Sidney. Victoria Redstall, Yang Lu, Denis Claivaz, Linda Newcombe, Immy Jj and hubby Steve. Wilf, Robert Pothecary, Christopher Grist Marlow and Riki Read. Last but not least, my dear friend, Martin 'The MasterChef', Reverend Chris Richardson and Fr. John Maunder.

Hospitality and Travel and – *No!* I am not getting sponsored here – Cathay Pacific or Oman Airlines or Philippine Airlines come highly recommended. Oman International Airport is incredible as a stopover en route to Ninoy Aquino Airport, Manila.

If you visit 'Phil', I'd suggest that you get a very cheap taxi to the Oxford Suites Hotel in Burgos Street, Makati. Brilliant place and a very reasonable price for the super staff service they give. In Cebu City, opt for the Park Lane International. Again first-rate, cheap, and the finest buffet you'll ever find on Planet Earth. Then, one must visit Palawan and El Nido. The first-class Casa Kalwa resort with its sugar sand beaches and swaying coconut pals is minutes away from the airport, which is serviced by Swift Air – another first-rate airline. Although a tad pricey, the staff at Casa Kalwa will make your dream holiday come true.

Travelogue and Acknowledgements now done and dusted, it leaves me to thank every one of you for buying this book, but now is the time to get some red blood painted all over the walls and take a trip into murder most foul.

Happy days.
Christopher
CHRISTOPHER BERRY–DEE

Preface

The Gates of Hell are terrible to behold, are they not?
E. A. BUCCHIANERI, AUTHOR OF *FAUST: MY SOUL*
BE DAMNED FOR THE WORLD

I'm not fucking stupid. I'm not fucking stupid,
you know. The police say that what I did was criminal.
The doctors say the components of my mind are unsafe
... so, give me back my real brain, hand over
my intelligence, because all of you are taking away my
faith in anything.
PETER SUTCLIFFE, AKA, 'THE YORKSHIRE RIPPER', TO THE
AUTHOR AT INTERVIEW IN BROADMOOR HOSPITAL

Hello dear reader. I hope that I find you all-singing-and-
dancing physically fit, full of grace and mentally competent
– the latter, however, you may well not be when you reach the
last page because this book comes with a 'Health Warning'.

Do not read further if you have a weak constitution or about to eat your dinner. But, please ask yourself, what would it be like to be without morality, lacking a soul, to never feel compassion; have zero pity, or harbour any emotions at all towards your fellow man?

What must it feel like to be a homicidal sado-sexual psychopath; to become trapped in an ever escalating uncontrollable downward spiral of violence, to be psychopathologically compelled to inflict untold pain, torture and immeasurable suffering on the innocent: babies; young kids; the elderly, the weak, the vulnerable – the easiest of prey – for, unlike the majority of us, where there should be a conscience, inside the heads of the sado-sexual-serial-killing-for-kicks-murderers there is nothing but a void, a sinister black hole.

Serial murderers are the polar opposite to the virtuous and the honourable, for they are cowardly, weak-willed, ruinous, maleficent, lacking any moral compass, sexually discontent, subconsciously full of a twisted desire for revenge for the self-perceived injustices and sorrows that society as a whole has, they feel, heaped upon them. Worse, many of these mentally distorted monsters are possessed of predetermined schemes and black plans to kill again and again.

In my view, they are way beyond evil, yet they fascinate so many of us at the same time.

Close to hand is my well-read copy of *When I Was at Scotland Yard* by Chief Inspector James Berrett, CID, New Scotland Yard, published in 1932. DCI Berrett starts his Preface with:

'Crime is a matter of universal interest. It always has been and it always will be. In itself, it represents to the millions of conventional people the unconventional, which they despise but still fascinates them. They like to read about it and hear about it.'

That was penned by a distinguished, highly decorated, long-serving police officer and what he says still holds good today. Moreover, James Berrett ends his Preface with, 'Now let me try to entertain you,' so with tongue in cheek let me try to sort-of entertain you – with an admission to make first of all, because hopefully it will give you this book's *raison d'être*.

There are countless tens-of-thousands of books, magazine and professional journal papers, newspaper articles, compendiums, *Wikipedia* and other websites, TV documentaries and movies concerning serial killers and their crimes. In fact, the world is awash with this stuff, and, quite often, at least twenty or thirty publications of any sort or mix cover the same criminal and his crimes and this is no bad thing either. With serial killers being relatively few and far between, it therefore comes with the territory that we true-crime writers are often accused of rehashing old stuff just for the sake of it. Everyone is entitled to his or her opinions, of course we are, and we writers must respect the thoughts of our critics, but please make this criticism peer-to-peer and not an hysterical rant from the totally uneducated in my subject, most especially those who have never met a serial killer in their lifetime, let alone written some thirty-seven books on the subject as I have most exhaustively done over decades.

Nevertheless, the plus side of this repetition gives us writers oft-times different slants on a given case, which, all combined, allow us a greater store of criminological knowledge, and to study even more, especially when fresh material unexpectedly comes to light.

For instance, in this book, I cover, amongst other serial killers, Peter Kürten, and, by gosh his has to be amongst the case histories most widely and comprehensively written about. Well, before you reach for your pen and fire off a letter headed 'A rehash', let me say that this book is not about 'rehashing' stuff, it is all about getting inside these killers' heads – and they are not nice places to be.

To even try to understand; even begin to attempt to study, communicate, interview or interrogate homicidal psychopaths, you have to think like them so that they can identify with you. It is of little use sitting at the edge of the abyss and peering over – one has to take the plunge to become one with their warped mindset – then they identify with you, and you 'get it' with them – but it is no bed of roses, for theirs is a sickening, stinking, infernal underworld, the dread place of the dead.

When you are interviewing these vicious criminals, they will often study you through unblinking eyes. They sniff the air, your smell, fear and weaknesses. Sometimes I have felt their evil tentacles of thought squirming their way into my head. It's as if they are, lizard-like, tasting you, and if you upset them, more often than not their hatred for all that you stand for comes radiating towards you as hot as a kitchen stove.

If you get it wrong, if you push the wrong buttons, these killers can lose the plot. They could rip your head off. When dealing up close and very personal with these highly unpredictable people your own death could be only a heartbeat away.

Often has been the case when I am alone in a small locked room with these unshackled killers; if they'd erupted

I could have been killed before the guards could even have unlocked the door to get me out. And for them there is some kudos to gain from 'taking you out' – well, it won't affect their prison sentence or death-row status at all, will it? Therefore, it really boils down to the instinctive matter of 'psychological checks and balances'. While they are weighing you up and down, you are measuring them too, and, as each killer is so psychopathologically different, the gameplay/mutual interactions are equally diverse every time.

Many of the killers I have interviewed boast, gloat, smirk, giggle and laugh as they go into minute detail about their crimes. They revel in their notoriety. Bathe in it. Other serial murderers glare, snarl and give one the eyeball as if to say, 'Don't you fuck about with me.' This is close-up and personal time with the psychopath trying to exert control; intimidate, threaten and bully.

None of this has ever fazed me because, you see, deep down they are weak, pathetic, little people and cowards at heart. The trick is to just look back with a blank expression and say, 'So what?' while thinking What an asshole. After a short while they get it. Period! They realise that all they say and do during the interview doesn't impress one jot. They imagine they have control – while the fact remains that *you* do. They are staying behind bars while you can breeze out any time you wish. They are eating crap prison food while you are off to a restaurant for a fine meal and cold beer. Their next holiday will be yard time for an hour while you are off to sugar-sand beaches, clear azure seas and swaying palms (the Philippines, of course!).

This is what this book is all about. I am going to try and

take you right into the heads of several of these psycho-sick individuals and see what make them tick; to attempt to show you how they became what they are. And, if you were one of them how would your brain work – what homicidal thoughts would turn you on, and what would switch you off when the deadly deeds are done? – so be prepared to be shocked with a few smiles along the way

> I'm sorry I did not write for a month. I have been very busy and there is a lot of football on TV… Stress? Fuckin' shite! The stress is in my head, so I know where FUCKING STRESS is. The fuckin' gnawing in there. The doctor says there's nothing fuckin' wrong with my head. FUCKIN' QUACK C★★T!
>
> THE UNSHACKLED, ONE-LEGGED KILLER
> AND KIDNAPPER MICHAEL SAMS, ABOUT TO
> LOSE HIS TEMPER DURING AN INTERVIEW WITH
> THE AUTHOR AT HMP FULL SUTTON

This book takes the reader along 'Murder Road' – to those dark, desolate crossroads, often in the dead of night, to the blood-drenched crime scenes. It's all about getting to know the personalities of the innocent, now dead in shallow graves with the sides caving in. It is about the humanoid beasts that moved on to be arrested, tried in a court of law, convicted, some later to be fried in 'Ole Sparky' or strapped to a gurney and given the 'Goodnight Juice', or even dropped through a trap with a hangman's halter around their necks.

Having interviewed over thirty of these twisted murderers, whose homicidal craft and skills involve: strangulation; suffocating; knifing; bludgeoning to death; setting their prey on fire alive; shooting; injecting with caustic agents and just about every other tortuous means of extinguishing life known to deviant man, I attempt to go further than ever before in this book by inviting you to the Gates of Hell - a far cry from Heaven's door. Therefore, the book is not for the squeamish. It will not make for a comfortable bedtime read because it is solely intended to put you inside the heads of those killers who thrive on pure evil.

I make no excuses for my language, and as my loyal readers already know, I'm not one for dishing out large helpings of 'professional' psychobabble – the stuff used by many of the shrinks who have spent years pontificating about what makes these killers tick when the nearest they have got to interviewing such a criminal is teaching criminology at some university wearing a tweed jacket, cavalry twill trousers and down-at-heel brogues.

I say it as it is. I speak for the victims who have suffered at the hands of these monsters with two faces. I speak for the next-of-kin who have lost loved ones. I speak for the cops who have to clear up the goddamn awful mess these serial killers leave behind . . . the pathetic brutalised bodies dumped like so much trash.

Of course if you disagree with my way of thinking then you'll be a person who is willing to forgive a sex monster who has snatched your wife, your partner or child from the streets, used them, abused them and then killed them without a care in the world when they dump the corpse in some ditch someplace out there in the cold to rot. No doubt you'll get over the grief one day, perhaps even pray for the beast's soul, but then you will be one of a rare breed because most of us would want that person put in a pine box as soon as possible.

So, here we are and now I am going to gently lead you to the edge of the abyss and throw you in so that you can say 'Hi' to the serial killers – first, however, to the tropical Philippines.

Introduction

To escape and sit quietly on the beach –
that's my idea of paradise.
EMILIA WICKSTEAD,
NEW ZEALAND FASHION DESIGNER

Every design, every book, every painting, every poem and almost everything we do in life starts with a blank page. This book is no exception, so right now I am sitting – very large ice-cold gin and tonic and a fat cigar at hand – in a lounger on the sun-kissed veranda of my favourite Philippine resort.

The sugar sand is so hot, even under the shady coconut palms it will melt one's feet. This is paradise and a far cry from bustling Manila; yet even here there are gun-toting cops all over the place. Seventy-plus tourist-friendly armed officers patrolling the grounds 24/7/365 . . . there is a police boat lazily bobbing up and down a few hundred yards offshore in the calm Sulu Sea. A gentle surf sparkles like trillions of diamonds as the sun settles behind the numerous limestone islands and cliffs. There are coral reefs, secret lagoons and fish filled waters. Palawan is a paradise on earth.

Forget the laws on human rights. If I make it to the presidential palace, I will do just what I did as mayor. You drug pushers, hold-up men and do-nothings, you better go out. Because I will kill you. I'll dump all of you into Manila Bay, and fatten the fish there.

RODRIGO DUTERTE'S 2016 PRESIDENTIAL ELECTION
CAMPAIGN WARNING ADDRESS TO DRUG LORDS

Now president of the Philippines, Rodrigo 'Rody' Roa Duterte is as good as his word. Killers, drug-traffickers – such criminals get very short shrift indeed.

And foreign criminals in the Far East and in South East Asia need not think that because they are westerners they will somehow get away with it . . .

Fuck asking for a pardon. They won't hang me cos I'm British.

BRITISH SERIAL KILLER, JOHN MARTIN SCRIPPS AT
INTERVIEW WITH THE AUTHOR AT CHANGI PRISON,
SINGAPORE, JUST DAYS BEFORE HE WAS HANGED

John Martin Scripps, aka the 'Tourist from Hell', was born in the UK. I extensively covered his case in my book *Talking with Serial Killers*. A serial killer and drug dealer motivated by monetary gain, he was hanged, at the age of thirty-six, in Singapore, on Friday, 19 April 1996, between two Thai bandits. I witnessed his execution and his cremation at Sing Sing Drive. He refused to be weighed for the 'long drop' and this error on his part ensured that his head was almost ripped off when he plunged to his doom.

Of course, Scripps knew all too well that he could be hanged for not only the Singapore drug offences and the brutal dismemberment of South African businessman Gerald Lowe in Singapore's River View Hotel; or shot for the murder of mother and son, Sheila and Darin Damude, in Phuket, Thailand – yet this handsome young Brit sailed on regardless with a 'fuck you society' attitude written all over his smug face.

Well, he deserved all that he got if you ask me, because Scripps had killed several times in other countries before, and, as lead investigator Superintendent Gerald Lim told me: 'In Singapore there are warnings everywhere informing people that if they break our drug and murder laws we will execute you no matter what age, gender, breed, religion or creed you are.'

Effectively, Scripps hanged himself. The Singapore authorities merely provided the rope!

In the UK we adopt a more 'lenient' attitude to those who commit serial homicide. Modern facilities, all mod-cons, good diet, health care, TV, internet connection, free illegal drugs – because our prison system is awash with them – yet still the inmates bicker, moan and complain.

For example, Joanne Dennehy. The subject of my book *A Love of Blood*, over several days this monster stabbed three men to death in what can only be described as bloodbaths. Then, not satisfied with this orgy she went on to stab two other men – dog walkers, chosen at random – in broad daylight, for heaven's sake – with one guy suffering over forty wounds. He survived for a few years then died. So, where is Dennehy now?

Miss Dennehy is enjoying all of the luxuries the privately run HMP Bronzefield can afford her. Since her incarceration, she has made two escape attempts, tried to murder another female inmate, and planned to cut off the finger of a prison officer. She has spent months in solitary confinement, and for this she tried and failed to sue the government in the High Court for violating the European Human Rights Convention, at the taxpayer's expense; while at the time of writing (November 2018) she is seeking £7,000 in Legal Aid – again at your expense – so that she can marry her lesbian jailbird lover.

Well, you could not make this up if you tried! Hands up anyone who wants to donate to the cake and wedding dress.

Society makes laws we all have to abide by and we are obliged to live within those laws. If we do not, law and order break down.

If you fail to yield at a stop sign or a red light then expect to be fined. If you commit aggravated murder you can expect to be executed. If you fail to take heed then the punishment can be very severe. These are decisions the individual has to make, not me!

His Honour Thomas M. Stark, New York
State judge (1925–2014) to the author at
interview, September 1974

Christopher Berry-Dee
Southsea, Hampshire, UK; El Nido, Palawan, Philippines

1

What is a Serial Killer?

I believe the only way to reform people is to kill them.
CARL PANZRAM, AMERICAN SERIAL KILLER, RAPIST,
ARSONIST, ROBBER AND BURGLAR (1882–1930)

Time and again I read a book or some other form of literature where a serial killer is erroneously called a 'mass murderer' and vice versa, yet the differences between the two categories are as chalk and cheese.

Collins English Dictionary defines 'series' as: 'a group or connected succession of similar or related things, usually arranged in order', whereas 'mass', as far as homicide is concerned means killing en masse.

Although most of you will know what a serial killer is, it is worth remembering that such a person is defined as an offender who has committed three or more slayings with cooling-off periods lasting days, weeks, months or even years between the 'events'.

A mass murderer kills en masse at a single location, as in the case of Ronald 'Butch' DeFeo Jr. Aged twenty-three, armed with a Marlin rifle, he shot to death his entire family of six as they slept in their home at 112 Ocean Avenue, Amityville, Long Island, NY, during the night of 13/14 November 1974. There is no 'cooling-off period' when a mass killer commits his crimes, because it is one continuous act.

More recently, Dylann Storm Roof, the baby-faced white supremacist-cum-domestic-terrorist, at the age of twenty-one, armed himself with a Glock pistol and shot dead nine worshippers during a service at the Emanuel African Methodist Episcopal Church, Charleston, South Carolina, on Wednesday, 17 June 2015.

A spree/rampage killer is altogether a different kettle of fish. He, or she, would, as defined by the US Bureau of Justice Statistics, be an individual who kills two or more victims in a short time at several locations with almost no time break between the murders. Armed-to-the teeth Michael Robert Ryan fatally shot sixteen people and injured some fifteen more in and around the sleepy Berkshire town of Hungerford, before hiding in a school and then taking his own life on Wednesday, 19 August 1987. Ryan used a Beretta pistol, a type 56 semi-automatic rifle and an M1 carbine during his spree.

An example of two homicidal spree/rampage murderers working together would be John Allen Muhammad (forty-one) and Lee/John Boyd Malvo (seventeen). Over a three-week period in October 2012, they shot ten people at Baton Rouge – Louisiana, Maryland –Virginia, and Washington DC, primarily using a Bushmaster hunting rifle. These murders were dubbed 'The DC Beltway Sniper Shootings' by the media. Muhammad was executed by lethal injection, Tuesday, 10 November 2009, at the Greensville Correctional Center, Virginia.

Therefore, there are distinct differences between serial killers, mass murderers and spree/rampage killers, but they all have one thing in common: they take the lives of many people and, in every case, they strike without warning. In this respect I liken them to Exocet missiles. They come in under the radar and, without conscience, rain down death and destruction.

Mass-murderers and spree killers are mostly driven by a self-perceived political or religious or personal grudge as in hate crimes. Sexual serial killers, however, are motivated by an overwhelming need for sex and the dehumanising of their victims at whatever the cost, so, for the purposes of this book, we will not concern ourselves with the motivations behind mass murderers or spree killers for we are about to focus in on sado-sexual serial killers ,who are altogether an entirely different breed.

With serial murderers we find several sub-groups; however, we need only concern ourselves with two types: 'organised' and 'disorganised' offenders and we will find examples of both throughout the following pages.

An organised serial murderer will be one who plans his crimes – often methodically. He will first carefully select his preferred victim type, which could be based on the person's appearance – for example, a blonde-haired woman or a red-haired man – or age-group –a child, young man or an elderly person – or perhaps a prostitute, or a person walking on their own in the dark, a gay man, a gay woman, an adolescent boy or girl . . . There is usually a sexual motivation, for most serial killers get consciously or subconsciously 'turned on' when they see their victim type; then comes the stalking phase, from which the offender receives a 'thrill' and an ever-increasing sense of sexual satisfaction. Many leading psychologists and psychiatrists conclude that the offender often gets more of a 'kick' from this stalking and covert observational experience than the actual kill. This I entirely agree with.

The second aspect worth considering when examining the modi operandi (MO) of an organised serial killer is the development of what is commonly called a 'murder kit'. They will start their killing time as a 'novice'; learning with each event what 'tools' are best to use. A change of clothing, perhaps a length of washing line or police handcuffs to restrain their prey? Some of the killers I have interviewed brought with them plastic sheeting to place on the back seat or in the boot of their car – in a calculated attempt to prevent blood, death-struggle vomiting, urine and excreta soiling the vehicle. Murder most foul is not like 'as seen on TV' – it can be literally foul.

However, most organised offenders, just like disorganised killers, stick to a particular means of extinguishing life – the one that pleases them the most. It could be a firearm, a hammer, knife or even a garrotte, whilst others like to get up very close and personal to strangle their victim with their bare hands or with a ligature.

They were dead as soon as I saw them, I think!
MICHAEL BRUCE ROSS ON HIS VICTIMS. FILMED
INTERVIEW WITH THE AUTHOR ON DEATH ROW, OSBORN
CORRECTIONAL INSTITUTE, SOMERS, CONNECTICUT,
MONDAY, 26 SEPTEMBER 1994

Albeit a disorganised offender, sado-sexual psychopath, Michael Bruce Ross, used his hands to strangle his prey. In fact, as he himself admitted to me during a filmed interview, he could only ejaculate when he watched the 'light of life go from their eyes'. To prolong this experience, to arouse himself even further, Ross part strangled some of his young female victims, then released his grasp to watch them writhe around, moan, cry, beg for mercy, only to reapply his grip. This he did several times, at once boasting to me that his hands would cramp up so he had to massage his fingers every now and then. This caused multiple marks around the throats of some of his prey about which he said, giggling, '. . . uh, the medical examiner couldn't understand the multiple bruising, an' I gotta kinda got a kick outa that.'

A disorganised killer is one who comes upon a victim almost by happenstance, as did Ross, who carried no murder kit at all as his hands were all he needed for the intended task; Ted Bundy was such a murderer, as was sexual sadist Kenneth Allen McDuff from Texas; so were Henry Lee Lucas and his sidekick, Ottis Toole, as were Arthur 'Art' John Shawcross (who strangled) out of New York State, and Harvey 'The Hammer' Louis Carignan, who killed right across a swathe of the US – all were disorganised offenders.

Bundy used a blunt object, sometimes a tree limb to bludgeon, as did Carignan, who also used a tyre lever or a crowbar. While McDuff had used a firearm in much earlier kills, he later used his massive hands, on one occasion a broomstick, to snap necks, or a tree branch to smash skulls to fragments. And, there is something here that I picked up on while interviewing so many other serial killers including Harvey Carignan, Kenneth Bianchi, and examining the MO's of Peter Sutcliffe and Ted Bundy – they all secretly hated women with a passion. Harvey Carignan, for instance, told me that women had always played games with his head, so I elicited an exclusive confession from him where he claimed that he was destroying the very part of women – their brains/ minds – that had plagued him the most. In fact, after he had fallen out with one girlfriend, he rammed her head into a lamp post, smashed an iron drain cover into her skull, then fed her to pigs.

She really had pissed him off, I guess!

Well, I expect that you are getting my drift by now so I will not labour on this any longer other than to add that there are the 'Inbetweeners' – a type of pick-and-mix of organised and disorganised in terms of MO and victim type. However, I will leave it to you, the reader, to study the victim and MO of any serial killer who piques your interest because in doing so you will begin to learn a bit more about what makes these monsters tick.

2

Can you Spot a Serial Murderer?

I'm the most cold-blooded son-of-a-bitch you'll
ever meet. There are people like me who could be
living next door to you. Society wants to believe it
can identify evil people, or bad or harmful people, but
it's not practical. There are no stereotypes.
We serial killers are your sons, we are your husbands . . .
we are everywhere. And there will be more of your
children dead tomorrow.
THEODORE 'TED' ROBERT BUNDY

Before we get into the nitty-gritty of the book, I need to
tackle a few questions; the most common being Can one spot
a homicidal psychopath before he (these offenders are mostly
males) strikes? It may also often be asked: How can I protect
oneself against such a person in that event? Well, I have to
tell you that, despite those books and articles that detail
characteristics to look for to identify a homicidal psychopath,
you cannot! It is completely out of the question, as this book

11

will reveal. I cannot say it more pointedly than the end of a bayonet. If a killer strikes you will not be given a moment's warning – it *will be too late*. And, chillingly, if such a killer zeroes in on you, you will not suspect a thing. He may have been watching you for days or weeks. Whichever way, he, or she, will just come out of the blue.

You could read every single guide on how to safeguard yourself from serial killers. You may take just about every precaution known, but the downside is that once a serial killer has picked his victim, that individual is probably a dead person walking. As this book will show, you can lock all your windows and doors but a determined killer will find a way to get to you, and this book will explain a lot more about how their brains tick. And, don't just simply take my word for it. Ask any homicide cop and they will tell you exactly the same thing.

On a final note, never feel anything for these killers for they cry crocodile tears. They only feel sorry for the predicament they find themselves in. These tears, however convincing they may appear to be, are selfishly designed to elicit compassion from you. In reality they don't care a damn about the suffering they have caused. During my decades working with and studying serial killers, I have not yet met or corresponded with a law-enforcement officer, lawyer or judge, who will disagree with me on this.

3

Interviewing Serial Killers

I don't believe in man, God nor Devil. I hate the whole
damned human race, including myself . . . I prey upon
the weak, the harmless and the unsuspecting. This
lesson I was taught by others: might makes right.

GARY RIDGWAY AKA THE
'GREEN RIVER KILLER' (1949–)

Let's not mince words here because sado–sexual serial killers
are humankind's pond-life bottom-feeders. They are utterly
amoral, conscienceless and heartless people who can terrorise
our societies day and night. They are a social disease; their
numbers and the awfulness of their crimes only increase in
intensity, so what is it like to meet them? In prison, that is.

'Chris, what is it like to interview a serial killer in the flesh
and does it affect you?' are two questions I am asked time and
again, and they are reasonable questions to be sure, followed
up by:

'Are you scared when you interview a serial killer?' 'Do

TALKING WITH PSYCHOPATHS AND SAVAGES: BEYOND EVIL

you suffer from nightmares after hearing about their awful crimes?' 'Do you struggle to maintain any form of personal relationships with normal people?' 'Was your hair always white?' 'Writing is quite a sedentary career, so have you ever considered a 5:2 diet'? 'Do you have any Facebook friends apart from yourself?' and, 'Is there any truth in the rumour that the only Christmas cards you receive are from homicidal maniacs?'

Then comes that old chestnut: 'I'd love to interview a serial killer but they would scare me shitless.'

Well, the answers to some of these questions, or others you may wish to pitch my way will become positively clear as we turn each page. So, may I try to cut to the chase . . . for the sake of keeping your sanity in one piece, it is important to have researched the killers' back-history – the knowledge you gain will stand you in good stead.

Kick off with their parents; birth, formative years; schooling; relationships personal and workwise; employment; all of their criminal antecedents no matter large or small, conviction/s; custodial sentences to the present day; you will need to know every detail. You will need to add to this how, where and why he or she committed their crimes – their method of operation (modus operandi), their way of living (modus vivendi), their victim-type preference and any relationship between offender and victim/s, and what turns these psychopathic conscienceless killers' minds on or off – what pushes their buttons or not. All this before you even start communicating with them in the first place.

All of this is a given and certainly not criminology-related rocket science.

In a nutshell, before you even begin to think about

visitation you will need to know more about the killer who will be soon sitting in front of you than he, or she, does.

I kind of think of one going through immigration at Moscow's Sheremetyevo International Airport, something I have done many times. I can tell you that when those Russian officials look at you wearing that 'never been to a charm school doctor's receptionist expression', then glance at your passport, then their computer screens, they'll know more about you than you do.

That is how analytical and suspicious you should be. Don't be a 'Ms 'Lonely Halfwit' Doris Jones, aged sixty-five, seeking a meaningful and loving relationship with a deep-thinking homicidal predator serving a natural life term, or one on death row about to meet the Grim Reaper. You cannot change such killers, you cannot reform them; any expressions of remorse are to be viewed with suspicion as being born of the criminal's self-interest and cunning; any death-bed repentance is probably instigated by the shadow of the Grim Reaper's scythe ...

The world is full of these well-meaning but to my mind seriously deluded individuals – men and women – who devote their time and their savings, to some mentally disorientated character whose criminal CV is more richly illuminated with serious crime than Blackpool's seaside promenade has lights at Christmas.

We call these lovestruck pen pals 'Murder Groupies', and, of course beauty is in the eye of the beholder. But c'mon, guys and gals, give Christopher a break here, please. Let's say it as it is because one has to be frantically desperate and as dumb as fuck to spend hours upon hours trawling the internet for a sexually-inclined sado-psychopathic soul mate who has spread enough human blood to paint the Golden Gate Bridge twice – okay, maybe just the once then – and a multiple murderer who has apparently suddenly found Jesus Christ when all of his appeals have been shot out of the window.

These murder groupies do stick in my craw, and I have encountered many of them on my travels along 'Murder Road'. Truly, it does make me want me to query their sanity almost as much as that of the killers themselves. Do not think you can change them, persuade them to 'see the light', lead them along any righteous path. And take their claims of innocence or redemption with a handful of salt.

Enough said. But nevertheless, permit me to take just long enough to warn any soft-hearted ladies who may respond to such as Henry Alexander Davis (Florida DC # 358319) DOB 25 April 1965, a cold-blooded killer, who murdered in the furtherance of a robbery.

He advertised himself on an online 'lonely hearts' website as seeking 'potential friends', modestly describing himself as 'Florida's Finest Chocolate' (he is black).

Hi, my name is Henry [he writes], I am now 53 years of age. I have been incarcerated for nearly three decades and I am an innocent man. My desire to develop friendship beyond this edifice of political smoke and mirrors is, in part, because I need to dispel the myth that I am void of humanity and, in part, because most of my family and friends are either deceased or have faded away.

Wrestling clumsily with his vocabulary and losing the battle, Henry continues:'...my basic interests are Law, philosophy, and spirituality. My desire is to meet people who are objectively cogitative upon which they can develop a mutually inspiring relationship through some engaging mental intercourse.'

Rambling on and on, he eventually concludes with this self-effacing description of himself: 'I welcome woman of all races. I weigh 210lbs. Solid as a rock "smile", healthy, compassionate, sincere, loving, honest and good-looking. For prompt response please send me $US150 because I am keen to learn new things.'

I bet he is!

Were Mr Davis a resident of the United Kingdom, he would be guilty of contravening the Trades Description Act, or, at best, being extremely economical with the truth as British train timetables are these days, for 'Florida's Finest Chocolate' is, after all, proclaiming his virtues from a super-max prison. He is also serving two life sentences, one for the use of a firearm in the execution of his civic duty as an armed robber, while the other is for burglary. Two more sentences, each of five years, seem almost too trivial to mention.

His lack of success hitherto in gaining more potential females than he has done thus far, may be due to would-be applicants having read the small print on this particular chocolate wrapper. On the other hand, it could be that they have trouble understanding what he is talking about!

Then we have the life-incarcerated emerging serial killer John David Guise Cannan, who, according to him, was descended from Knights Templar. At the time of writing this book, a letter he had written to a female pen friend was leaked (by police) to the media . . . to the *Birmingham Mail* to be precise. In this letter John promises to buy his besotted admirer a Spanish villa when he has never had a pot to piss in, nor ever will. Notwithstanding the fact that here we find an incredibly violent rapist, a robber, a conman extraordinaire and most certainly the killer of three women: Sandra Court, estate agent Suzy Lamplugh and Bristol lass, Shirley Banks, this lovestruck woman (name omitted for legal reasons) is, I suggest, in need of her head examined more than is Cannan.

But please don't take my word for all of this. There are thousands of women and men 'seeking objectively cogitative mutually inspiring relationships through some engaging mental intercourse' with homicidal maniacs via the internet. Well, maybe you can, for my book, *Murder.Com*, written with the total cooperation of the FBI, CIA and Russian State Police, is, if not seriously mind-blowing, oft-times downright hilarious – except that the outcomes were often lethal for the suckers who fell in love with a behind-bars sociopath who was subsequently released – covers many such cases.

The problem, it seems to me, is that the folk who should be educating themselves by reading that book do not. Those who do, don't get it either, for never a day goes by when even more people go online seeking love on the internet only to find themselves fleeced of all they had, presently have, or will ever have, to paraphrase the words of steel-blue-eyed, Clint Eastwood, playing Bill Munny, in the 1992 movie *Unforgiven*: 'It's a hell of a thing, killing a man. You take away all he's got and all he's ever gonna have.'

And, indeed, many women looking for love on the internet fall prey to serial killers, as did the victims of Mr John Edward 'JR' Robinson, who, in brief, conned, 'hired' or abducted women whom he defrauded, mistreated and used as slaves, before disposing of them. In 1993 he discovered the internet and, calling himself 'Slavemaster', roamed various social sites to pick up his victims. Sometimes called the internet's first serial killer, he is on death row, at the El Dorado Correctional Facility, Kansas.

Having got that off of my chest, I testify that I have walked many a death row where the smell is always the same – not a delicate fusion of summer blooms to be sure. What, in fact, hits you is the reek of disinfectant, bleach, cooking fat, stale urine, faeces and human sweat, permeating every brick of the so-called 'Green Mile'. And that's just the smell. The racket, can at times, be deafening, like feeding time at the monkey enclosure of a zoo.

With nothing better to do, the inmates (it is PC not to call them 'convicts' these days) howl, grunt, gibber, chatter, whoop and screech. If they happen to take a dislike to you, or anyone for that matter, they will throw their faeces at you or urinate through the bars. If the cells only have solid steel doors they piss all over their cell floors and wipe their shit on the walls.

I think some monkeys do that, too!

For security reasons in the US if you visit a death row or a prisoner in Hi-Seg (high segregation), the whole penitentiary is placed under lockdown. Inmates tasked with cleaning the corridors move silently, the only sounds being the swish and slop of grey soapy water as they mop floors, with not a word passing between the cons or the correctional officers, whose orders are curt and to the point. 'STAND STILL. PRESS YOUR FUCKIN' NOSES AGAINST THE WALL!' There is no eyeballing here in the 'Big Houses' or 'Pens'.

In the UK we don't have death rows or 'green miles'. The last executions in the United Kingdom were by hanging, and took place in 1964, prior to capital punishment being abolished (in 1965 in Great Britain and in 1973 in Northern Ireland).

> You ask if the term 'Correctional Facility' applies to UK prisons. Fuck, no!
>
> Correctional? Don't make me laugh, mate. They are in and out and in and out. I have a little weasel of a man on my wing who beat his kids to death and then crashed his car in an effort to say it was a road accident. It was all because his wife was leaving him and he never wanted her to see her kids again ... I am obliged to call him 'sir'.
>
> Fancy a game of pool?
>
> PRISON OFFICER EMPLOYED BY A PRIVATE
FIRM, INTERVIEW WITH THE AUTHOR,
MONDAY, 20 AUGUST 2018.

Having interviewed many UK prison officers – that is those who are employed in the 'private sector', whose main aim is to satisfy their shareholders and screw the interests of penal reform (please excuse the pun here), I have found that as a whole these prison officers are at their wits' ends.

Can you believe it – and this is a fact which the Home Office will never comment upon – privately run prisons are paid a bonus for the time inmates are kept out of their cells, for recreation or simply mingling? Make of that if you will, but this includes the most heinous of serial killers – simply for fear of breaching their human rights. And here is another titbit of correctional information. These days in the UK, the strict Home Office protocol is to address inmates with a courteous 'Sir' or 'Mr', or 'Mrs' or 'Miss', while in the US penitentiaries it is, 'Hey fuckwit, haul ass over here!' There is none of this leftie human rights stuff .

In the US when a 'dead man walking' is brought before me for an interview, which frequently turns into subtle interrogation – unbeknownst to them sometimes a hard interrogation – he will be shackled, cuffed to a waist chain with ankle manacles permitting only an unsteady gait. Unless, that is, I have felt it to be desirable and safe enough for me to ask that his restraints be removed. He'll be flanked by four close-control officers; burly men, immaculately dressed to impress you, the privileged visitor – one guard either each side holding an arm, one guard behind and the senior officer in front leading the way as each security door hisses open then clangs shut.

These men have come from the 'belly of the beast' – their interviews with me probably their last contact with the outside world, after which they are returned to death row, deep within the human storage facilities containing the most deadly men and women alive, and where the smell is always the same.

So, it goes without saying that the safest place to meet a serial killer face-to-face is in a prison. If you bump into one on the 'out' the chances are high that you are fucked and up the proverbial creek without a paddle.

Although I have interviewed many highly dangerous killers (some thirty in all) most times I prefer them unshackled, making it more comfortable for them and moderately uncomfortable for me. They do lose their tempers sometimes; you can see the rage starting to simmer as their faces turn bat-skin tight and beads of sweat start trickling down their foreheads staining wet the collars of their shirts. But, they never attack, you see, because they are cowards at heart. They are all mouth and prison-issue trousers – baby killers, child killers, vulnerable-women killers; these monsters are truly the scum of the earth. So never expect to meet a real-life Hannibal Lecter type. They don't exist.

4

All Shapes and Sizes

Quite obviously, serial killers come in all shapes and sizes – ranging from overweight, blubbery lumps of lard like bisexual serial killer John Wayne Gacy, to the scrawny, ferret physique of dripping-gunge-one-eyed Henry Lee Lucas – both of whom I've interviewed. They were both on death row at the time: Gacy at Menard Correctional Center in Chester, Illinois; and Lucas at Ellis Unit, Texas. Gacy was executed by lethal injection on Tuesday, 10 May 1994 at the Stateville Correctional Center, Crest Hill, Illinois; Lucas had his death sentence commuted to life imprisonment. He died of natural causes on 12 March 2001.

Unlike these two, some of the killers I've interviewed are as fit for purpose as any athlete; others, however, were certainly a long way from Greek gods. Arthur John Shawcross, for instance, when I saw him, was physically quite a strange assemblage of bits and pieces. A large head, thinning hair, porcine ever-blinking eyes, rubbery nose, bullish neck sitting on very sloping shoulders, all leading down to a massive belly which fell over his trouser belt, going further south to short, stumpy legs and the smallest size feet I had ever seen in an adult. One got the impression that Shawcross had never been genetically programmed with speed in mind, however, I was assured that he did move like the wind when being chased around at 'Yard Time' by a lot of angry Crips or Bloods (members of two notorious rival African-American street gangs), all very keen to rip the head off this fat, white, child murderer and serial killer.

Some are super-intelligent. Cocky Connecticut serial murderer, Michael Bruce Ross, with his IQ of 150, could have still been a free man today had he not pitted his wits against super-sleuth State Trooper Detective Mike Malchik, and opened his mouth too wide – not once but twice – to pretty much convict himself. On the other hand, there is Ronald Joseph 'Butch' DeFeo Jr, with his massive ego supported by two skinny legs with nothing except a 'To Let – Vacant without Possession' sign between his ears.

I've been fuckin' waiting for two hours for you. Who'd do ya think I am? I got better things to do.

> RONALD 'BUTCH' DEFEO JR, AKA
> THE AMITYVILLE HORROR, TO THE AUTHOR,
> GREEN HAVEN CORRECTIONAL FACILITY,
> STORMVILLE, NEW YORK, FRIDAY,
> 23 SEPTEMBER 1994

DeFeo (born 1951), was and still is an utter moron. He stands about 5 foot 5 inches tall and bathes in ill-deserved fame thanks to the 1979 horror movie *The Amityville Horror* (plus several equally appalling sequels and spin-off), infamy like a slimy frog peering out of a pond waiting to see if a book, or a movie royalty cheque is coming his way – which for decades one hasn't, never has, actually!

This mass murderer, as mentioned earlier, shot to death his entire family of six as they slept in their 112 Ocean Avenue, Amityville, Long Island, home, so it must have taken a lot of homicidal skill to load up his high-powered .35-calibre Marlin hunting rifle and blast them to kingdom come at point-blank range. Brave man is our Ron.

Casting aside for the moment that this fool DeFeo had a confession beaten the hell out of him by Detectives Dennis Rafferty and Lt Robert Dunn (both big guys whom I interviewed at the Suffolk County police HQ in Yaphank), using of all things a Long Island telephone directory (big heavy books those are too), Ron was dumb enough to lead cops to the exact places where he dumped several items of crucial evidence. The idiot even pointed to the precise spot where he threw the rifle into the dock behind his house. He actually drew a map so police divers could find it in less than 40 seconds – almost before they got wet.

Then DeFeo pleaded total innocence at trial.

I truly mean you could not make this up if you tried – which he was, and found guilty and sentenced to circa forty years on each count.

But, it is the killers' eyes that I enjoy peering into when I interview them; some being like the black eyes of a Great White shark, as are Bianchi's when he is trying to psych someone out and stare them down. 'Mr Unshackled Fit as Uber Alpha Male' was radiating hatred at me. This was serious eyeball-to-eyeball stuff. My response was to lean forward across the table, place my hand on his shoulder and whisper in his ear: 'Hey, you miserable son-of-a-fuckin' bitch, give me a smile.' He cracked and I had a one-hour interview with one of the evil Hillside Stranglers.

'Chris, you touched one of these monsters . . . ?'

Well, it goes without saying that it would be quite unwise to invade a homicidal maniac's personal space unless one has the measure of the man. Some of these killers are very unpredictable. In a millisecond they can flip and rip one's head off before the guards can even think about intervening. But, in my limited experience to a greater degree it comes down to 'mind control'. A quiet word, leaning forward with a smile, showing them that they don't intimidate you up-ends their mental processing ability – if they possess any. One can almost hear the billions of electrochemical microcircuits fizzing away in their heads, all in a very confused state, to then falling back to the default position, with the killer thinking: 'What the fuck do I do now?'

Other killers rant and rave, as did a heavily shackled Douglas Daniel Clark, aka the 'Sunset Slayer', when I interviewed him at San Quentin State Prison (SQ), in 1995. He was not angry with me though: he was furious at the prison authorities for some minor sleight. You can find most of the unedited video of my interview with Doug on the internet. I liked him a lot because he didn't mince his words, his language becoming quite blue at times. Besides, the cops well and truly, according to him, stitched him up.

So, these killers would be no threat to you if you had the inclination to go and meet one of them in prison: your reason being, perhaps, sheer curiosity; maybe you have in mind a long, loving and meaningful relationship or, possibly, like me, for professional reasons.

Oops, silly Christopher. I almost forgot to tell you th[...]
you live in the UK, or pretty much anywhere else for [...]
matter, and want to meet someone in a US super-max facility
you'd have a fondness for travelling…a lot of it and lots more,
because they build their prisons in the middle of nowhere,
which can be located in a place not far from The Twilight
Zone, where I think a lot of American prison officers come
from too.

In the UK, our prisons are built with inmates' visitors'
convenience in mind – take for example HMP Parkhurst, or
HMP Albany on the Isle of Wight. Buy an ice cream, hop
onto the hydrofoil or hovercraft, and you step ashore on
the island in ten minutes flat. Grab a taxi or jump on a bus
and you are at the clink very soon thereafter. Visit done and
dusted, you'll find a country pub less than a breath away . . . a
ploughman's lunch, washed down with real ale makes visiting
prisons in the UK a very enjoyable day out, it seems to me.
Bring the kids too.

Now try the same thing again in the US – take the
previously mentioned Washington State Penitentiary at Walla
Walla as one gruelling example. This place isn't set in some
verdant holiday destination surrounded by sandy beaches
and blue seas, and there are no gift shops selling crap, no art
galleries selling crap, or any up-your-backside Royal Yacht
Squadron close by. The heck there isn't.

As an aside, the etymology of Walla Walla comes from the
Native American name meaning 'Place of Many Waters'.
According to *Wikipedia*, tourists to Walla Walla are often told
that it is a, 'town so nice they named it twice'. For crying out
loud! I cannot see why. For Heaven's sake it's a city, anyway!
And, like all US cities or towns or reservations, mostly

unlike the UK, flagging up places such as Milton Keynes or Basingstoke, there has to be a blood bath featuring someplace in its history. Walla Walla is no exception.

As history has it, one Dr Marcus Whitman and his pinched-faced wife Narcissa were settlers who led a group of like-minded folk riding in and on those old 'prairie schooners' along the Oregon Trail, which the local Cayuse tribespeople took great exception to. And for a very good reason. I am led to understand: the settlers not only hauled with them all the necessities for settling such as the indispensable Holy Bible, and a sewing kit, sundry pots and pans and sacks of beans, they also brought a whole lot of infectious diseases and maladies including measles. Despite the doctor's efforts to tend to the sick braves, squaws and children, they died in their droves and were pretty much wiped out – all but achieving what a hostile neighbouring tribe had been struggling to do for years with bows and arrows. The local peoples held a deep suspicion of 'medicine men' so this was not the place for the Whitmans to be. In a nutshell, the remaining Cayuse carried out a massacre and Marcus and Narcissa were killed . . . But I have digressed. Walla Walla's original name, 'Steptoeville' was to commemorate Edward Jenner Steptoe, a West Point highly decorated, battle-hardened US Army soldier signally remembered for his abject defeat at the Battle of Pine Creek on 17 May 1858 – later to be dubbed the 'Steptoe Disaster'.

Like Dr Whitman, it was a case of being in the wrong place at the wrong time, for Steptoe, with 164 troopers, picked a fight with over 1000 'Indian' warriors. Fortunately, the then Brevet Lieutenant-Colonel Steptoe escaped with his life. Mentally disorientated (and wouldn't you be?) he went on sick leave only to be promoted to Lieutenant-Colonel, shortly to resign it on the grounds of ill health. He died in 1865, never knowing that a very, very small unincorporated town in Whitman County – yes, named after the very same Dr Whitman – would be named in honour of his cock-up at Pine Creek. Neither did he know that a butte, and then a valley, would also be named after him; the latter because he once he rode through it on a horse. Oh, and he has a post office named after him, too!

Getting to the Washington State Penitentiary by air is a trip not for the fainthearted. When it's foggy, flying from Seattle to the airstrip at Walla Walla can bring about a very close encounter with one of North America's most active volcanoes, and possibly the most dangerous, Mount St Helens. By road it's at least a lifelong drive and there is not a single pub en route. What is the world coming to? Yes, the massive winding Columbia River is all very nice – great views across to the Rattlesnake Hills and Saddle Mountains relieve the tedium – but after some 2,000 kilometres passing through places with names like Turdsville and Drownded Man's Gulch [*sic*], the drive gets a bit repetitious, this much I can confirm. So travelling to visit a serial killer is an exercise one must consider carefully.

> I should never have been convicted of anything more serious than running a cemetery without a licence.
>
> JOHN WAYNE GACY (1942–1994), DEATH ROW,
> MENARD CORRECTIONAL CENTER. 1965.

En route to see Mr Gacy, with a film crew headed by my longtime friend, producer Frazer Ashford, I visited 'Olde Worlde' Chester, parked on a steep grassy bluff over the banks of the Mississippi River. Way, way back, Chester was a favourite stopping place for the river men and paddleboat passengers. Charles Dickens and his wife Catherine stayed here on 11 April 1842.

Mark Twain, author of *The Adventures of Tom Sawyer*, was a paddleboat pilot on 'Ole Miss' from 1857 through to the Civil War; supposedly staying on several occasions at Cliff House, then a fine river hostelry.

E. C. Segar, creator of Popeye the Sailor Man, was born here on 8 December 1894. It was in Chester that Segar invented many of his cartoon characters based on local folk. Chester has also featured as filming locations in the movies *In the Heat of the Night* (1967) and *The Fugitive* (1993). Pretty good going for a small town (population circa 8,562), I think we can all agree?

But I have digressed, as all of my loyal readers know I am wont to do.

Despite their ill-deserved media notoriety, once killers are incarcerated, they are reduced to mere identity numbers. Amongst the cases we find in this book there will be no movie stereotypes such 'Dr Hannibal Lecter', no 'Joe Chill' out of the Batman movies, no wide-eyed 'Anton Chigurh' played by Javier Bardem in *No Country for Old Men*.

Aside from the movie stuff, once locked up, sexual psychopath killers become non-persons destined to spend the remainder of their worthless days in what are loosely called 'Correctional Facilities' – soulless human warehouses reeking of cheap disinfectant, urine, stale food – and precisely the correct places to house 'The Legion of the Damned' they are, too.

'Correctional' be damned for there is nothing correctional

about these super-max facilities, nor is there anything correctional about the death rows with perhaps one exception ...

We correct all the ailments that cause stone-cold killers to kidnap, rape, torture and murder our men, women and children. We execute them and that corrects them for good!

ASSISTANT WARDEN-IN-CHARGE OF
EXECUTIONS, NEIL HODGES,
THE WALLS PRISON, HUNTSVILLE, TEXAS,
TO THE AUTHOR, MAY 1995

As a 'special treat' for me, Neil gave me a dummy run from the holding cell to strap-down in the death chamber. Six burly guards – no priest around this time – and I was immobilised on the gurney within 30 seconds flat!

Murder is not about lust and it's not about violence. It's about possession. When you feel the last breath of life coming out of the woman, you look into her eyes. At the point, it's being God.

SERIAL KILLER THEODORE 'TED'
ROBERT BUNDY (1946–1989)

Yeah! I want a fried chicken dinner with gravy on the taters, I want to shit in your hat, and I got to have Mae West sit on my face, because I am one horny motherfucker!

TOOT-TOOT, PLAYED BY THE MUCH-MISSED
LATE HARRY DEAN STANTON (1926–2017).
QUOTE FROM *THE GREEN MILE*, 1999

5

Some Men You Just Can't Reach

If you possess the correct credentials you can visit a death row, of course you can, however modern death rows rarely have lime-green walkways and rough brick walls as portrayed on the set of the Stephen King movie *The Green Mile* starring Tom Hanks as Officer Paul Edgecombe and with the late Michael Clarke Duncan as the enormous, almost lovable John Coffey. Most, if not all death rows are now decorated in pastel shades allegedly pleasing and calming to the eye. But there is an exception: 'Condemned Row' at the old Connecticut Somers Prison (where I visited Michael Ross) was painted a dirty chocolate-brown. Come to that, it seemed that the entire place was painted in the same colour inside and out.

Go, cowboy, go!
JESSE TAFERO'S (1946–1990) LAST WORDS BEFORE
HE CAUGHT FIRE IN FLORIDA'S ELECTRIC CHAIR

For my part, I think that along with prison movies such as *The Shawshank Redemption* and *Cool Hand Luke*, *The Green Mile* almost hits death row on the head; most especially the lighting up in 'Old Sparky' of Michael Jeter, who played 'Eduard Delacroix'; reminding one of the several occasions when the convicted have been fried alive – John Louis Evans III, for instance, who met Alabama's 'Yellow Mama', 22 April 1983, or Jesse Tafero, who, in 1990, like his predecessor, caught fire. His hair went up in flames with ashes singeing his shirt.

From *Cool Hand Luke* I have chosen a quote that seems to me to be particularly apt for this book:

> What we've got here is . . . failure to communicate. Some men you just can't reach.
>
> THE CAPTAIN, PLAYED BY STROTHER MARTIN
> (1919–1980) IN THE 1967 MOVIE *COOL HAND LUKE*,
> STARRING PAUL NEWMAN

'Failure to communicate . . . some men you just can't reach'? So who are these killers we cannot reach or really communicate with? What precisely goes on inside their heads?

To start the ball rolling, they don't have any morality that's for sure. Where there should be understanding, a compassionate caring for their fellow man, there is zilch. You can witness this when sitting talking to them face-to-face as I have done more times than I can count or care to remember. Many of these socially dysfunctional people exude glibness and superficial charm. They are, in the main, pathological liars. They can be very convincing ones at that, as evidenced by the beautiful, convicted one-off killer, Jodi Ann Arias (b.1980) who is now serving a life sentence without the possibility of parole for the horrendous slaughter of 'all-American hunk' Travis Victor Alexander, aged thirty, at his home in June 2008.

Despite being proven guilty beyond any doubt; having admitted her culpability at trial, at other times pleading innocence, whenever it suits her purpose, she now has millions of internet supporters. When I saw her in ASPA-PV State Prison Complex, Perryville, Arizona on 16 January 2018, this is what she said to me: 'Christopher, I did not kill Travis. I would be thrilled to write my whole story with you.'

Thanks, but no thanks, Jodi!

Professor Robert Hare's *Psychopathy Checklist Revised* describes psychopaths as being 'callous; showing a lack of empathy, all traits akin to cold-heartedness', and Robert Hare has got it spot-on, for the criteria for a dissocial personality disorder include a total unconcern for the feelings of others. Psychopaths' brains have been found to have weak connections among the components of the brain's emotional systems. These disconnects are partly responsible for the psychopath's inability to feel emotions deeply.

It is also said by many psychiatrists and psychologists that psychopaths and sociopaths are not good at detecting fear in the faces of other people – nonetheless, most of the serial killers I've interviewed gain an immense amount of depraved sexual gratification from seeing the terror on their victims' faces when they are being tortured, often for hours or days of unrelenting pain and suffering that only cease when death mercifully intervenes.

Without going into the finer detail, we need look no further than the sado-sexual serial killers Frederick and Rose West, who tormented some of their victims for hours. Another of this type would be the appropriately named Florida redneck auxiliary cop, David Alan Gore. As far as torture and the causing of indescribable human suffering goes, Gore made Fred West seem like a saint. This man abducted his many female victims, stripped them, hung them up in a barn, raped them, slowly skinned them, often cutting into their breasts while they were alive – becoming perhaps one of the most disgusting psychopaths ever to have walked the earth in my opinion. His exclusive sickening written confessions to me – which I passed on to the prosecuting authorities – helped fast-track his execution on 12 April 2012.

Balding and bespectacled Californian Phillip Carl Jablonski is a man who slit throats, sodomised and even cannibalised his victims. I got to know this monster very well and like many others of his ilk he seems to have few regrets for his actions.

I have no remorse for the murders, rapes or pimping of adolescent boys and girls. I am proud I raped my slut sister and mother. Maybe my slut mother will rot in hell – they both died in 1986. There are other unsolved murders I have committed, and a few of them are over twenty years old. By the way, I have a son called Christopher.

PHILLIP JABLONSKI, DEATH ROW LETTER
TO THE AUTHOR, 28 JANUARY 2008

This man is fascinated by the British serial killer John Reginald Christie, saying to me: 'A friend of mine sent me a photo of Christie and I look just like him.'

Thanks for the info, Phillip!

And, mere words cannot even begin to depict the brutal murders committed by serial murderer Gary Ray Bowles (six known victims, but perhaps as many as twenty-five). The crimes scenes were blood baths, but does he have any remorse?

> I had sex with thousands of men for money, probably at least two [thousand] for money, and I probably had sex with at least 100 women on my own. I had a lot of fun, but I also ended up spending over half of my life in prison.
>
> GARY RAY BOWLES. LETTER TO THE AUTHOR
> FROM DEATH ROW, UNION CORRECTIONAL
> INSTITUTION, FLORIDA, 30 SEPTEMBER 2009

Well, perhaps Gary is prone to exaggerating here, gilding the lily if you prefer, but all serial killers try to pull a fast one from time to time, just to impress, you see!

In other words, many of these evil people thrive on the pain and suffering caused by their own hands. Indeed, oft times they have been smirkingly gleeful when describing their crimes to me during interviews.

> Yes, sir. Several days after I dumped her in the creek I went back an' I cut the vagina out of her [June Cicero, aged thirty-four]. It was frozen so I thawed it under the car heater then ate it. Threw the bone part away then went to Dunkin Donuts where I talked to the cops about who was doing all the killing.
>
> ARTHUR JOHN SHAWCROSS (1945–2008)
> AT INTERVIEW WITH THE AUTHOR AT THE
> SULLIVAN CORRECTIONAL FACILITY, FALLSBURG,
> NEW YORK, FRIDAY 30 SEPTEMBER 1994

All of which brings me to the homicidal brain.

6

The Homicidal Brain

Human morality is unthinkable without empathy.
DUTCH PRIMATOLOGIST AND ETHOLOGIST,
FRANS DE WAAL (B. 1948)

Quite naturally, the emotion of disgust plays an important role on our socially inclined ethical senses. The majority of us find certain types of unprincipled actions disgusting, which keeps us from engaging in them ourselves and, through our expressions of revulsion and disapproval of them, discourages others. But psychopaths have extremely high thresholds for revulsion, as measured by their responses when shown mind-numbing photographs of mutilated faces and when exposed to foul smells.

When subjected to such awful images and nauseating olfactory onslaughts, the majority of good folk would grimace or reach for a nearby bucket in which to throw up, but not the people we are discussing in this book, far from it. This is why so many serial sex killers – despite the pervasive stench of decomposition – return to the rotting corpses or skeletal remains of their victims, to gloat, sometimes to commit necrophiliac acts. So imagine innocently stumbling across such a grim, moonlight Stephen King type scene. Bejeezus, that would even scare the hell out of me!

Using functional magnetic resonance imaging (fMRI), researchers in the United States, Germany and elsewhere have started taking scans of the brains of psychopaths while the criminals view horrific images, such as photographs of bloody stabbings, shootings, or evisceration. When normal people view these images, fMRI scans light up to indicate heavy brain activity in sections of the emotion-generating limbic system, primarily the amygdalae, a pair of almond-shaped structures in the brain, which are believed to generate feelings of empathy. But in psychopathic patients these sections of the amygdalae remain dark, showing greatly reduced activity, or none at all. This phenomenon, known as limbic under-activation, may indicate that these people lack the ability to generate the basic emotions that keep the primitive killer instincts in check.

I'm full of romance and love and I wear my heart on my sleve [sic]. I am a hopeless romantic ... But can also stand my ground.

MICHAEL RAFFERTY'S FACEBOOK
AND PLENTY OF FISH PROFILE

One example of this reaction deficit can be found during the police interviews of twenty-eight-year-old Michael Rafferty who, along with his truly evil girlfriend, Terri-Lynne McClintic (aged eighteen), both high on OxyContin prescription pills, at end-of-school time on Wednesday, 8

April 2009, abducted an eight-year-old Woodstock schoolgirl called Victoria Elizabeth Marie 'Tori' Stafford. They drove Tori in Rafferty's mother's borrowed car to a rural area near Mount Forest, Ontario, where she was brutally raped by Rafferty, then beaten to death by McClintic using a claw hammer purchased by her at a Walmart store after Tori was taken. During the killing, Tori's head was covered with a black plastic bin liner, also purchased by McClintic at the same time as the hammer, to prevent the splatter of blood and brain matter.

Conman, viewer of internet clickety-click child porn, womaniser Rafferty who enjoyed sexual choking and torture sex, and dropout McClintic, whom he pimped out for drug money, were arrested on Tuesday, 19 May 2009.

Over two days Rafferty and McClintic were interviewed by legendary Ontario Provincial Police (OPP) Detective Staff Sergeant Jim Smyth along with Detective Staff Sergeant Chris Loam and Constable Gordon Johnson. Despite hours of 'hard cop/soft cop' questioning, using every trick in the interrogator's book including the proven 'Reid Technique', and with irrefutable evidence piling up, cold-as-ice Rafferty showed not a moment of emotion throughout, although McClintic eventually cracked. Denying any guilt, Rafferty's only concern was for himself, at once cockily arguing that the police were fools, that he had an alibi – one he could never prove existed.

Both killers were sentenced to serve life in prison in 2012.

Perhaps the best way I can describe these fundamental emotional issues from a layperson's perspective is to look at the function of the amygdala. There are two amygdalae, each located close to the hippocampus, situated in the frontal portion of the temporal lobe on each side – the left and the right – of the brain. Your amygdalae are essential to your ability, or inability, to feel certain emotions and to perceive them in other people. This includes fear, or lack of fear, and the many changes that it causes in the body.

Deficits in the expression of fear occur in psychopaths and in people who have damaged amygdalae. Some of the serial killers I have interviewed had suffered some form of frontal lobe impact during the early stages of their lives. Although this is not the be-all and end-all of it, it must be considered as a contributory factor of psychopathy, one not to be lightly dismissed.

As an example: Kenneth Alessio Bianchi, aka one of the notorious 'Hillside Stranglers' (whom I corresponded with for several years before I interviewed him at the Washington State Penitentiary), fell from a kiddies' playground slide and bashed the front of his skull. Later he plunged down a flight of steel steps onto concrete paving. Countering this is a comment made to me by Professor Elliott Leyton. 'So what? Millions of kids bump their heads, but they all don't turn into homicidal maniacs, do they?' He has a valid point.

Nevertheless, revealing experiments by Drs Jari Tiihonen and Kent Kjehl – the latter the author of an amazing and insightful book *The Psychopath Whisperer* – and colleagues verify the contributory importance of the amygdala in affective disorders. They find, for example, that '. . . psychopaths actually have smaller-sized amygdalae (volume is reduced from normal), presumably accounting for the reduction of amygdala function and fear.' I call it a 'mental impairment' of sorts.

Whatever the case, the amygdalae appear to have much to

answer for, as many neurological circuits control psychopathic traits, including those involved with dopamine production and its distribution around the brain, such as with the frontal lobes that have interconnections with the dopamine centres of the brain and with the amygdalae.

Without labouring on the physiological technicalities, along with a bunch of other hormones the neurotransmitter dopamine is a chemical messenger that zips between brain cells, playing an important role in executive functions, motor control, motivation, arousal, reinforcement and reward, as well as low-level functions including lactation, sexual gratification and nausea. So if low levels of dopamine are being produced and the amygdalae are not getting the right amount of it, expect to suffer depression, inability to handle stress, fatigue, mood swings, and an incapability to concentrate, all of which is not at all good for you or anyone else nearby if you suddenly lose your temper.

And, this may also partly explain why some people are prone to sudden outbursts of seemingly inexplicable anger. They unexpectedly flip, as in 'road rage', for example. You all know the feeling when someone cuts in front of you on the highway. You toot your horn and they give the finger in return and that is the end of the matter. Usually. But, looking at the case of Kenneth Noye 'Mr Goldfinger', here we have an excellent example of what can happen when someone loses his or her rag big time.

On Sunday, 19 May 1996, Mr Noye, who was on release from prison on life licence, was involved in a road-rage incident with twenty-one-year-old motorist Stephen Cameron, on a slip road of the M25 motorway, near Swanley in the county of Kent. During the 'altercation' Mr Noye pulled a knife with which he stabbed Cameron to death. Then Noye, a crooked gold dealer, fled the country to Spain from where he was extradited to the UK.

Noye's is a fascinating story with criminal narrative bettering any motion picture plot by miles and, at the time of writing, he is at HM Prison Standford Hill on the Isle of Sheppey – a low-level facility with a day-release provision for inmates. On that note, you will understand why I am referring to Kenneth Noye as 'Mr', because this man never forgets, and one questions whether or not – with his still loyal criminal fraternity connections still in place – his anger-management issues have yet been resolved because his amygdalae may not still be up to scratch ... if you catch my drift?

Sorry for the delay. We are just waiting to clear a drunk dancing topless man from the tunnel. The rest of the line is stuffed.

LONDON UNDERGROUND TRAIN DRIVER TO
PASSENGERS, WEDNESDAY, 2 AUGUST 2017

Another analogy I will use is the London Underground network, the Tube. If you are an American reader, let's try New York City's subway system – the seventh busiest rapid transit system in the world. Most often these systems, with their multitude of stations, interconnecting points, engineering competence seasoned with some incompetence, and complicated timetables should run smoothly like clockwork despite the countless trillions of electrical signals whizzing around every millisecond of every day.

RIGHT, NOW, you want to get from A to B. Your dinner is waiting at home; maybe you have an urgent business appointment to meet. Your grandmother is being buried. If you miss the interment your family will never speak to you again, but someplace along your route the 'Auto-triggered Diagnosis System' kicks in because of a track or signal failure. It could be that a mega-stressed-out someone has – inconveniently to you and tens-of-thousands of other passengers – thrown themselves onto a live rail. Things slow to a crawl, if not stop completely, and are you getting tense and angry? Of course you are! And you would not be alone in your frustrations. Just ask any of the 1,379 million London Tube passengers who use this network every year. I'll put money on it they will mostly agree, for when one single part of the system jams up the knock-on effect, like falling dominoes, affects the whole works. Put another way; like the electricity that powers the Tube, if the dopamine inside your head powers down and your amygdalae aren't getting enough 'juice', expect to suffer stress.

The amygdalae, therefore, are of central importance because of their inhibitory influence on fear and aggression, and also because countless emotional signals of all sorts, like the Tube's electricity, converge at this site, thus shunting critical information throughout the central nervous system.

The amygdalae are also essential in adverse (inhibitory) learning so it appears that the absence of fear is a major diagnostic criterion of psychopathic competence. It essentially frees the individual from inhibiting responses, blunts empathy, guilt, nostalgia and remorse. This reduction of amygdala-fear enables many behaviours to occur that otherwise would defeat the agenda of individual psychopaths, in an 'I couldn't give a shit' sort of way, as did Colonel David Russell Williams who didn't give a damn when he was running amok, and I know that the Canadian police who dealt with him would say precisely the same thing.

> I hit her with a flashlight . . . Restrained her . . . I raped her but couldn't ejaculate. I gave her oral sex and then made her do it to me. Then I wrapped duct tape around her mouth and her nose and watched her suffocate to death . . . then I went back to work. I was addicted to sex. It was like a switch I couldn't turn off.
>
> English-born Colonel David Russell Williams, Canadian Forces Base Trenton, to Detective Staff-Sergeant Jim Smyth, Sunday, 7 February 2010, on the murder of Marie-France Comeau

Moving swiftly on, let's take a look at the hypothalamus and, just as with the amygdala, if it malfunctions step back and wait for a big bang, at least a dull thud.

In humans the hypothalamus, a small region of the brain, weighs about 4 grams (about four pinches of salt) in an average human brain of around 1,400 grams (about half as heavy as a standard brick). Ever so tiny – proving that size doesn't always count – the hypothalamus, made up of distinct nuclei as well as less anatomically distinct areas, plays a pivotal role in an astounding number of functional and behavioural activities that are essential for the day-to-day survival of you and me and, lo and behold, it hasn't even a clue about anything.

Furthermore, your hypothalamus never gets any credit for the work it does to keep you up to speed 24/7/365 every moment from cradle to grave, for it not only enables hormone release, but also dishes out all manner of stimulation, olfactory stimuli, blood-born stimuli, a whole bunch of steroids and control of food intake, to name but a few. Yet, here is the neat thing about this unassuming minuscule part of the brain: it doesn't even know why it is there; how it came to be inside your head in the first place; what its use is, or why it even exists at all – and even less does it expect to receive any medals for doing the sterling work that it does on your behalf. Now, I call that being modest, don't you?

The hypothalamus region of the limbic system is also the most primitive, primeval and perhaps one of the most important parts of the semi-spongy grey matter residing between our ears. It is one of the production centres of dopamine because the hypothalamus serves the body tissues by attempting to maintain its metabolic equilibrium and providing a mechanism for the immediate discharge of tensions. Indeed, it appears to act rather like an on/off sensor; on the one hand, seeking or maintaining the experience of pleasure and, on the other hand, escaping or avoiding unpleasant, noxious conditions. Hence, feelings elicited by this part of the brain are very short-lived.

The hypothalamus has no conscience, neither can it bear a grudge, and the feelings generated throughout you may disappear completely after just a few seconds, although they may last a tad longer. This is much the same way as military colonel-cum-multiple-rapist-cum killer Colonel David Williams, and so many of his type, have described their thoughts. 'One minute the evil thoughts are there, the next moment they vanish into thin air like a fart in the wind,' as it was vividly described to me by US serial killer, Keith Hunter Jesperson, aka the 'Happy Face Killer'.

So the limbic system mediates a wide range of simple emotions. Because it controls the ability to feel pleasure and displeasure it is able to generate and use these emotions to meet a variety of needs, be they sexual, nutritional or emotional. That is, it can reward or punish the entire brain – thus the individual – with the amygdalae and the hypothalamus not having a clue as to what they are doing or what's going on.

If, for example, the hypothalamus experiences pleasure, be it from satisfying a craving for chocolate, drugs or sex – or the need for sadistic sex and murder – it will switch on 'reward' feelings so that the person continues engaging in the activity desired. In the case of the priapic serial murderer, Michael Ross, this 'switch' was jammed halfway it seems to me. He was a compulsive masturbator. Even as a very young boy he gained immense sexual satisfaction from masturbating after watching his father wring the necks of the deformed chicks on his father's Connecticut poultry farm. Later, while studying agriculture at Cornell University he spent much of his free time 'working himself off' and even then he demanded sex from his girlfriend, Connie, at least four times a day, and, furthermore, he was an avid reader of hardcore porn magazines While he was on death row, his prison counsellor, Ann Cornoyer, told my film crew and me that 'Michael masturbates at least forty times a day to the degree that he has sores on his penis.' Now, this guy was not stupid. He had an IQ of 150, all proving that you don't have to be a village idiot to metamorphose into a homicidal maniac.

In the cases of sexual psychopathic killers where the switch jams halfway, so to speak, the limbic system's needs go unmet, dopamine levels drop and the individual will experience depression, anger, mood swings even murderous rage. And here is another snippet of food for thought: as the chocoholic 'needs' their chocolate and then more, so do rapists and sexual killers become addicted to committing their crimes, hence the propensity for their offences to escalate.

If it pleases you, let's take a step back for a moment and, using a laterally alternative psychology, consider this: say, for example, that you are a serious chocoholic. You are not really hungry but you have a sudden craving for it and here is a bar of the finest Swiss chocolate placed in front of you, but your partner says 'NO! Watch your diet'. The thing is that you might not have wanted the chocolate until you'd seen it on the table. Chocoholics insist that it is habit-forming, that it produces an instant feeling of wellbeing, and even that abstinence leads to withdrawal symptoms for when we eat sweet and high-fat foods, including chocolate, serotonin is released, making us feel happier.

But your craving for chocolate intensifies and you need it NOW! You may feel agitated. Your dopamine levels are plummeting. You are starting to feel mildly angry with your partner who is preventing you from satisfying your needs. In extremis you argue. To settle matters, the chocolate is given to you, and your needs being unexpectedly met, all is calm again.

Now, to be honest with you, I have never come across an example of a person killing someone over a bar of chocolate but there are those who have committed murder over the price of a meal.

On Saturday, 14 October 1989, forty-two-year-old Steven Kenneth Staley, with guests Tracey Duke and his girlfriend Brenda Rayburn, sat down for a bite to eat at the Fort Worth Steak and Ale restaurant. At the time he was an escapee from a halfway house in Denver following a four-state crime spree. By all accounts, Staley and his cohorts were unhappy with the meal (after having eaten everything put in front of them) and the service they received. Nevertheless, instead of registering their complaint in the accepted way, he and his companions expressed their dissatisfaction by pulling out an arsenal of semi-automatic weapons and rounding up the restaurant's entire clientele (thirty customers), along with all six staff.

To Staley's warped mind, some compensation was required so the trio ordered everyone to hand over their wallets, and then Staley commanded the manager, thirty-five-year-old Robert Dorsey Read, to open the safe and deposit the takings in a briefcase.

An employee who managed to escape alerted police, and squad cars soon surrounded the building at 7101 Highway 80 West, but the three robbers took Read hostage as the police arrived, then hijacked a car and fled with cops in hot pursuit.

As might be expected, all three villains were caught and arrested after a high-speed chase which ended with their car breaking down. Sadly, Robert Read had already been shot dead. He had been killed by the mindless Staley the moment he was dragged into the car.

The bill for this extravagant night out was extremely high. Staley received the death sentence. The other two were given thirty years each. But this was not quite the end of the matter. After fifteen years on the 'Green Mile' Staley's execution was stayed because his attorney argued that his client was 'incompetent to be put to death'. Allegedly he was psychotic and believed, among other things, that the polygraph machines were controlling and torturing him. To resolve the matter the State of Texas prescribed the condemned man drugs to make him competent and this has caused a furore simply because the legal argument is that one of forbidding a person who is forced to take drugs to make himself better to get executed. Work that one out if you can!

But I am a fair man, so it would be remiss of me not to mention Staley's long history of mental illness, to include paranoid schizophrenia and depression. According to him, his mother – who was also mentally ill – abused him as a child when he was six or seven by trying to pound a wooden stake through his chest. His father was an alcoholic.

Again according to Staley, he tried to kill himself as a teenager. Indeed, doctors who have examined Staley on death row have said that he talks in a robot-like monotone yet has 'grandiose and paranoid' delusions. He says he invented the first motorcar and marketed a character from *Star Trek*. He has given himself black eyes and self-inflicted lacerations and has been found spreading faeces and soaking himself with urine. Now medicated with the anti-psychotic drug Haldol, Staley complained of paralysis and sometimes appeared to be in a catatonic state. For years he has had a bald spot from lying on the floor of his cell night and day.

If ever Staley gets his judicial desserts, he'll probably complain about his last meal too!

A similar denial scenario might apply to drug addicts. Their addiction, their cravings for a particular drug become so intense that they will beg, rob and steal any way they can to satisfy their emotional needs whatever the cost, even if it entails committing burglary, robbery, or even murder.

It may be of interest to note that hard-nosed law enforcement interrogators sometimes – although not so much nowadays – use a similar form of 'emotional denial' when interviewing suspected offenders.

Picture this: here are the cops sitting drinking coffee across a table while munching through a box of doughnuts and, even if they don't smoke, there could be a pack of cigarettes in front of them while you, the interviewee – a three–pack–a–day man – gets zilch!

In this untidy event, out of your comfort zone, you, the suspect, will be stressed. You need comfort food (which is denied) and the smell of hot coffee (also denied) merely adds to the anxiety. God, if you smoke, wouldn't you just love a puff right now! Added to which, this is the cops' playground. They are in complete control of you, and right now they even control what you drink, eat or smoke, when you take a leak, whether you go back home or spend a long time behind bars.

What the suspect doesn't know is that the cops are subconsciously interfering with your senses to feel pleasure or displeasure. In a roundabout way they are jamming up your reward feelings, which can only be fulfilled with a sugary doughnut and coffee-fix if and only if you play their game, with (in US parlance) 'STOP THE FUCK JACKIN' US AROUND – here's a donut, asshole, so stop blowin' smoke in our yard!" coming in short order.

Continuing this analogy, and forgive me for doing so, but for even the average diet–defaming true UK or US male (vegetarians and vegans excluded), getting a whiff of sizzling bacon, gently frying eggs, beans, tomatoes, fried bread and coffee, will make you hungry even if you are not. Then, if your missus orders you to forget it cos you are gonna, sometime later, have a Lo-Cal salad because your mother-in-law has suggested that you should adopt the 5:2 diet . . . hey, guys, killing the both of them could be the way to go.

Well, of course it isn't – but, there are hundreds of killers who have committed murder for even less sensible culinary motives. It's just that a few people go into overdrive, as into extremis, and there is basically nothing complicated at all about it.

Give this some thought next time you smell bacon and eggs!

What I have touched upon in very simplistic terms above is very much confirmed by the general science writer and blogger Carl Zimmer who published a short yet concise article in the US popular science magazine *Discover*, in 2009. 'The Brain: Where Does Sex Live in the Brain? From Top to Bottom' reviewed the origins of research into sex and it provided a summary of the then current thinking of neuroscience's attempts to pinpoint where sex lives in the brain. And live in the brain it certainly does.

It would be redundant of me to include all of Zimmer's piece here because it might throw the reader way off course, nevertheless, 'The Brain: Where Does Sex Live in the Brain? From Top to Bottom' is of interest as it serves, quoting Zimmer: 'to introduce the lay person into the hitherto unexplored neural terrain of sex'.

Further reading of this article may be of some interest to you or it may not; notwithstanding this, and I will be impertinent here by further quoting: 'Sexual desire is defined as the behavioral drive that motivates individuals to *fantasise* about or to seek out sexual activity.' [My italics]'

And this clinical definition from psychologist Annabel Aisha Alley (in Quora.com):

Sexual desire is the culmination of several different neural mechanisms, each is controlled in different areas of the brain and is activated at different times of the sexual experience. The *euphoric* and *pleasurable* experience of sex stems primarily from the limbic system, which is the colloquial term for areas including the amygdala, hippocampus and limbic lobe (dentate and cingulate gyrus). This area is common to all mammals and is considered one of the oldest areas of the brain. *It regulates emotion and encourages the avoidance of painful of aversive stimuli and the repetition of pleasurable experiences.* [My italics]

'Fantasise', 'the repetition of pleasurable experiences' – these resonate, do they not, when we specifically examine the homicidal, morbid psychopathology of individual serial killers who are addicted to committing sexually driven homicide? Their limbic systems, the brain's moral regulating emotional structures, are wired up quite differently from yours and mine.

Putting this another way, let's think of a display of computers on sale in a store. They are all packaged the same way. Upon opening they all look identical and should function as designed. Yet, one single, almost microscopic microcircuit within a chip will cause one particular computer to malfunction. The human brain is prone to malfunction in much the same way.

This, I recognise, is most definitely a layman's analogy (critics take note), nonetheless, the human brain is the most advanced machine that will ever be created. And, while we are programmed to produce 'good' results, in a minority an error, a glitch, in the coding will produce antisocial calculations and serious fuck-ups from time-to-time. Which brings me conveniently to John Christie, the subject of our next chapter.

7

John Reginald Halliday Christie

> For years I knew I had to kill just ten women
> then my work would be finished.
> JOHN CHRISTIE (1899–1953)

From our cradles to our graves, as we meander through life we all have a narrative; a chronicle either good, middling, bad, or most normally a mixture of all three, to become our life's story. But allow me to flesh this out a bit if I may by starting with the following – and this is all backed up by masses of social and criminology research, and the FBI – all coming down to the subject of Nurture and Nature.

It used to be Nurture v. Nature, but that is, more-or-less, old hat these days.

Category 1. Most people have their formative years bedded deep with decent parents from good gene pools. They enjoy a healthy home life, diet, suitable schooling – in other words they are lovingly nurtured from the outset, enabling them to mature into adulthood and become moral, law abiding members of society.

Category 2. Unfortunately, others have their early days built on shifting sands – having to endure troublesome childhoods, abusive or violent parents; perhaps an absent or overbearing father or mother. To even witness alcohol and/ or drug abuse, to live with disrupted schooling, poor diets: all of this can seriously impact on the developing mind, possibly sowing the seeds for what the child grows to perceives as normal behaviour, for him or her to re-enact in the decades to follow. I might say that this would be 'negative parental conditioning', leading to delinquency, an early criminal record and, as ever more lenient prison terms are meted out, this unchecked antisocial behaviour will inevitably lead to an ever-growing spiral of criminal activity – all of which negatively impacts on us all.

As obvious as this may seem, throughout our lives, hour upon hour, day upon day, month after month and year after year, we are faced with a multitude of choices and decisions to make. Those from category 1 (above) are far better equipped to make those determinations in a sensibly informed manner. However, many of the individuals from category 2 are neither mentally healthy nor morally able to make wise, prudent moves. Thus we find that people from this group are more likely to break the law, even commit violent crime, than others; simply because they have been socially programmed to do otherwise. But there are many exceptions, of course there are, so I would foolish to place all my eggs in one basket here, as the account (p. 165) of Colonel Williams will show.

More to the point, when researching any highly dangerous offender's back history – his or her narrative – one should be looking for the 'markers', or the 'way points', let's say, occasions where the individual has gone off course, so, we might be asking ourselves questions, such as:

What brought him to this junction?
Why did he make the decision he chose?
What were the consequences for him and society?
Did he learn from his mistake?
Did he feel or exhibit any genuine remorse?
Did he stop misbehaving and did he reform?

Once we start looking at these issues in depth, we begin to gain a better understanding about what is going on inside a serial killer's head.

During my career as a criminologist, I have spent thousands of hours researching sexually motivated murderers dating back over a century, so very briefly let's take a look at a few of the most notorious, starting with Britain's John Reginald 'Reg' Halliday Christie.

In Christie we have an alleged necrophile – although strictly speaking this was never legally proven – who murdered at least eight women during the 1940s and early 1950s.

In Christie we will discover a man who, while superficially holding himself in high esteem, subconsciously knew otherwise. Like so many criminal psychopaths he was a narcissist who wore many different masks, wearing each one for his particular needs at suitably given times.

To start with, photographs of Christie taken circa the

period encompassing his murders and trial do not show an attractive specimen of manhood. With a high balding dome, a man finding it difficult to smile, a bit priggish and certainly nervous, bordering on anally retentive is what I see. From the looks of him, we might perceive that deep down in his twisted psyche he was afraid of women, for it would seem he had little to no sex with his wife – whom he later killed anyway – added to which, to all intents and purposes he was sexually impotent.

Christie has a criminal antecedent narrative worth further reading; however, there has been very little written, let alone documented about Christie's state of mind, yet his historical narrative undoubtedly tells us that he was a low-achiever; later holding down a menial job as a ledger clerk at the time of his murders, all of which did nothing to support his own self-inflated, high and mighty opinion of himself. Underlying his psychopathology was sexual frustration. The only way he could gain release was having a female under his total control – very much like Michael Ross did as I have briefly explained earlier. Thereafter, the victims became 'disposable', killed then dumped like so much trash.

> Having a cup of tea seems as much a part of my murder career as whisky is with other murderers. For me a corpse has a beauty and dignity, which a living body could never hold. There is a peace about death that soothes me.
>
> JOHN CHRISTIE.

This grim statement from Christie resonates almost precisely with the gruesome remarks made by the likes of American sado-sexual serial killer, Jeffery Lionel Dahmer (1960–1994), aka 'The Milwaukee Monster'. Dahmer committed the rape, murder, and dismemberment of seventeen men and boys between 1978 and 1991.

Dennis Andrew Nilsen (1945–2018) was born in Fraserburgh, Scotland, and, like Dahmer, he was a true necrophile. 'Des' strangled at least twelve young men using a ligature – usually a tie – then he dismembered them.

The only motive that there ever was, was to completely control a person; a person I found physically attractive. And keep them with me as long as possible, even if it meant just keeping a part of them. Then I separated the joints, the arm joints, the leg joints, and had to do two boilings. I think I used four boxes of Soilex for each one, put in the upper portion of the body and boiled that for about two hours and then the lower portion for another two hours. The Soilex removes all the flesh, turns it into a jelly like-like substance and it just rinses off. Then I laid the clean bones in a light bleach solution, left them there for a day and spread them out on either newspaper or cloth and let them dry for about a week in the bedroom.

JEFFERY DAHMER

I could only relate to a dead image of the person I could love. The image of my dead grandfather would be the model of him at his most striking in my mind. It seems necessary for them to have been dead in order that I could express those feelings which were the feelings I held sacred for my grandfather ... it was a pseudo-sexual, infantile love which had not yet developed and matured. The sight of them [my victims] brought me a bitter sweetness and a temporary peace and fulfilment.

DENNIS NILSEN, QUOTED BY BRIAN MASTERS
IN *KILLING FOR COMPANY* (2011)

Using similar kill methods to Dahmer and Nilsen, Christie strangled his victims to death with a ligature after he had rendered them unconscious with domestic gas. Others he raped then strangled as they lay out cold. So whether he was a true necrophile – one who enjoys sex with dead bodies – is a matter still open for debate.

It is true of course that he killed a baby and, a few years later, his own wife, Ethel, but *they* were not objects of his sexual perversions. They were murdered simply for expediency's sake – then, for much the same reason, he allowed Beryl's husband, twenty-five-year-old Timothy Evans, to go to the gallows for the murder of his own wife and his baby daughter Geraldine, when this somewhat simple backward patsy, with the mental age of an eleven-year-old, had killed no one.

Eventually, Christie got his just desserts. He was hanged by Albert Pierrepoint at HM Prison Pentonville, London, on Wednesday, 15 July 1953. His physical particulars and the clothes he'd been wearing when he plunged through the trap were washed clean of excrement and urine, then sent to Madame Tussaud's, in London.

Height: 5ft 7.5 ins.
Size in hats: 6
Waist: 33 ins.
Chest: 36 ins.
Size in shoes: 7 ½.

Colour of eyes: Pale blue-grey.

Name and address of tailors: Reg Faire,
    Portobello Road, W11.

Suit: Blue-grey rough material with large herringbone
    pattern.

Shirt: Bonart. Very pale lilac grey with faint red-stripe.

Shoes: Very round toe-cap; old and in bad condition.

Tie: Very cheap imitation club stripe.

The Sixth Commandment – 'Thou Shalt Not Kill' –
fascinated me . . . I always knew that some day I
should defy it.

. . . My first murder was thrilling because I had embarked
on the career I had chosen for myself, the career of
murder.

JOHN CHRISTIE

We can learn a little more about Christie's psychopathology
when we look back over his life's narrative.

His father, Ernest John Christie, a dour disciplinarian and
ardent churchgoer, was a designer at Crossley Carpets at Dean
Clough Mills. He was the first Superintendent of the St John
Ambulance Brigade, Halifax branch, and as a member of the
Conservative Party, was also a leading light in the Primrose
League. Founded in 1883, this was an organisation that
promoted Conservative principles and patriotism, and on
joining, members had to sign a pledge:

I declare on my honour and faith that I will devote my
best ability to the maintenance of religion, of the estates
of the realm, and of the imperial ascendancy of the

British Empire; and that, consistently with my allegiance to the sovereign of these realms, I will promote with discretion and fidelity the above objects, being those of the Primrose League.

The League was disbanded in 2004.

Mrs Mary Hannah Christie, the daughter of a local businessman and Liberal councillor, was known as 'Beauty Halliday' before her marriage. She was keen on amateur dramatics.

John Christie was born on 8 April 1899, the second youngest of seven – five girls and two boys, the others being Percy (the eldest), Florence ('Cissie'), Effie, Elsie, Winifred and Phyllis ('Dolly'). While very little is known about Elsie, other than that she left home as a youngster to work in Morley, and is believed to have died before 1953, all the other siblings are known to have gone on to be 'normal' people leading normal lives. Percy, the eldest, became a bank manager in Leeds, and died in 1970, Florence died in 1949, Effie in 1918, Winifred in 1968 and Phyllis in 1973.

Percy was to tell the *Yorkshire Post*, following Christie's arrest (on 31 March 1953): 'I have, or had, a brother called John Reginald Christie. But neither myself nor any members of the family have seen or heard of him since he disappeared from Halifax thirty-three years ago.'

All had their mother's maiden name, thus John Christie was John Reginald Halliday Christie; he, and he alone, received a larger share of his mother's attention. He was the runt of the brood. Other children rarely played with him. He dreaded his mean, ill-tempered disciplinarian father and was quick to run to his mother, to hide behind her skirts when Ernest came down hard.

Young John sang in the school choir. He became a scout, then an assistant scoutmaster. He was top of his class in arithmetic and algebra. He was good with his hands, able to repair watches and make toys. To all intents and purposes, everything was pretty good thus far, but it was not long before he started to fall off track.

It seems that there were several occasions in his early youth that had a negative formative influence on Christie, the first of which occurred when he was eight years old. His maternal grandfather died and he viewed the body that had been laid out on a trestle table in the parlour – a common practice back then. This was similar to the experience that Dennis Nilsen had when his grandfather passed away. Christie later described the trembling sensation he felt as both 'fascinating and pleasure', much in the same way as Nilsen had done.

The seeds of morbid curiosity had now been sown.

A second influence was the ongoing dominance his sisters had over him. They, like Christie Sr, were always bossing him about.

The third came in his teens after he had left school and was working in Halifax's Gem Cinema. One day, he with friends went down a lover's lane known as the 'Monkey Run'. They paired off, and Christie ended up with a girl more sexually experienced than him. He could not perform the sexual act, word got around and he became known as 'Reggie-no-Dick' or 'Can't-do-it-Reggie'. He would never forget that humiliation.

The seeds of sexual impotence had been sown.

Aged seventeen, he was working as a clerk for the local police when he was caught stealing tomatoes. Although he was never charged with theft, he lost his job. The overly strict Christie Sr was so mortified that he banned John, who had brought shame on this puritanical family, from the house.

In Christie's mind, the final seeds of family disgrace had now been sown. The runt had been kicked out of the brood and he'd have to fend for himself.

Job after job now followed; in short order he became a drifter, clerk, shoemaker, then clerk again, with intermittent periods of unemployment in between. Sometimes he slept on his father's allotment and his mother would take him food.

If anything could have straightened up Christie it should have been the army, and when he was eighteen, he was called up for service in the First World War and sent to France. Two years later, in June 1918, he was gassed, though exactly how seriously has never been determined. Nevertheless, for a short while he received a military pension, but it is said that a leopard never changes its spots – neither did the black marks writ large over John Christie.

On Thursday, 20 May 1920, he married the placid, passive, dumpy, ultimately ill-fated Ethel Waddington. The couple remained childless until the day he strangled her in bed and buried her under the living-room floorboards thirty-two years later. The motive was probably that he suspected that she had finally cottoned on that he was a killer, or at least up to no good, and intended to leave him, perhaps report what she knew about his dirty secrets to the police. In addition, Christie would have noticed that life was more to his taste on those occasions when she was away visiting family – making this absence permanent was the obvious next step.

And the police certainly knew all about John Christie because:

JOHN REGINALD HALLIDAY CHRISTIE

In 1921, while working as a postman, he was caught stealing money out of letters and was jailed for nine months.

He now had a criminal record.

In 1923, he was arrested for posing as a military officer. This time he was given a break and treated more leniently after claiming he'd been gassed by the Germans during the war. Magistrates bound him over to keep the peace but put him on probation for a violent assault.

Now we know he was a short-tempered and violent man.

The following year Christie was jailed for another nine months, this time at Uxbridge Petty Sessions for larceny.

Christie's criminal narrative was starting to gain pace, although accounts of his next few years vary, his wife had deserted him and he was back into his drifter's life once more.

In 1929, he was again before the courts for attacking a prostitute with whom he was living. The magistrates called it a 'murderous attack' – a portent of things to come – and handed him six months hard labour.

In 1933, after yet another spell behind bars for stealing a car from a Roman Catholic priest who had befriended him in prison, Christie wrote to Ethel. He begged her to come to him, which she did at once, making the biggest mistake of her totally decent life. Then, for who knows what reason, in 1939 he applied as a volunteer with the War Reserve Police and was accepted, becoming a police special constable, which role he held until 1943. This brought him into contact with prostitutes over whom he now held 'power'. You might rightly ask, 'What for fuck's sake was the Metropolitan Police thinking about, employing a man they've been locking up for years? And they give him a uniform too!'

I mean you could not make that up if you tried . . . Sadly, however, it now becomes 'killing time'.

Despite his claims to respectability as a uniformed part-time police officer, a war hero, and also of being a man self-allegedly possessed of some 'medical knowledge', Christie was now spending much of his time in low-class pubs and cafés where he held forth as being someone he wasn't. The people he mingled with were drifters, as were the majority of his victims, who were prostitutes – or, to use the American euphemism, working girls, which sounds kinder. This was the period of post-war rationing and Britain was only just recovering from suffering serious food shortages with folk living through austere times.

Pretty seventeen-year-old Ruth Fuerst lived in a single furnished room in Oxford Gardens. She was an Austrian-born girl who had moved to England in June 1939; a munitions factory worker who sometimes sold her body to make ends meet. In August 1943, Christie strangled her at his home, 10 Rillington Place, Notting Hill, and buried her in his back garden. His wife was away at the time. Not long after, he resigned from the police and found a job at a radio factory in Acton.

Christie gassed and strangled thirty-one-year-old Muriel Amelia Eady, in October 1944, while Ethel was, again, visiting family. Muriel was living with an aunt in Putney and had found work in the same radio factory in Acton. It seems that she was suffering from catarrh, and her kind colleague, Mr Christie, claiming some medical knowledge, invited her to his home, suggesting she try his special inhaler. Her corpse joined Ruth Fuerst's rotting remains.

JOHN REGINALD HALLIDAY CHRISTIE

On Tuesday, 8 November 1949, twenty-year-old Beryl Susanna Evans was strangled to death. Two days later her fourteen-month-old baby daughter, Geraldine, was killed. (The two share a grave at Plot G179 Gunnersbury Cemetery, Acton, Borough of Ealing, West London.)

> When I murdered my wife I removed the one obstacle which for ten years had apparently held me in check. After she had gone the way was clear for me to fulfil my destiny.
>
> JOHN CHRISTIE

Ethel Christie was strangled in her bed in December 1952. She was buried under the living-room floorboards.

With Ethel now out of the way, the killings intensified with three murders committed within as many months.

Pretty twenty-six-year-old Southampton prostitute, Kathleen Maloney, met Christie in a London pub. She was lured back to 10 Rillington Place where she was gassed and strangled in January 1953. Her corpse was concealed in the kitchen alcove.

Rita Nelson from Belfast, twenty-three years old, pregnant and a prostitute, bumped into Christie in a café. She was lured back to Christie's home on the pretence that he could perform an abortion and there she, too, was gassed and strangled. Her body went in the kitchen alcove with Kathleen's.

Finally came Hectorina MacLennan. Scottish-born, the twenty-six-year-old brunette was seeking a room when she knocked on Christie's door. She had seen a 'Room to Let' sign outside. She was gassed and strangled on Friday, 6 March 1953. Her body would join the other two victims in the kitchen alcove – which was pretty much filled up by now.

Hectorina now shares a pauper's grave in Gunnersbury Cemetery, in West London. In most accounts, her age is given as twenty-six, but on the gravestone she is twenty-seven.

It is commonly acknowledged that throughout his life Christie paid a meticulous, overweening attention to detail. I suggest this was a 'superficial' trait, not uncommon amongst psychopathic killers for it becomes part of the 'mask of normality' they wish to present to the outside world, when, psychologically, they are all too different inside. In truth they are pretending to be what are not, and we will see an excellent example of this when we look at Neville Heath shortly.

When Christie was in the army, one of his instructors asked him to leave his exercise book behind as an example of care and neatness for other recruits.

When he was in prison, his fellow cons quickly learnt of his obsession with physical cleanliness. On one occasion an inmate offered him a drag on a cigarette. Christie replied, 'No thanks; it's been in your mouth. No offence of course, but you mustn't judge me by how I look at the moment, my boy. These aren't my proper clothes. I even keep my personal linen spotless.'

For me, this almost insignificant wave-of-the-hand response to the offer of a puff on a cigarette must tell us more about Christie's psychopathology than at first sight; indeed it really allows us another opportunity to drill down into the mindset of someone who has a fragile ego and subconsciously a very low opinion of himself altogether. This affected manner is almost always found amongst charlatans and con artists. Here, Christie is using speech and behaviour not natural to him and solely designed to impress others – his fellow inmates – whom he deemed much lower in the social order than himself.

All taken together, this points to him also having an obsessive-compulsive disorder (OCD); a mental anxiety disorder characterised by uncontrollable, unwanted thoughts and ritualised, repetitive behaviours one feels compelled to perform. OCD affects people of all ages and walks of life, and occurs when an individual gets caught in a cycle of obsessions and compulsions. Obsessions, by their very nature, are unwanted intrusive thoughts, images or urges that trigger intensely distressing feelings. In a person such as Christie, with him knowing that he wasn't the achiever he strived to be, it was as if he were subconsciously and compulsively trying to wash his own bullshit away.

And I will take this all-that-glitters-is-not-gold superficiality a little further by drawing a comparison between Christie and the British killer John David Guise Cannan. My book, *Ladykiller* (1993), written with Robin Odell, is the definitive work on this sexually motivated murderer. What, however, struck me when researching *Ladykiller* was his chameleon-like personality. Well-dressed, well educated, from a solid middle-class family, tall, handsome, romantic to a fault, beautifully spoken; a man of impeccable tastes – he was, at face value, a real ladykiller, with women swooning over him. Nevertheless, behind this façade was a highly dangerous, violent, cold-blooded psychopathic sexual predator with numerous rapes, two confirmed kills and probably a few more come to that in his extensive criminal history.

He was also broke. My examination of his banking records supplied to me by the Avon and Somerset Constabulary proved that he was not just well overdrawn but skint. He didn't have a pot to piss in. John was bouncing cheques all over the place.

In this respect of shallowness, I was drawn to the shiny black BMW car he drove. It was the bottom of the range 'entry model', the sort of car people buy just for the badge and to be able to boast, 'Yes, but I own a BMW!' You know the type, I am sure. However, just like Cannan himself – all fancy shop-front window but full of cheap crap inside – his 'Beemer' was the same, for when I opened the boot I found it jampacked with rubbish and clutter; a pair of handcuffs were discovered in the jack-well, an imitation revolver in the glove compartment along with lengths of white washing line which he used to tie up his victims. It was an utter mess; enough to completely fill two large plastic bin liners, all very much in line with Cannan's psychopathology.

The same applied to Cannan's flat at Foye House in Bristol. Yes, it was neat and tidy. Yes, it was tastefully furnished, I'll give him that, but this was all show; a place to entertain his many conquests and where he could demonstrate his cooking skills, pop a champagne cork or two, yet, what was in his garage? A hastily repainted Mini Clubman, fitted with the false number plates SLP 386S. The original tax disc was for a vehicle - index No. HWL 507N, expiry date Monday, 29 February 1988. No. 2665371. This was found by police in his attaché case. Shirley Anne Banks, the owner of the car had been in Cannan's flat. He killed her and dumped her battered body in a stream. The phony number plate, SLP 386S, was a spiteful nod to the missing, presumed murdered London estate agent, Suzy Lamplugh, being his third victim and who disappeared in 1986.

We can see almost precisely the same shallow behavioural traits being exhibited by John Christie who boasted to his drinking companions and colleagues that he was a substantial property owner with a nice neat back garden. He was someone of importance in the community. He let rooms and his tenants held him in high esteem. Indeed, one of his neighbours, Mrs Patricia Pichler, who, then aged eleven, lived at No. 3 Rillington Place, a few doors down from Christie, told Nick Duerden, writing for the *Independent* on Monday, 5 December 2016: 'Mr Christie was the poshest man on the street, the smartest. He was someone to be respected. Honestly, I only have good memories of him. Really, no one suspected a thing. '

You can see further inside his head now, yes? If you can, you know by now that he was the consummate liar– 'All mouth and no trousers', as the saying goes. The 'property' was a stinking shambles, and although he was merely a tenant himself who illegally sub-let other rooms, his 'tenants' could expect little by the way of privacy.. The stairs were so narrow that two people couldn't pass on them at the same time. The only lavatory was in the junk-filled barren back garden.

Cramped inside their tiny terraced homes, the residents of Rillington Place gathered on the road to relax and gossip. Strangers would most certainly have given cause to comment, but Christie's aloofness and veneer of respectability protected him from the prying eyes of his neighbours.

Christie, however, was not above sticking his nose into the affairs of others. He bored a hole in the wall above his kitchen door so that he could watch all callers to the house. It was through this hole he leched over the goings and comings of pretty Beryl Evans; to then creep out and secretly watch her sashay up the stairs to her rooms. What a devious little man he was!

Now, what of this serial killer's victimology (in this instance to mean the preferred type of victim), his modus operandi and his modus vivendi?

Just like so many homicidal sexual psychopaths, John Christie found easy, gullible prey in the vulnerable. For decades, all across the world, thousands of prostitutes have provided for easy pickings because they are self-employed in the 'oldest profession'. By the very nature of their 'work', these 'working girls' often place themselves at great risk of being abused, beaten, raped and even killed. John Christie knew this. Even as a mere WRC (War Reserve Constable) he'd had the power to arrest prostitutes, harass and cajole them; even advise and, comfort them; he knew their failings and weaknesses. Even after he'd left the police, he had the patter and would have been quick to let them know he was a former police officer, and with his wife frequently away visiting relatives, he was well able to invite the down-on-their-luck women back to his home for a few nights – food thrown in for free He was allegedly a man with medical knowledge, so who could distrust him? To think that his intentions were anything but honourable or murderous would have been the last thing on their minds. To these women he must have seemed like a blessing in disguise.

It goes without saying that not all of Christie's victims were street girls. Ruth Fuerst, Kathleen Maloney, Rita Nelson and Hectorina MacLennan certainly had prior convictions for prostitution. On the other hand, Muriel Eady was a work colleague who made the mistake of trusting Christie.

As far as is known, Christie committed no further murders for the five years following the Muriel's killing, probably solely because of Ethel's presence – as his words quoted earlier make chillingly clear. His next confirmed murder was that of Beryl Evans. It took place during the daytime of Tuesday, 8 November 1949, in the top-floor bedroom occupied by her, her husband Timothy, and their baby daughter. The lecher in Christie became particularly fascinated by the pretty, petite young woman and he zeroed in. This sexual fantasist wanted to have sex with her and that was that. Yet, he would patiently wait until it would be offered up on a plate to him, and it soon was.

In the summer of 1949, Beryl fell pregnant for the second time. She was dismayed. The couple were all but on the breadline. Timothy liked his drink. There was rent to pay. The baby had her needs to be met, they had little money coming in, added to which there were hire-purchase payments to make, so she decided to have an abortion.

None of today's free counselling services existed back then. The National Health Service had only been set up in 1948, concentrating on physical ailments, basic mental care, dental care and spectacles. It was not geared to subjects like abortion or illiteracy, and the dim-witted Timothy Evans certainly was illiterate: he could hardly read or write.

Now faced with Beryl's determination to abort the pregnancy, Timothy Evans had no one to turn to. He was trapped between his staunchly Roman Catholic background and Christie's charlatan expertise as an allegedly decorated soldier who had served and had been gassed in the war. 'Mr Christie' was – Evans believed - his landlord. He had been a police officer, he possessed 'medical knowledge on matters of abortion', which remained illegal in Britain until 1967. These medical matters were known 'only to doctors and learned medical men', whispered the perverted Christie.

After making enquiries, Beryl found that there was a back-street abortionist just a few miles away in the Edgware Road who would help her on payment of £1.00, a sum the Evans could ill-afford, so she told several people about this – including Mr Christie.

Now Christie's trap was closing for he had convinced Beryl that he could perform an abortion on her in the house. It was all totally illegal, he stressed. It had its risks, he told her as she looked with tearful trust into his eyes.

When Beryl discussed this with her husband, he spoke to Christie who showed him what he called 'one of my medical books'.

Evans stared at it.

This 'medical book' was nothing more than a St John's Brigade first-aid manual (of which organisation, ironically, his father had been a superintendent when Christie was a child). But Christie knew that Evans couldn't read. Moreover, the drawings would impress him. To naive Tim the medical illustrations looked 'professional'.

Timothy Evans reluctantly agreed to the kind offer from sly Christie, who, in his self-appointed role of 'landlord', had also told the couple that if they had another child they would be evicted, therefore he would also be unable to furnish them with landlord references when they sought future accommodation.

The trap had been sprung!

Shortly, thereafter, while Evans was a minute's walk away at work at a local baker's on the corner of St Mark's Road and Rillington Place, Christie laid Beryl on her bed, covered her face with a mask. He told her that the procedure would numb any pain, then he piped coal gas through a rubber tube into a water solution, suffocating her to death. During her wide-eyed gasping death struggle he probably ejaculated. Whether he had sex with her dead body is unknown.

Two days later, Christie strangled to death Beryl's baby girl.

Sadly, there is no room in this book for the flight, arrest, trial and conviction and hanging of the innocent Timothy Evans. This is best left for the reader to study at another time. However, I strongly recommend *10 Rillington Place* written by my late friend Ludovic Kennedy. Even better, watch the 1971 movie of the same name starring Richard Attenborough (Christie), John Hurt (Timothy Evans) and Judy Geeson (Beryl Evans). It is an absolute bum-on-seats must-watch!

Ludovic Kennedy believed Christie was a necrophiliac. With what evidence that is available I would somewhat sit on the fence here, and we heatedly debated the issue over lunch at Langan's Brasserie in Mayfair many years before dear Ludo passed away. Nevertheless, at the time of the case the consensus of public opinion was that Christie was mad when, by every legal definition, he most certainly was not.

Referring back to the very start of this chapter I mentioned that there are times in our lives, our histories, when decisions have to be made. We can unwittingly, or deliberately, make totally antisocial choices – the latter which Christie certainly did perhaps more times than we know about.

Could Christie have corrected himself? Of course he could have, and he should have, yet he sailed on regardless. In doing so he knew what the consequences would be if he were found out – '. . . to be hanged by the neck until you be dead', which he was. Indeed, after effectively sending the innocent Timothy Evans to the gallows, he, the pillar of the community, 'Mr Christie', believed himself untouchable and kept on killing. But so many 'organised' serial killers who carefully plan their crimes, more often than not fail to give the same detail of consideration to concealing the deed now done, and Christie was no exception.

It would be fair to say that he escaped by the skin of his teeth after killing Beryl Evans and her child, thanks largely to police incompetence. What a breath-taking relief that would have been to him. He'd outwitted the law and justice itself. So now this arrogant man went from bad to worse, being stupid enough to leave decomposing bodies all around his property for the next horrified tenant of 10 Rillington Place to sniff out and for the police to find.

It was a bit late in the day when, on 18 October 1966, Timothy John Evans was granted a free posthumous pardon. His remains were recovered from within the grim walls of HMP Pentonville and moved to a new consecrated grave at St Patrick's Catholic Cemetery, Leytonstone in Essex. Perhaps it would have been more appropriate for him, Beryl and their baby daughter to have been laid to rest as a family – which, in their tragically short life together they certainly were.

According to Home Office Burial Records, Christie's Pentonville Prison grave, aka the Pentonville Prison Cemetery, Islington, London, remains unmarked. It is close to the exercise yard and up against the prison wall. After autopsy, due to lack of space his body was placed into a hessian sack and dumped on top of other corpses, all of which will slowly turn to dust then fade away. 'Rillington Place' was changed to 'Ruston Mews' in 1954. All of the original houses were finally demolished in 1970.

8

Peter Kürten

I am often asked the somewhat vague question: 'Who do you think is the worst serial killer of all time?' and my answer usually is: 'They are all truly evil but if you look up the meaning of "evil" in a dictionary you might find Peter Kürten's face staring back at you.' And, for this reason I have included him in this book. Indeed, Kürten transcends evil by miles for if ever there were a *real* monster, Peter Kürten was he. Even his psychiatrist, Dr Karl Berg, labelled him the 'King of Sexual Perverts', so we cannot really judge Kürten as anything but a homicidal sado-sexual maniac. By my reckoning he has to be amongst the worst of the Devil's Spawn. He can also be thought of as the first psychologically studied and interviewed serial killer of the twentieth century.

The word 'sadism' comes from the erotic and licentious writings of the Marquis de Sade, a French nobleman born in 1740. Up until his death in 1814, aged seventy-four, de

Sade scandalised his contemporaries by advocating the free expression of sexual instincts.

At the age of eighteen, de Sade was sentenced to a year's imprisonment for the flagrant mistreatment and use of a young prostitute. After being imprisoned in the Bastille, he relieved his boredom – most likely also his sexual frustrations – by reliving his fantasies in writing sexually explicit plays and novels.

Of further interest is that we find this 'use of prostitutes' (working girls, if you prefer) to satisfy men's 'secret' sexual/ fantasy needs – services not available at home with a wife or a partner – running through all working-girl killings. It is that 'use and abuse' scenario being played out time and again right up until the present day.

With sadomasochists, the suffering may be real or it may just be fantasised, yet those fantasies, as we see so often, form part of the graduation from fantasising, as in reading or watching internet porn depicting violent sexual scenes, to stalking, sexual assault, rape, serial rape, then on to sexually-motivated homicide. Yet, it has to be said that sadomasochism is found in heterosexual and homosexual relations too.

Masochists seem to outnumber sadists. For this reason, 'bondage' and 'discipline' services are widely on offer as a form of prostitution. For some masochists, self-inflicted pain can be a stimulus for sexual arousal – though for the average sexually healthy person it might seem a bit extreme to have to be tied up in chains, struggling into a black plastic suit, donning a mask, have an orange stuck in one's mouth and being well and truly thrashed by a twenty-six-stone bleach-blonde Miss Whiplash just to get one's 'rocks off'!

Most of the time, however, sadism and masochism are

restricted to fantasy or simulation. But some sadists do commit murder and mutilate. Nonetheless, the typical sadistic killer can often be an introverted and timid person, which Kürten was not. In a male, he may be preoccupied with what he sees as his own inadequate or poorly developed genitalia. His actual sexual performance with a partner may be poor and he may inflict pain to assure himself of his power, and we can include the despicable Peter Kürten in this category.

> In the case of [Rosa] Ohliger, I also sucked blood from the wound on her temple, and from [Rudolf] Scheer from the stab in his neck. From the girl [Gertrude] Schulte I only licked the blood from her hands. It was the same with the swan in the Hofgarten. I used to stroll at night through the Hofgarten very often, and in the spring of 1930 I noticed a swan sleeping at the edge of the lake. I cut its throat. The blood spurted up and I drank from the stump and ejaculated.
>
> PETER KÜRTEN (1883–1931)

Kürten, a German serial murderer, was dubbed by the media the 'Vampire of Düsseldorf', or the 'Düsseldorf Monster'. Here we find a sado-sexual opportunist killer harbouring a morbid love of blood; a sexual predator who committed a series of murders and sexual assaults in and around the city, with his victim-types and MO varying over time.

> I have no remorse. As to whether recollection of my deeds makes me feel ashamed, I will tell you. Thinking back to all the details is not all unpleasant. I rather enjoy it.
>
> PETER KÜRTEN

Although much has already been written about Peter Kürten, we will see that some aspects of his work and domestic life match with those of John Christie, for, at face value, he was polite, soft-spoken, seemingly well-educated, and just like Christie he was fastidious in his dress and appearance. To all intents and purposes, Kürten, like Christie, appeared to be a 'non-threatening' individual, and, as with most serial murderers, you would not have glanced twice at him if he passed you in the street.

This is precisely what makes this killer breed so lethally dangerous.

Again, almost mirroring Christie, Kürten was married and lived quietly with Frau Kürten in a small apartment at 71 Mettmanner Straße, while always maintaining a lifestyle of respectable mediocrity. Again, like Christie, this was all a front. However, here we find slight difference between the marital arrangements, for although both men rarely had sex with their wives (mainly because they were both fixated on only getting sexual satisfaction through killing their helpless victims), Christie's marriage was one of convenience and for appearance's sake, while Kürten actually 'doted' on his spouse, and we will see more of this shortly.

Teach your children moral behaviour or they'll be in court all the time.

JUDGE JUDITH 'JUDY' SCHEINDLIN

Peter Kürten came into this world on Saturday, 26 May 1883 at Mulheim am Rhein, across the river from Stadtkreis Köln (Cologne) in what is now the state of Nordrhein-Westfalen, Germany,. Born to a dirt-poor family, he was the eldest of thirteen children, two of whom died at an early age, and they all lived in a cluttered one-bedroomed apartment. Various sources ascribe to him as being the third sibling, elsewhere he is the fifth child and other times he was the eldest, so, please make of this as you will.

Nevertheless, the matriarch was occasionally with the drink to drown her sorrows because the patriarch who was a sand-caster (moulder) in a timber factory by trade and a brutal out-and-out alcoholic.

Aside from this, it comes down to us that Frau Kürten was a sort of mother hen to her clutch of kids. Herr Kürten, on the other hand, when in his cups, often forced his wife and children into a room before ordering her to strip naked and raping her as the kids looked on. Therefore, we can be sure that she suffered from extreme physical and psychological abuse throughout her married life, as did the children from the moment they were born. Indeed, she was so miserable that she openly begged her husband to kill her to end it all; however, she didn't want to leave her children behind so she just got on with life as best she could.

According to testimony Kürten later gave to his psychiatrist, Professor Karl Berg, he was already a killer aged nine; claiming that he had murdered two of his playmates while rafting on the River Rhine. He had pushed one lad into the water knowing he couldn't swim and, when his playmate attempted to save him, Kürten pushed the kid's head under the water. There is no doubt that two of Kürten's pals did drown; however, with him denying it, and telling police the two kids had simply fallen into the water, it was ruled as two accidental deaths.

Although he was a good scholar, Kürten certainly had a dysfunctional childhood, and we can't take that away from him, for his formative years were an unmitigated disaster. Indeed, he had the worst childhood that anyone could wish for, added to which he had been initiated into bestiality by the local authority's dogcatcher who lodged in the same building as the Kürtens. It was he who taught the young lad how to torture the animals he caught. Taken together, there can be no doubt in anyone's mind that these extreme forms of abuse had negatively impacted on the lad's mind.

To escape his father's mistreatment, young Kürten often ran away from home; sometimes he was away for days, even weeks. Constant absenteeism from school or running away from home is another marker of emerging juvenile delinquency, and this is supported by us knowing that during these periods he lived rough on the streets; mixing with pettifoggers and thieves; stealing whatever wasn't nailed down to clothe himself and eke out an existence.

At the risk of repeating myself, I refer to the previous chapter, on John Christie, where I wrote:

Unfortunately, others have their early days built on shifting sands – having to endure troublesome childhoods, abusive or violent parents; perhaps an absent or overbearing father or mother. To even witness alcohol and/or drug abuse, to live with disrupted schooling, poor diets: all of this can seriously impact on the developing mind, possibly sowing the seeds for what the child grows to perceive as normal behaviour for him, or her, to re-enact in the decades to follow. I might say that this would be 'negative parental conditioning', leading to delinquency, an early criminal record and, as ever more lenient prison terms are meted out, this unchecked antisocial behaviour

will inevitably lead to an ever-growing spiral of criminal
activity, all of which negatively impacts on us all.

One of the FBI's predictors for a young child developing a
serious antisocial personality disorder as he or she matures is
most likely to be by the way he or she is treated by his or her
parents during the formative years. Therefore, it is during this
precious time that a child's brain soaks up information like a
sponge; drinking in every bit the kid can take. Therefore, it is
this 'parental imprinting'; this 'indoctrination' of everything
that is going on around the child that will form the basis – the
psychological foundations – for all that is to come.

Although it is not a scenario to be cast in stone, I look at
this from a 'layer cake' perspective: day-after-day, week-after-
week, month-in-month-out, a child from a dysfunctional
form is subjected to layer upon layer of different forms of
psychological and physical abuse until it begins to accept
maltreatment as being the norm. In other words, the child
becomes numbed to it. I use the term 'indoctrination' because
we are inescapably shaped by familial and cultural context,
and thus some degree of indoctrination/learning – be it
good or bad – in parent-child social-imprinting relationships
all have an essential function in the formation of any child's
development in becoming a good person, or a bad person, in
the years to come.

Solely for the purposes of this book, there is a fine line
to be drawn between 'indoctrination' and 'learning' and
this distinction often lies in the eyes of the beholder. Some
authorities distinguish 'indoctrination' from 'education' on the
basis that the indoctrinated person is expected not to question
or critically examine the doctrine they are being exposed to.

We find this with cults and extreme religious factions where brain- or mind-washing takes place.

Where I find this particularly applicable in young children who metamorphose into criminals is that most youngsters are simply not in the position to question or critically examine their parents or their teachers even when the adults are wrong. The young child learns from, is taught by, its parents; the Latin word for 'to teach', *docere*, being the root of 'indoctrinate', and originally this is exactly what it meant.

FBI offender profiler, John Douglas, says that Peter Kürten's overall behaviour exhibited all of the signs of a serial killer, based on the fact that he 'reacted to a chronically abusive upbringing when he engaged in violence toward animals and set fires. He abused animals because it gave him control, something he did not have as the victim of his father's beatings.' Douglas adds, 'He set fires because it also gave him sense of control over other people.'

John Douglas's observation can rightly be applied to the majority of fully emerged serial killers and this is why, out of the hundreds of case histories concerning these monsters, we see the same 'victim control' psychopathology running throughout, and that is why Kürten is such an excellent example for us to study.

Therefore, if there is any mitigation for Kürten's later horrendous rape and killing time – which there really isn't – we are obliged at least to take his early years, the physical and psychological abuse he suffered, into consideration because if anyone was born on the wrong side of the tracks, he was! To quote C. L. Swinney, author of *Monster: The True Story of Serial Killer Peter Kürten*: 'Of course he [Kürten] needed to be held responsible for his acts, and I would never condone his behavior, but those wishing not to acknowledge the contributing factors [abusive childhood] to creating one of Europe's most vile serial killers are fooling themselves.'

In 1896, thirteen-year-old Kürten met a girl of his own age. Somewhat echoing his imprinted experiences when his mother was forced to undress and have sex with her husband in front of Peter and his siblings, we might assume that young Kürten became quasi-erotic during these events for he asked this girl to undress and have sex with him. While at first seeming happy to comply – probably brought about by some form of coercion – she denied him sex. To satisfy himself Kürten resorted to committing bestiality with sheep, pigs and goats to achieve ejaculation – an offence that had been made illegal in the German Empire in 1871. It was now a crime punishable by imprisonment, but this did not deter young Kürten, who at such a young age was already an emerging sexual sadist. Years later, after his arrest for serial homicide, Kürten told his psychiatrist that he could only achieve an orgasm with these animals by stabbing and slashing them to death with increasing ferocity.

In our more enlightened times, clinicians and therapists refer to this condition a hypersexuality disorder, a disorder that affects both men and women to varying degrees, and is commonly known as 'satyriasis' in men and 'nymphomania' in women. Some medical professionals do not acknowledge such pathology exists, asserting that the condition merely reflects a cultural dislike of exceptional sexual behaviour, so there is debate over it. Nevertheless, what we do find in Peter Kürten's psychopathology are compulsive masturbation; compulsive sexual behaviour; hyperphilia; problematic hypersexuality; sexual addiction; sexual compulsivity; sexual dependency; out-of-control sexual antisocial behaviour and paraphilia. Link all of that to bestiality and his utterly dysfunctional earlier years and to the fact that he had already murdered two of his schoolmates when he was just nine, we have pretty much a fully-blown homicidal psychopath who is bound to wreak havoc on society in the very near future.

This is a chilling scenario, indeed, and, when we delve deep into the heads of most sexually motivated predatory serial murderers past or present, John Christie, for example, or Michael Ross, Henry Lee Lucas, John Wayne Gacy, Ted Bundy, Kenneth Bianchi, Harvey Carignan, Arthur Shawcross, Peter Sutcliffe and more, we can find similar back-narratives running through all of their sick minds like threads of steel wire in a type of almost overwhelming sexually compulsive homicidal sexual disorder, an obsessive–compulsive disorder (OCD) of a most extreme sort.

It was 1897. Peter Kürten at the age of fourteen years old had finished school. He then ran away from home repeatedly until his father, sick and tired of this, got him a woodwork apprenticeship at his own place of work. To repay his father, young Peter, after a year or so there, broke into the place and stole around 300 marks (*roughly* equivalent to £3,600 or US$4,700), a not inconsiderable sum in those impoverished times. Four days after the burglary he was arrested and sent to a juvenile detention centre where he spent one month in custody. In November 1899 – according to Kürten's 1930 confessions – he strangled a young woman while they were having sex in a wood and left her for dead. As no body was ever found, and no complaint against Kürten was made, it is to be presumed that she survived, recovered and chose to say nothing about her experience.

But now it was time for Kürten Sr to get his comeuppance. During the course of Peter's burglary investigation, police interviewed Frau Kürten and her children and, in doing so, they learned that he had been forcing himself on his thirteen-year-old daughter. He was arrested and sent to prison for three years. This was the break Frau Kürten had been praying for. She obtained a separation order, relocated to Düsseldorf, and, years later, remarried, none of which was any good for young Peter.

After his short stint at the reform school Kürten continued his career in crime, adding arson to his repertoire. He set ablaze haylofts and barns; thrilled to bits as everything went up in flames and smoke while hoping that a tramp may have been sleeping in the hay.

There is no doubt that Kürten was not just a pyromaniac – that is to say a person who has a compulsive desire to set fire to things – but also suffered from pyrophilia – becoming sexually aroused by setting fires. Kürten admitted as much, telling his psychiatrist: 'I got pleasure from the glow of the fire, the cries of help. It gave me so much pleasure that I got sexual satisfaction.'

In 1996 I interviewed the US serial killer Henry Lee Lucas on death row in Texas. Henry told me that he and his sidekick, Ottis Toole, set fires just for the fun of it – to stand back then masturbate as they watched the fire services rush to the scene and extinguish the flames. With Kürten, it was the same, as he carried out part of the 'revenge' on society that, while in custody, he'd vowed to take.

He was a very angry young man, indeed he was; he attempted eight strangulations, carried out two axe attacks and numerous acts of arson. He was in prison for a large part of twenty years, the longest stretch lasting from 1905 until 1913. And German society wouldn't have to wait too long after his release before he struck again and he did so with a ferocity that is more terrifying than any inventive horror screenplay writer could come up with.

Kürten's first confirmed murder was of ten-year-old Christine Klein. Her savvy businessman father, Peter, was the owner of the 'Wirtshaus Peter Klein Schenke', a three-storey tavern/inn at one corner of a busy Mülheim an der Ruhr intersection, making it a popular place to drink and to stay.

Thirty-year-old Kürten had been robbing places for months and as a customer he knew landlord Klein. This, however, did not deter him from attempting to burgle the place. During the night of Sunday, 25 May 1913, he carried out his intention to break into the premises in order to take whatever jewellery and cash he could lay his hands on.

The Kleins were asleep and he crept around the place until he suddenly spied ten-year-old Christine in bed. She was wearing pyjamas and tucked up under thick covers. Almost instantly he dismissed the idea of robbing the premises and decided to rape and kill the little girl. For a few seconds Christine might have thought that she was having a nightmare because after his arrest Kürten recalled that she woke up and struggled for some time as he strangled her with his bare hands while rocking her head backwards and forwards. He then slit her throat from ear to ear. The sight of the gaping wound, its now vivid blood-red colour and the gurgling noise it made sent Kürten into a sexual frenzy. He began cuddling the dead child while masturbating until he ejaculated over her – then he quietly left. Ironically, Kürten dropped his handkerchief embroidered with the initials 'PK', thus initially throwing suspicion upon the distraught Peter Klein of murdering his own daughter.

> I broke into a house in the Wolfstrasse – an inn owned by Klein . . . I went up to the first floor. I opened different doors and found nothing worth stealing; but in the bed I saw a sleeping girl of about ten covered with a thick feather bed . . . I drew her head over the edge of the bed and penetrated her [genitals] with my fingers.
>
> I had a small but sharp pocket knife with me and I held the child's head and cut her throat. I heard the blood spurt and drip on the mat beside the bed. It spurted in an arch, right over my hand. The whole thing lasted about three minutes. Then I went, locked the door and went back home to Düsseldorf.
>
> PETER KÜRTEN'S RECOLLECTION OF THE
> MURDER OF CHRISTINE KLEIN

The following day he returned and sat drinking a beer in a café directly opposite Klein's inn at once gloating at all of the police activity going on around him. This was a practice he would later repeat time and again; moreover, we often see this perverse behaviour acted out by many other serial killers too.

If anything could have put Kürten back on track it should have been military service. The year was 1914, and war had broken out; Kürten was thirty-one-years old when conscripted into the Kaiser's Imperial German Army (Deutsches Heer). It is fair to say that he went willingly but after seeing men dying in deplorable numbers he deserted. He hated his own country. He detested just about everyone he came across and he did not like being ordered about because it reminded him of how his father had treated him as a youngster.

When he was finally caught he was sent to a military prison where he spent the remainder of the war. But did prison change him, did it, heck? During his incarceration he was the most troublesome of inmates. He spent much of his time in solitary confinement where he enjoyed being left alone and away from everyone else. Very much like Christie, he looked down on the guards and fellow prisoners alike, believing that he was intellectually and socially above all others, with him later saying: 'I'd think about attacking staff and inmates, setting the place on fire. Actually, I'd like to sabotage the railways to kill as many people as possible.' He was freed in 1921 aged thirty-eight.

Immediately after his release from prison, Kürten went to his sister's home in Altenburg. Using devious tactics employed by so many serial killers, he reinvented himself as a former 'prisoner of war' – which tongue-in-cheek he was in a sense – and declared that he had been recently released by the Russians. He stayed for several years and it was here that he met his future wife.

The polar opposite of the prim and proper Ethel Christie, it has to be said that Kürten's wife-to-be was no shrinking violet. She had been a prostitute and had been jailed for four years for shooting a man who jilted her after promising marriage. Nevertheless, she had recanted her sins; now believing that whatever fate came forth it was her duty to endure in order to redeem her sinful past – surely her marriage to Kürten would not be one made in heaven? Nevertheless, she accepted Kürten's offer of wedlock, later accepting his infidelities and criminality apparently without complaint. From where we sit now, and with the great gift of hindsight, it seems to us obvious that she thought that dapper Peter was about the best she would ever get, and did she pick a 'wrong-un', oh yes, she did!

According to statements Frau Kürten later made to police, her husband never treated her badly which is somewhat at odds with what others close to the couple were to claim; Kürten himself was adamant that it had only been possible to have very infrequent sex with his wife by fantasising about violent sex with someone else.

In 1925, it seems that Kürten made a, let's say superficial, effort to reform. I say 'superficial effort' simply because dyed-in-the-wool sociopaths can never change their spots as they are not psychologically wired up to do so.

For a while he returned to his former work as a moulder in a large woodworking factory. He became a trade unionist and was politically active – well, after all is said and done, he now had a wife to support – but he still went out on the prowl seeking brutal sexual encounters.

Can you now see this Jekyll and Hyde character at large just like Christie – even Peter Sutcliffe, aka the 'Yorkshire Ripper', and countless more of their ilk because their homicidal mindsets, without a single exception, take to wearing masks of 'normality' while hiding the beasts sleeping within?

Needless to say, Altenburg was too small a town to contain this pervert's desires. In 1925 the Kürtens made the decision to move to Düsseldorf. Unfortunately, history does not tell us why the couple made this move but I suggest it was because he had not long been charged with sexual assault. His wife had intervened to save him from further proceedings and the quiet, sleepy Altenburg was no longer the place to be.

> The place where I attacked Frau Kühn I visited again that same evening twice and later several times. In doing so, I sometimes had an orgasm.
>
> PETER KÜRTEN ON THE ATTACK
> ON FRAU KÜHN

Sunday, 3 February 1929: while walking through a snowy Düsseldorf during his lunch break Kürten spotted elderly Frau Maria Kühn. He followed her for a while and felt an erection forming in his trousers. Swiftly he grabbed her by the lapels and managed to pull her into bushes. In all, he stabbed her at least twenty-four times, with scissors, but she managed to survive because although many of the stabs he inflicted went so deep they impacted on bone.

> When that morning I poured petrol over the child Ohliger and set fire to her, I had an orgasm at the height of the fire.
>
> PETER KÜRTEN TO POLICE ON THE
> MURDER OF ROSA OHLIGER

On Saturday, 9 February 1929, eight-year-old Rosa Ohliger had been playing near her home when Kürten noticed her. He waited for a chance to pounce, which he did when she strayed a little too far. He grabbed her from behind cupping her mouth and trying to choke her unconscious. Carrying her some fifty yards into a nearby heavily wooded area he took out his scissors and stabbed Rosa three times in the neck and heart killing her almost instantly. Now possessed with having sex with the dead body, despite already having had an orgasm, something made him stop. He had a sixth animal sense he was being watched. He panicked. He didn't want to get caught so he moved her body a little further away and pushed Rosa under a hedge. He then, according to his own account, went to the cinema before going home. Early in the morning he crept out of bed and, picking up a bottle of petrol, returned to the child's body, doused her and set her alight, hoping to burn away any evidence connecting him to the killing. As she started to catch fire the smell of the sizzling flesh gave him another erection. Then he made a run for it using trees as cover and was back home in minutes.

Later that morning he returned to the area. Drinking Altbier in a nearby tavern, he watched the public and police commotion and he even went as far as talking to an officer for twenty minutes about what had occurred.

Although Rosa's body was badly burned, at autopsy it was determined that her killer had also stabbed her in the stomach, temple and genitalia, spontaneously ejaculating as he stabbed the child and spilling his semen over her knickers and inserting it into her vagina with his smeared fingers.

Thursday, 14 February 1929: the Flingern-Nord suburb of Düsseldorf became the location for the next murder scene when the dead body of forty-five-year-old Rudolf Scheer was found lying by the side of a road. Apparently, Scheer was a well-respected mechanic. He had been stabbed to death. Once again Kürten brazenly revisited the crime scene and ingratiated himself with the police, saying: 'I hope you catch the bastard soon.'

This ingratiating himself with police reminds me of the post-killing behaviour of New York serial killer Arthur 'Art' John Shawcross whom I interviewed at the Sullivan Correctional Facility, Fallsburg, NY, on 29 and 30 September 1994. I have extensively covered the life and crimes of 'Art' in my *Talking with Serial Killers* (2003, 2018).

After several of his murders, Shawcross would drive to places where the cops were eating and chat to them about the sex slayings now terrorising the city of Rochester. Indeed, he told me that he enjoyed the feelings of power and control he gained from this; secretly gloating that there he was chatting to police and they hadn't a single clue as to who he really was.

Between February and August 1929, Peter Kürten took a relative break from his killing – half-strangling four women before returning to his murderous ways – but he hadn't really started yet. Indeed, he wasn't even off the starting blocks . . .

Sunday, 11 August 1929 witnessed the strangulation and stabbing homicide of pretty Maria Hahn. Some writers say Maria was eleven; however, the truth is that she was a young woman of about twenty, who worked as a domestic servant; according to Kürten he came across the young woman, sitting on a street bench, on Thursday, 8 August, describing her as 'a girl looking for marriage'. He stopped and they chatted briefly, but before parting company, they had arranged to meet on the 11th, which was her day off. Once again the literature on Kürten is confusing at best. One published source has her being murdered on Thursday, 29 August, while another true-crime writer suggests that she was killed on the 14th or 15th. As the killer himself was absolutely clear that he killed Maria Hahn on the 11th – and as Sundays were often, by tradition, a domestic servant's day off, which was doubtless why they agreed on that day – I think I will run with Sunday, 11 August. The murder weapon is another object of uncertainty, with some claiming that it was a knife, others that it was a pair of scissors. The confusion is unsurprising considering that her body was not found for three months. Forensic evidence, however, shows that the stab wounds administered to her throat, breast and head were inflicted with scissors – and this was supported by Kürten's testimony.

Kürten's recollections of every detail of his gruesome murders, the dates, places and times were always bang on the nail. He was fastidious about this, although he occasionally came up with two different versions of the same event. And he stated that during his first meeting with Maria on 8 August they had arranged to meet up in the Neanderthal district of Düsseldorf the following Sunday. It would become a rendezvous with death.

The couple spent a couple of hours together that sunny Sunday, then Kürten lured this young woman, whom he described as 'a loose-living domestic servant who was willing to offer me quite a lot', into a meadow so that he could kill her. According to this monster, she had repeatedly pleaded with him to spare her life as he alternately strangled her, stabbed her in the chest and head and sat astride her waiting for her to die. He later buried Maria's body in a cornfield, only to return to her corpse many times to masturbate – behaviour similar to that of the Connecticut serial murderer, Michael Bruce Ross with several of his victims – and with the sickening intention of nailing her rotting remains to a tree in a mock crucifixion to shock and disgust the public.

Ross dumped one of his naked victim's bodies in the wooded grounds of the Connecticut State Police Headquarters. Kenneth Bianchi and Angelo Buono left naked bodies of women, and two young girls spreadeagled, legs apart, around the hills surrounding Los Angeles. Joanne Dennehy, the thirty-three-year-old British serial killer, dumped the almost naked corpses of three men in water-filled ditches near Peterborough. One victim, Kevin Lee, was wearing a black, sequined dress now pulled up over his buttocks. An aerosol can was inserted into his anus – there for the world to see.

Canadian-born Keith Hunter Jesperson, aka 'The Happy Face Killer', whom I spent several years corresponding with, was more subtle. Yes, he did dump six of his victims out in the sticks, but his last kill he tied to the rear axle of the heavy rig he was driving and dragged until just the frayed end of the rope was left and the girl was spread bit-by-bit along twelve or so miles of highway.

In the case of Maria, according to Kürten her corpse proved too heavy to lift; besides it was, by now quite literally falling to pieces, so he opened up the shallow grave to embrace and caress her as he lay underneath her corpse. Well, you would not wish to come upon such a terrible scene in the dead of night, would you?

During the early morning of Wednesday, 21 August, Kürten randomly stabbed an eighteen-year-old girl, a thirty-year-old man, and a thirty-seven-year-old woman in separate attacks. All three were seriously wounded, and they told police their assailant had not spoken a word before he attacked them. Then, on Saturday, 24 August, Kürten noticed Gertrude Hamacher (five) and her foster sister Luise Lenzen (fourteen).

It was the time of the annual fair along the banks of the River Rhine. Kürten was hunting through the bustling crowds of visitors for a victim when he spotted the two girls as they were walking home through the relatively quiet Flehe district of Düsseldorf. It was about 10.30 p.m., and not really the time of night for parents to allow their little kids to wander around. Furthermore, the girls were using unlit back alleys to avoid the busy streets. They were walking into a death trap, from which escape would have proved impossible. He swooped.

Kürten appeared as if from nowhere in front of the girls and politely asked Luise to run an errand for him. 'Would you please go and buy some cigarettes for me?' pointing to the fair. 'I'll look after the little girl.' Although Luise was slightly taken aback, she had been raised to do as her elders told her so she took some money from Kürten and ran off to find cigarettes.

Within seconds Kürten picked Gertrude up in his arms, then walked out of the alleyway over to bushes bordering an allotment. Here, in a patch of runner beans, he began strangling her with such force he later said he felt as though her eyes might pop from her skull. He then pulled a knife out of his pocket and slit her throat, killing her almost instantly.

Luise had run quickly back to the alley, stopping short when she saw the stranger and that Gertrude wasn't there. 'Did you get my cigarettes?' Kürten asked smiling. As she handed the pack to him, in a flash he grabbed her wrist. Within moments she had been dragged struggling to where the body of Gertrude now lay dead and covered with blood.

Giggling, he choked the girl, fondled her breasts and vagina. Finally, after having an orgasm, he used his knife to slice her throat from ear-to-ear in one slow, very deliberate motion, almost decapitating her. At post mortem it was also discovered that she had been stabbed about the torso with one stab penetrating the aorta.

Kürten later described how he had watched the blood seep from Gertrude's neck. First he touched it with his fingers and rubbed his fingers together staring at it. He explained to a horrified court how Luise's blood felt, and told them the colour made him 'happy again because I wanted to know what it tasted like'. It was alleged by police that he also bit Luise around the knife wound in the left side of her neck indicating that he was trying to either eat her skin or suck her blood. Whether or not on this occasion it was true, at least several times Kürten admitted to sucking blood from the necks of his victims – one of which was a swan he'd killed. Be that as it may, Kürten lay on the ground masturbating over the dead children for some time before calmly folding his knife and walking away without a care in the world.

The following day when Gertrude Hamacher's and Luise Lenzen's bodies were found, he strangled and drowned a girl only known as 'Anni', and tried the same with Christine Heerstrausse; then went on to stab Anna Goldhausen, Frau Mantel and Gustav Kornblum. Then he hit on Gertrude Schulte.

Various writers attribute various dates to the attack on Gertrude Schulte; however, I am satisfied that it actually took place on Sunday, 25 August 1929. I stand to be corrected.

Hello. You are very beautiful. My name is Fritz Baumgart.
PETER KÜRTEN ON MEETING GERTRUDE SCHULTE

Indeed Gertrude, with seductive eyes and full lips, was a raven-haired beauty to be sure. Aged twenty-seven at the time, she made her living by helping a family with housework, doing domestic chores and looking after their children at their home near Neuss, just outside of Düsseldorf.

At about 2 p.m. on that Sunday, she finished her work and went to meet a few friends. This was a get-together that she'd never make, for on her way Gertrude met Kürten, who she first thought was not unattractive.

Kürten, like Christie, had always possessed a confidence about him that seemingly attracted women. Whether that is true or not is another matter; however, he did take care of his physical appearance by eating properly and he stayed fit. Indeed, many who knew him described him as quite handsome, and some went as far as saying he was debonair.

For her part, Gertrude's looks and figure attracted many men. But she was a streetwise young woman and rarely took up their advances because she knew that all that they wanted was her body.

Kürten's opening gambit of, 'Hello. You are very beautiful. My name is Fritz Baumgart', fell on deaf ears. There was something about him that was creepy, so Gertrude politely rejected him. Nevertheless, getting more sexually aroused by the second, he persisted with a charm offensive never likely to knock any woman off her feet: 'Let's say we go somewhere and have sex,' he suggested bluntly.

Gertrude's reply was cutting in every sense of the word: 'I'd rather die,' she said as she turned her back to walk away.

'Die then,' snapped the now enraged Kürten. He closed with her and stabbed her in the back thirteen times. He let her fall to her knees and left her to die. But she didn't.

Despite a massive manhunt for the as yet unidentified serial killer, there was still no respite for the folk of Düsseldorf throughout September. In an effort to throw detectives off course by using a different MO, he changed his attack weapon from scissors to a hammer, sometimes using a rope to choke his victims into unconsciousness. He attacked Sofie Rückl, according to him with a chisel, and tried to strangle Maria Rad; both were lucky to escape with their lives. Then Kürten bludgeoned Ida Reuter to death with a hammer. In her case, once again, various accounts give conflicting times and dates.

One source has it that on Friday, 6 September 1929, 'thirteen-year-old' Ida Reuter (she was much older) was found dead, face down with her panties tugged off, in a field in Flehe. Unlike the previous homicides Kürten had committed, this source continued, he did not strangle or stab Ida, but this time he had shaken and beaten her to death with his hands and fists. This account is a bit of a mystery as Ida Reuter was in fact a domestic worker aged thirty-one, and other sources state that she was killed on 29 September or the 30th, not on the 6th. The most accurate version of events must, however, surely be that of the police records, the forensic evidence and of the killer himself.

The official report tells us that at 7 a.m. on Monday 30 September, a woman's body was found in the meadows beside the Rhine, 'lying in a posture typical of sexual outrages', on the back, with her knickers pulled off. She had been raped –

probably after death had occurred. There was evidence that the body had been dragged a considerable distance.

What we know from Kürten's confession was that he met the youthful-looking thirty-one-year-old at Düsseldorf railway station. He persuaded her to accompany him to a café and afterwards they went for a stroll through Der Hofgarten close to the River Rhine. As darkness fell, Ida wanted to turn back – which they did, until they were out of the sight of other walkers when he pulled a hammer out of his pocket and hit her on the right temple and dragged her unconscious body further into the dark. There he dealt her more hammer blows about the head, and raped her. Becoming aware of people relatively nearby, Kürten then dragged the body further into the fields.

Dr Karl Berg's forensic report (published in his book *Der Sadist*, 1932) states that the injuries were consistent with 'repeated heavy hammer blows from a square-faced hammer'.

In October 1929, Elisabeth Dörrier was killed. Once again, published accounts vary as to details: some suggest that she was eleven years old, while others have her age as around twenty-two, which for more than one reason seems much more likely. At the root of this confusion may be a photograph that purports to be of Elisabeth Dörrier. The small grey snapshot of a girl's face could depict a girl of around eleven, or it could be of a fresh-faced young-looking woman in her twenties – besides which, it is undated and could have been taken years before Kürten killed her.

A number of sources state that the murder took place on Saturday 12 October, which it might just have, and some narratives report that Kürten picked up the servant girl as she walked along the pavement about a mile from her residence and walked her to nearby bushes where he suffocated her until she fell unconscious. He then, they say, stabbed her about twenty-two times until she bled out and died. Although plausible, this account directly contradicts both forensic evidence and Kürten's testimony.

It's all a bit of criminological mess I'm almost afraid to say, but it must be remembered that by now the city of Düsseldorf was in turmoil, with equal amounts of panic, speculation and theorising about the 'Vampire of Düsseldorf' (sometimes the 'Düsseldorf Monster'), abounding in the press and in the streets, so it is understandable that contemporary accounts might be inaccurate and contradictory. However, recourse to forensic reports and the account given by Kürten himself lead me to believe that the following account is the most accurate I can come up with. It is worth noting that the circumstances and MO closely reflect the murder of Ida Reuter not quite two weeks before.

At about 9 p.m. on Friday 11 October 1929, Kürten popped his hammer into his hip pocket and set off for a walk. As he passed by a theatre, he encountered Elisabeth Dörrier, a servant girl, and suggested they walk together. She was reluctant at first but accompanied him to a bar for a drink; they afterwards took a train to Grafenberg and went for a stroll along the Düssel – a small tributary of the River Rhine. As they walked along the path Kürten suddenly struck her once across her right temple with his hammer, she dropped to the ground instantly and he raped her, battering her about the head repeatedly with his hammer. She was found, horribly injured and unconscious, at 6.30 a.m. on 12 October and died the following day, the 13th, without regaining consciousness.

On Friday, 25 October 1929, Kürten attacked another two women with a hammer. Frau Meurer and Frau Wanders both survived – although in the second attack this was purely thanks to an act of God: the hammer handle broke. So I trust this brings you some relief because it certainly brought no comfort to them, or Kürten, come to that!

On Thursday, 7 November 1929 – this is a date agreed upon by everyone – and Kürten had been stalking five-year-old, blue-eyed Gertrude Albermann for several weeks. He knew that her parents often took her to play in a Flingern district park near their home. He had also noticed that her parents spent much time gossiping with other folk, all of which allowed the curious little girl to explore, sometimes briefly stray though not too far away. Now, on this day, he was hiding in bushes sexually primed and ready to pounce.

Then she was there . . . he grabbed her; cupping her mouth so she couldn't scream out, then calmly he walked her almost a mile to an area he had selected as his killing place. Choking her into unconsciousness he pulled out his knife (some erroneously say it was scissors) and stabbed Gertrude thirty-six times until she bled out. Kürten later told police that he had stared at her for some time. He went back and forth in his mind whether he should sexually violate her or set her on fire. He chose a much different path. Picking up the body he carried her almost half a mile to a nearby factory, where, outside the walls, he told Dr Berg, he stabbed her again and raped her. The autopsy results support his account. He then made a makeshift grave for her out of rubbish and bricks. And he calmly walked away.

Two days after Gertrude's distraught parents had reported

her as missing to police, an editor at a local newspaper received a cryptic letter, headed 'Murder at Pappendelle'; the content of which indicated that the body could be found near a factory wall. Enclosed also was roughly drawn map marked with an 'X'. Almost immediately police believed that the writer was the child's killer. They rushed to the scene and amongst nettles they found her body.

In February 1930, Kürten tried to strangle a woman known only as 'Hilda'. On Sunday, 30 March, he attempted to strangle two women known only as 'Maria' and 'Irma', then on Wednesday, 30 April, came the attempted throttling of Sibilla Hau, and another girl whose name is unknown, followed by an attack on Charlotte Ulrich who sustained serious injuries, and several other young women – all on the same day!

Kürten's last encounter, on 16 May, was with Gertrude Bell, with whom he had sexual relations but whom he did not hurt; indeed, according to her testimony he told her she was 'too good' for him and that he was a bad man . . . Nevertheless, she was deemed to be a victim by the authorities, and it is very possible that he would have killed her had they not sought shelter from the rain in her room in the home of her employer.

It was the previous encounter, however, that proved to be his undoing. .On Wednesday, 14 May 1930, Maria Budlick (aka Budleis/Butlies), a twenty-year-old unemployed domestic servant, had taken a train from Cologne to Düsseldorf in search of employment. At Düsseldorf Central Station she was approached by a man who offered to help her find a hostel and it was this unlikely turn of events that would soon put

Kurten's neck under the guillotine's razor-sharp blade with his head dropping into a burlap sack.

The stranger was a presentable sort of chap, but Maria was sceptical; nevertheless, she agreed to follow him; not feeling afraid, and as they walked and talked she noticed that they were heading south down Die Ellerstraße towards the Volksgarten Park. It was now getting dark when the pfennig dropped. Maria suddenly recalled the terrible stories about the Düsseldorf Monster, the hair went up on the back of her neck and she told the stranger that she would now find her own way to a hostel. They began to argue.

By chance, standing close by was Peter Kürten who then intervened.

Even referring to Kürten's own account, piecing together what followed has not been an easy task, but it seems she accepted his offer of assistance when he told Maria that she could stay at his rooms on Mettmanner Straße. However, when they arrived he tried his luck and she refused him saying that she didn't want sex and could he please find her another place to sleep.

Seemingly Kürten agreed.

Kürten later told his psychiatrist that they walked along Worringer Platz, that he led the confused and very scared young woman deep into the Grafenberg Woods where he suddenly grabbed her hand and asked, 'Can I have you?' It seems that under duress she agreed. Nevertheless, adding to his account, he went on:

I thought that under the circumstances she would agree and my opinion was right. Afterwards, I took her back to the tram, but I did not accompany her right to it because

I was afraid she might inform the police officer who was standing there. I had no intention of killing Budlick as she had offered no resistance.

Unsurprisingly, this rape and close call with death greatly upset Maria, who returned almost immediate to Cologne where she fretted for a few days. Then, on Saturday, 17 May, she wrote a letter to her friend, a Frau Bruckner, and Kürten's looming fate intervened again. A Frau Brugmann opened the envelope in error. She read the contents describing the rape and the man and his rooms in great detail, so the public-spirited woman contacted the police.

When police finally tracked Maria Budlick down on the 22nd, she described a brass nameplate that read '71 Mettmanner Straße'. Lieutenant Inspector Ernst Gennat then persuaded her to accompany him and other officers to the address where he knocked, entered and climbed the creaking stairs to search the building for evidence. At some point Kürten spotted Maria and panicked. He tore down the stairs right past two policemen and into the street where he vanished into the night. Gennat and his men gave chase but Kürten had slipped away yet again.

Ernst August Ferdinand Gennat (1880–1939) was a gifted criminologist, a 'super cop', later to become Director of Berlin's Criminal Police. Indeed, his *Wikipedia* page makes for absolutely fascinating reading, and it is here and elsewhere that I learned something new.

I had always believed that the definition of 'serial killer' was commonly attributed to former FBI Special Agent Robert Ressler who first used the term 'serial homicide' in 1974, in a lecture at the UK's Bramshill Police College. Author Ann Rule, however, postulates in her book *Kiss Me, Kill Me* (2004), that the credit for coining 'serial killer' goes to LAPD Detective Pierce Books, who created the Violent Apprehension Programme (ViCAP) system in 1985.

In truth it was the stolid Ernst Gennat who developed most of what we know today as 'Offender Profiling'. His work is documented in articles designed for public reading, such as his 1930 paper on Peter Kürten, *Die Düsseldorfer Sexualverbrechen* (*The Düsseldorf Sex Crimes*), in which Gennat becomes the very first law enforcement officer to come up with the term 'Serienmörder' (Serial Killer).

Peter Kürten was now on the run. Hundreds of police officers were trying to hunt him down. A deadly earnest Lieutenant Inspector Ernst Gennat was leading them. He was determined to get his man .

The cunning Kürten meanwhile contemplated his next move.

Throughout the night I walked about. On Thursday 22nd of May, I saw my wife in the morning in the flat and so I fetched my things away in a bag and rented a room in the Alderstrasse, I slept quietly until Friday morning.

It would be fair to say that at this stage Kürten was confused and, once again, he made a simple mistake. The rape of Maria Budlick was, as far as the police were concerned, a one-off incident. It hadn't even crossed their minds that the man they were looking for was the media-dubbed 'Düsseldorf Monster'.

In fact, according to Kürten's own testimony he had convinced himself that although they most likely did not suspect him, it wouldn't take too long before they did. But what if they had suspected him? What evidence did the police have to link him to the serial killings? Not much at all seems to be the case. If he kept his mouth shut, then there was a very good probability that he would have been only charged with raping Maria Budlick, and that would have been a tenuous charge in any event. Any lawyer worth his salt would have presented a defence arguing that Maria had gone willingly with him to his apartment and then into the woods for consensual sex . . . besides, why did she not go straight to the police afterwards? There was an office standing next to the tram stop so why did she not report the rape there and then – was it because she feared stigma and shame? It would have all come down to her word against his.

> Today, the 23rd, in the morning, I told my wife that I was also responsible for the Schulte affair, adding my usual remark that it would mean ten years or more separation for us, probably forever. At that, my wife was inconsolable. She spoke of unemployment, lack of means and starvation in old age. She raved that I should take my own life then she would do the same, since her future was completely without hope. Then, in the late afternoon, I told my wife that I could help her.
>
> PETER KÜRTEN, PARTIAL WRITTEN CONFESSION

What little conscience Kürten had left now focused upon his loyal and devoted wife who had struggled through thick and thin with him for many years. He suggested that she turn him in to collect what amounted to a very substantial reward – money enough to last her for years. Reluctantly, she agreed. Therefore, on Saturday, 24 May, Frau Kürten went to the police and told them everything. She explained that she was planning to meet Peter at 3 p.m. outside of the Rochus Kirche in Düsseldorf. When he turned up, armed officers arrested him and he went meekly into custody, saying with a wink, 'There is no need to be afraid.'

> After my head has been chopped off, will I still be able to hear, at least for a moment, the sound of my own blood gushing from my neck? That would be the best pleasure to end all pleasures.
>
> PETER KÜRTEN

Peter Kürten's execution was fixed for 6 a.m., Wednesday, 2 July 1930. For his last meal he ordered Wiener schnitzel, fried potatoes and white wine. Aged forty-eight, and accepting his fate with equanimity, he at least went to the guillotine with a fully belly.

Professor Karl Johann Theodor Berg (1868–1936) a doctor, psychologist and Professor of Forensic Medicine gained Kürten's confidence in the months between his arrest and execution. Kürten spoke frankly of his acts and the motivation behind them. Berg concluded that, though sane under German law (which is not dissimilar to the prevailing UK's M'Naghten Rule), Kürten was a narcissistic psychopath interested only in his own gratification (very much the subject of the prequel to this book, *Talking with Psychopaths and Savages*, 2017).

Kürten's narcissism is all too obvious in his recitation of his deeds before an audience, as Dr Berg wrote in his account:

He was not accused of these crimes one by one, but reeled them off on his own account, beginning with No. 1 and ending with No. 79, every single case, dictating them, in fact, to the stenographer and even showing enjoyment at the horrified faces of the many police officers who listened to his recital, day by day. ['No. 1' was the unknown girl left for dead by Kurten in 1899; 'No. 79' was Gertrude Bell.]

Karl Berg, the fifth of fifteen children of the pastor Ludwig Berg, attended the grammar school in Pyrzyce, Poland. Later he studied at the University of Königsberg (now Kaliningrad, Russia); Wroclaw in Poland, Leipzig and Berlin. In 1905 he was a court physician in Essen; from 1906 in Düsseldorf, then during the First World War, he was employed as a medical officer in Belgium, France, Russia, Siberia – later again in Düsseldorf as Professor of Forensic Medicine and medico-legal officer at Düsseldorf Criminal Court. Professor Berg's book about the Kürten case, *Der Sadist*, first published in 1932 (English translation published in 1938), remains one of the major texts of criminal psychology. It is a fascinating read if you have the stomach for it.

So, where do we go from here?

Undoubtedly Peter Kürten suffered from one of the most abusive childhoods one can imagine, but does any of that mitigate his dreadful crimes? I think not. After he had committed his first sexually related offence, like John Christie who was also not an unintelligent man, Kürten must have realised that what he had done was morally wrong. However, as discussed earlier, whether it was 'Nature' or 'Nurture', or even Nature v. Nurture, or Nature and Nurture, he could never have been classified as 'insane' under the German equivalent of the M'Naghten Rule – the test for insanity – which states in broad terms, the determination whether a person was sane at the time of its commission and, therefore, criminally responsible for the wrongdoing.

A devastated Frau Kürten was given the reward – the equivalent of $1,000.00 which was a very substantial sum back then (very roughly, US$15,000 or £11,500 today) – and was never seen nor heard of again.

The location of Peter Kürten's grave is unknown, with the official record stating that his body is 'Lost or destroyed, specifically: Guillotined at Klingelpütz Prison in Germany'. Erected in 1838 as a city prison, star-shaped to allow the warders to observe the prisoners on all four wings from a central hub, the building was taken over by the Nazis after 1933 and became that main place for executions in the Rhineland. Over 1,000 people were executed at Klingelpütz before US forces liberated it in 1945. It has since been demolished and a memorial stone has been erected where it once stood.

For the movie buffs, Kürten case was the subject of the 1931 movie 'M' – *Eine Stadt sucht einen Mörder* starring Peter Lorre and directed by legendary German director Fritz Lang, who referred to 'M' as the best of all his movies.

9

Neville George Clevely Heath

They're weak and stupid. Basically crooked. That's why they're always attracted to rascals like me. They have the morals of alley cats and minds like sewers. They respond to flattery like a duck responds to water.
NEVILLE HEATH (1917–1946) ON WOMEN

I honestly don't give a damn what happens to me. I've faced death too often in the last six years to worry about it. Anyway, I've nothing left to live for since I lost my wife and child.
NEVILLE HEATH

It is universally agreed that most, if not all homicidal psychopaths, wear a mask of normality concealing the beast living within. And, while such a person can always change this guise their killer brains will never alter, for they are mentally programmed – irreversibly wired up with no conscience – in a completely different way to you and me. I hope!

Making a selection of which killers to include in this book has not been an easy task for there are many hundreds to choose from; therefore, I have been very picky and chosen carefully and, to my mind, I think that the emerging serial killer Neville Heath is well worthy of inclusion here, as I hope you will soon agree.

Heath was never a man satisfied with wearing just the one 'mask'. As an off-the-wall analogy, he was like a chameleon, which can change its outward appearance many times to suit its surroundings – for self-protection for survival, and also for hunting prey.

Recently I visited the Manila Ocean Park. It's the country's first world-class marine theme park, a premier educational facility and a fun place to be. Aside from fish, penguins and a seemingly bored alligator, there were many types of 'creepy-crawlies'; as in snakes, stick insects, lizards, etc, and this brought home to me just how these creatures can meld into their surroundings, to become almost undetectable to the eye. My eyesight is pretty good, yet peering hard up close to the glass, I was damned if I could spot anything except green leaves, brown twigs and, with the geckos, a little hump of sand with two little, unblinking eyes, staring in my direction. There they sit. Motionless. All but invisible to all around them, ready, in an instant, to strike and kill their prey.

It all reminded me of how serial killers can mask their outward appearance and Heath is just like that, but in humanoid form.

I would like you to bear this in mind as we move on, because in Neville Heath we find a man who wore a dozen masks. He adopted his own type of camouflage, being most able to change skins at a whim whenever it suited him – and military uniforms were his wardrobe, his outer skin. This makes Heath an unusual subject, who, like the aforementioned creepy-crawlies, had no conscience at all.

Born on Wednesday, 6 June 1917, Neville George Clevely Heath became a dashing chap who had grown up in a stable home in Iford, Essex. He was the first son of William, a hardworking barber at Waterloo Station who saved and invested his money wisely, and Bessie 'Betty' Heath. The lad was sent to a mixed convent school, although the family were not Catholic, and later to Rutlish, a fee-paying school situated on Rutlish Road, Merton Park, in south-west London.

Aged sixteen, he passed his School Certificate, but 'Nev's' marks were not high enough to qualify for the University of London matriculation. Rightly, his parents and teachers wanted him to re-sit the exam, but young Heath had other ideas. Like so many youngsters, he wanted to see life, as in *right now*!

School friends remember Heath as a precocious young fellow, who wore dapper suits and smoked a pipe. He looked older than his years and was an excellent athlete. However, Heath exhibited sadistic tendencies from an early age. As an omen of things to come, one day a girl at the desk next to him reached out her hand to pick up a dropped pencil. Without warning he stamped on her fingers. On another occasion a teacher found him viciously spanking a girl with a ruler while she screamed out in pain.

Heath's first job as a packer in a textile warehouse, he felt, was beneath him. He craved excitement, so as soon as he turned eighteen, he applied for a commission in the RAF. He showed a natural aptitude for flying and he had all the makings of an officer so, within a year, he was promoted to Flying Officer, being posted to No.19 Fighter Squadron RAF Duxford, where he flew Gloster Gladiators. It was at Duxford that he started to develop a more depraved side to his character in his relationships with women. One girl later recalled that when she had refused to spend the night with him he had suddenly lost control and began to hit her across the face and body. The girl broke free and ran for safety to a local hotel.

Furthermore, it was at Duxford that Heath's troubles really began, for, by this time, he was living beyond his means. His ego was bigger than his wallet, so to help fund his extravagant lifestyle, he began embezzling mess funds and bouncing cheques.

Now aged twenty, in March 1937, Heath won his pilot's wings and was posted to nearby RAF Mildenhall, from where he almost immediately deserted, returning to his parents' home in Wimbledon.

It would be three months before the RAF Police came to arrest Heath. As a gentleman he gave his word not to escape and, was allowed to remain under open arrest. One month later he stole a sergeant's car and fled.

From this time on, Heath earned a living through crime, all of which culminated in his appearance at the Old Bailey Central Criminal Court, London, on Tuesday, 12 July 1938. Rather than sending him to Wormwood Scrubs prison, Sir Gerald Dobson, MA, LLM, QC, Recorder of London, packed him off to a newly built borstal, where he would spend the next two months.

In October 1938, he enlisted in the Royal Army Service Corps. In early 1940 he was again commissioned, serving in the Middle East. Yet, a year later he was cashiered for the fraudulent use of a second pay book, as well as returning to his old habit of acquiring funds by bouncing cheques.

Sent back to England, Heath abandoned ship in Durban, South Africa. He travelled to Johannesburg where he introduced himself as Bruce Lockhart to eighteen-year-old Elizabeth Rivers, a member of a wealthy Johannesburg family. But her parents soon discovered that 'Bruce Lockhart' was not his real name and questioned him. He lied again, saying that his birth name was James Robert Cadogan Armstrong, and came up with some cock-and-bull story about his whole family having died and how it had become too painful for him to use the family name.

Unsurprisingly, Elizabeth's parents were sceptical, but Elizabeth was besotted and eloped with him. In February 1942 they married. The following September they had a son, whom they named Robert.

Over the next two years Heath rose to Captain in the South African Air Force and life was good. He showed himself to be a fond husband and father – furthermore he made no unusual sexual demands on his wife, doubtless because he was busying himself screwing any young piece of skirt he happened upon. This period indeed proved to be the most stable in Heath's life.

In May 1944, Heath was seconded to Bomber Command in England, and soon he was sliding into the bad old ways. Before long he was forging his flying logs to impress Wrens (WRNS, in the Women's Royal Naval Service) and issuing cheques he knew would be dishonoured. Six months later he returned to South Africa only to be arrested on charges of fraud.

By now his in-laws – who had never approved of Heath in the first place – were sick and tired of him. He was an utter cad and they wanted nothing more to do with him. If Heath would agree to a divorce, and to give custody of the child to Elizabeth, they would pay him a £2,000 lump sum just to see the back of him. Heath grabbed at the offer and was deported from South Africa, *tout de suite*!

Six months later he would find himself back in the Old Bailey on trial for murder most foul.

Thus far, here we have in Neville Heath, a man who took narcissism to another level, an officer and a self-alleged gentleman, a tall handsome young Air Force hero, home from the war/s; and to women his easy charm would soon become an utterly fatal attraction in more ways than one.

Heath's old-school-tie social world had been one of leather-covered chairs, polished tables, gin-and-tonics, handlebar moustaches, cigars, murmured discreet conversations in the gentlemen's clubs. He came across as a hail-fellow-well-met chappie. One for a firm handshake and a buddy-buddy slap-on-the back sort of guy before he metamorphosed into a fraudster, a charlatan, who developed an array of impressive sounding aliases and – with his fine physique, well-tailored dress sense and equally well-tailored gentlemanly charm, a smooth line of chat and cut-glass accent, and twinkling eyes – he had women falling at his feet: which two of them did literally, stone dead. For this suave gentleman was a sex maniac, one of the most violently depraved men the UK has known. In a few summer days, he haunted England's genteel south coast.

Welcome to Heath's world.

Heath's vicious streak (the beginnings of which were evident while he was still at school) developed, turning him into a full-blooded sadist who could only achieve full sexual satisfaction by performing, or imagining, acts involving female suffering and humiliation – very much like so many sexual predators, Michael Ross, John Christie and Peter Kürten amongst them. Indeed, at one point during his trial, which commenced at the Old Bailey on Tuesday, 24 September 1946, Heath admitted to his defence lawyer that he found sadistic acts with women more pleasurable than sexual intercourse. But of course there are some people who derive sexual satisfaction from sadomasochistic acts and are *not* driven to murder.

The appalling cruelty these psychopathic killers inflict seems to produce no remorse, pity or guilt. Indeed, the sight of their helpless victims serves only to add to their sexual frenzy, with hands-on-strangulation, or by using a ligature, being the one of their favoured methods of killing as the victim's suffering is prolonged. Therefore, it goes without saying that such offenders are highly dangerous. With any treatment once incarcerated being rarely effectual, the hangman's halter can prove extremely effective. Heath was hanged on Wednesday, 16 October 1946, at HM Prison Pentonville.

With some previous history of beating women, his two murder victims were thirty-two-year-old Margery Brownell Gardner née Wheat, at the Pembridge Court Hotel, Notting Hill Gate, London, on Monday, 20 June 1946; and twenty-one-year-old former Wren Doreen Margaret Marshall, who was killed at Branksome Chine, Bournemouth, on Sunday, 3 July 1946.

Heath's rake's progress, one that ended in two homicides, is of interest to us because police later pieced together details of his extraordinary career of crime – his previous criminal narrative – during which, in the course of a decade, he successfully managed to get himself commissioned and dishonourably discharged on no less than three occasions. In short it makes unedifying reading, as follows:

February 1936: Obtained a short-service commission in the RAF.

August 1937: Court-martialled for being absent without leave for nearly five months. Other charges included escaping while under arrest and 'borrowing' a non-commissioned officer's car without permission. Sentenced to be cashiered. Commuted subsequently to dismissal.

November 1937: Placed on probation on charges of fraudulently obtaining credit at a Nottingham hotel and attempting to obtain a car by false pretences. Eight other charges, including posing as 'Lord Dudley', taken into account.

July 1938: Sentenced to three years' borstal for housebreaking and stealing jewellery worth £51 from a friend and for obtaining clothing worth £27 by means of a forged banker's order. Ten other offences taken into account.

September 1939: Released from Hollesley Bay Colony because of the outbreak of war.

October 1939: Enlisted in the Royal Army Service Corps.

March 1940: Commissioned and posted to the Middle East.

July 1941: Placed under arrest after a dispute with a brigadier. Went absent without leave. Court-martialled for these offences and for obtaining a second pay book by making a false statement; for making a false statement to his commanding officer, enabling him to be absent from his unit; and on five charges relating to dishonoured cheques. Sentenced to be cashiered.

November 1941: Absconded from the troopship that was bringing him to England when it docked at Durban in South Africa. Went to Johannesburg where he passed himself off as a Captain Selway, MC, of the Argyll and Sutherland Highlanders.

December 1941: Enlisted in the South African Air Force under the name of 'Armstrong'. Commissioned.

May 1944: Seconded to the Royal Air Force. Shot down on the Dutch-German border while piloting a Mitchell bomber.

August 1945: Court-martialled and dismissed from service in South Africa on six charges; three of conduct prejudicial to good order and military discipline and three of wearing military decorations without authority.

February 1946: Arrived back in Britain.

It would later come to light that Heath had hardly stepped ashore in England when we come across him again, for, on Saturday, 23 February 1946, the manager of the Strand Palace Hotel, 373 Strand, London, burst into a bedroom to find Heath roundly thrashing a naked woman with a cane, both of them highly intoxicated. An electrician, who had heard screams of a woman begging a man to 'stop', had alerted the manager who knew Heath as having booked into the hotel as 'Captain James Cadogan Armstrong' of the South African Air Force.

Although the woman had allowed Heath to spreadeagle

her and tie her wrists and ankles to the bedposts in what amounted to sadomasochistic sex, her beating had been severe, as evident from the scarlet weals across her buttocks.

For his part, the suave Heath showed no embarrassment whatsoever. Indeed, he protested at the intrusion because it had 'spoiled' his fun and it was a 'private matter' anyway. The police attended, but the woman refused to prefer charges. Heath paid the hotel bill and they left together, smiling and giggling, apparently on good terms.

'All to his, or her own', it is said, and from this incident at the highly respectable Strand Palace Hotel where the woman was heard to be screaming, we may rightly assume that she was enjoying herself as much as Neville Heath. Besides, when she was spoken to by police she was in high spirits in every sense of the meaning; and, like Heath, she also resented the intrusion into their privacy.

Then, in April 1946, Neville Heath was fined at Wimbledon Magistrates' Court in South London for wearing a military uniform and decorations to which he was not entitled.

Thirty-two-year-old Margery Brownell Gardner had left her alcoholic husband and their baby daughter in Sheffield to seek fame and fortune in London. Occasionally a film extra, her gay bohemian social circle – a group of misfits now consisting of black-marketeers, pimps, thieves and ex-military officers on the make – knew her as 'Ocelot Margie' because of the fake fur coat she wore. Sexually submissive, she led a precarious lifestyle, moving from bedsit to bedsit, hotel to hotel, sleeping with men in return for a meal and a bed for the night – although, it has to be said, she was not what the police termed 'a common prostitute'.

During the day of Margery's murder, fantasy-driven Heath was 'on the make' in a Fleet Street public house drinking with journalists and offering to fly them abroad in his private plane. One reporter gave him £30 for a flight to Copenhagen, and, as soon as his back was turned, conman Heath fled. Now flush with the journalist's money in his wallet he went to a private club where he spent the afternoon. He then took a cab to the Trevor Arms, 231 & 233 Knightsbridge, St Margaret, Westminster, where he met Margery Gardner. The two were seen by people several times in various pubs, and then again having dinner at the Normandie Hotel, at 96 Sussex Gardens, Paddington, before moving on to the Panama Club, a seedy strip joint in Kensington. So, there was no doubt that Heath had been drinking heavily all day and would have had a very dangerous amount of booze for a sexually motivated psychopathic narcissist who already had lowered inhibitions aligned with no morals or conscience at all.

> The man asked how much the fare was. I said it was 1s 9d, and he gave me 2s 2d. Then they walked towards the hotel. He put his arm around the woman's waist and I saw them enter the hotel.
>
> HARRY HARTER, TAXICAB
> DRIVER, TO DETECTIVES

Although Heath later confirmed that he had been drinking with Margery Gardner during the evening of Wednesday, 19 June, the very attractive Margery and 'Man-about-Town 'Neville Heath – now calling himself 'Lieutenant-Colonel' Neville Heath – had definitely been dancing together at the Panama Club in Kensington during the late evening of the following day, the 20th. Around midnight they left the club together, hailed a taxi on the Old Brompton Road and asked the cabbie, Harry Harter, to take them to the nineteen-room Pembridge Court Hotel, 34 Pembridge Gardens, Notting Hill Gate, which he did, dropping them off about fifty yards from the foyer.

It was now Friday 21 June, and at 2 p.m. a chambermaid entered Room 4. In one of the single beds, she saw a young dark-haired woman covered up to the neck in bloodstained sheets and blankets and, who, with a bluish tinge about the face, was quite obviously dead.

Police from nearby Ladbroke Grove arrived within minutes. Sergeant Averill being the first officer on scene.

Sergeant Averill noted that the woman's clothes had been neatly folded over a chair. This indicated that the wearer had been relaxed and comfortable when she'd arrived there. A further discovery was that of a wartime identity card. This identified the victim as thirty-two-year-old Margery Aimee Brownell Gardner. Her rings were still on her fingers and the contents of her bag were untouched. A quick check of police records showed that Margery was 'known to police'. The previous September she had been travelling in a stolen motorcar that was chased by the law and stopped at Hyde Park Corner. Her explanation that she had no idea the car was stolen was accepted by detectives, but she was now on the files of Scotland Yard's 'Ghost Squad' suspects, a discreet elite unit set up to investigate post-war crime in London's West End.

The scenes-of-crime photographs show that Margery had been terribly mutilated. Her nipples had been all but bitten off. There are seventeen weals, apparently made by a leather whip that had a diamond-pattern weave and a metal tip.

In total there are nine lash marks on her back between her shoulder blades, six across the right breast and abdomen, and two on the forehead.

The woman had been bound hand and foot, with the right arm pinned beneath the back. Her face had been punched repeatedly. The ankles had been bound together with a white handkerchief bearing the name 'L. Kearns', and she had bled profusely from the vagina, which indicated that she was still alive when injuries to it were inflicted.

From looking at these dreadful photographs and the overall crime scene, the positioning of her clothes placed neatly over a chair, and the total absence of any defensive wounds on the deceased's fingers and hands, it appears likely that Margery was willing to be tied up – for her own sexual pleasure or, more probably, to please her handsome new boyfriend – sadly suffering the tragic consequences as the result of being now innocently under the control of a sado-sexual maniac.

Curiously, Margery's face had clearly been washed, although there were still traces of blood on her cheeks and in her nostrils. Blood on the second bed suggested that she had been killed there and her body moved after death – while interlacing markings on the pillowcase pointed to a bloodstained whip having been placed there.

It has been said that initially police thought that she had died of shock – hardly the likely cause of death – but upon subsequent post-mortem examination at Hammersmith Mortuary, the noted pathologist Professor Keith Simpson found asphyxia to be the cause – possibly through the use of a gag (later found to have been Heath's scarf) or by having her face pressed by a pillow. Simpson further stated that '... even without the seventeen lash marks the girl's injuries were appalling. Both nipples and some soft breast tissue had been bitten away and there was a seven-inch tear in her vagina and beyond caused by the short poker found in the fireplace.'

In summary: Margery had suffered terrible pain throughout her tortuous ordeal and death only mercifully intervened when Heath suffocated her.

The manhunt for Margery's savage killer was now on. Furthermore, if anything, Neville Heath was imprudent by nature. He was one of a serial killer type who spontaneously kills without any forethought or post-crime planning and, in this respect he had been far too clever for his own good.

The homicide cops asked to see the hotel's guest records and Mrs Alice Wyatt, who helped her father-in-law to run the place, provided them. The detectives noted that Room 4 – that same room – had been let the previous Sunday, the night of 16 June, to a man with a female companion (not Margery), and he'd signed the register 'Mr and Mrs N. G. C Heath', giving an address in Hampshire. Within hours, Detective Superintendent Thomas Barratt, who was in charge of the case, had established that Mr N. G. C. Heath was in fact Neville George Clevely Heath. Barratt instantly realised that Heath was a 'person of interest', and his name was flashed to every police agency in the country.

And, it is at this point one might rightly ask about the woman who was found in a bedroom of the Strand Palace Hotel being whipped by Heath. *Was* she Margery Gardner, as hotel staff and the press believed? In which case, why, after she had suffered such a beating at the hands of Heath as early as 23 February, would she want to see him again? Surely she would have known that he was a violent man; one prone to kinky sex? Yet, looking back at her London lifestyle, maybe she was into that too, people surmised. Police files covering that earlier incident, however, state clearly that the woman in question was not Margery Gardner. The actual woman probably, and understandably, decided that she would be well advised to keep quiet about her little adventure.

On Tuesday, 25 June 1946, police issued a 'Special Notice – Murder' to all police forces and exit ports in the country. It showed a previous tight-lipped mugshot of Heath looking to his right, a man whose face clearly had bitterness written all over it.

The notice, which was restricted to law enforcement for fear of tipping Heath off, reads, verbatim, as follows:

M.P. (FH). – It is desired to trace the after-described for interview respecting the death of MARGERY GARDNER, during the night of 20th-21st inst. – NEVILLE GEORGE CLEVELY HEATH, alias ARMSTRONG, BLYTH, DENVERS and GRAHAM, C.R.O. No. 28142-37, b. 1917, 5ft. 11 ½ in., c. fresh, e. blue, believed small fair moustache, h. and eyebrows fair, square face, broad forehead and nose, firm chin, good teeth, military gait; dress, lt. grey d.b. suit with pin stripe, dk. brown trilby, brown suede shoes, cream shirt with collar attached or fawn and white check sports jacket and grey flannel trousers. Nat. Reg. No CNP/2147191.

Has recent convictions for posing as Lt.-Col. of South African Air Force. A pilot and believed to possess an 'A' licence, has stated his intention of going abroad and may endeavour to secure passage on ship or plane as passenger or pilot. May stay at hotels with a woman.

Enquiries are also requested to trace the owner of a gent's white handkerchief with brown check border, bearing 'L. Kearns' in black ink on hem and stitched with large 'K' in blue cotton in centre.

A national police manhunt was on, but where was Neville Heath?

After killing Margery, Heath rinsed the leather diamond-weave whip and packed it into one of his two suitcases along with the scarf he'd used to gag her and the cloth that had tied her wrists, before wandering off into the night. He hailed a taxi, asking the driver to take him to London Victoria Station where he boarded an early-morning train to Brighton and Hove. Here, close by, at the Ocean Hotel in Worthing, he signed in under his real name. Then, without wasting a moment, Heath telephoned a girlfriend, Yvonne Symonds, to tell her that he was in Worthing. 'Could we meet up for lunch tomorrow?' he asked her. She readily agreed.

The two had met for the first time at a WRNS dance on Saturday, 15 June, in Chelsea. Heath had, with equally indecent haste, proposed to Yvonne the following evening in the Pembridge Court Hotel. To all intents and purposes, they were 'unofficially engaged', but we can presently remind ourselves that Yvonne was the 'unknown woman' who had stayed with Heath, who'd signed them into the Pembroke Court Hotel register as 'Mr and Mrs N. G. C. Heath', giving a false address in Hampshire.

Well, it is true that Yvonne had met Heath, as mentioned

above, at a dance in Chelsea the Sunday prior to Margery Gardner's murder. Afterwards, he'd taken her to his favourite nightspot, the Panama Club, where he soon suggested: 'Let's find a hotel and sleep together.' At this, Yvonne later told police, she refused. Nevertheless, the charming Heath spent the whole of the next day with Yvonne. She recalled that he was debonair and charming and that he 'fascinated her'. Then Heath proposed for the second time and they spent the night together because marrying a distinguished war hero and pilot was now on the cards. Her parents, Mrs and Mrs Symonds, would have been thrilled to bits!

This lunch in Worthing with Neville Heath proved 'memorable' for Yvonne Symonds, for at some time during the course of the meal, Heath suddenly said: 'Yvonne, there's been a nasty murder in London. Have you read about it in the papers?' She hadn't, so Heath dropped the subject, promising her that he would return to the issue later that night when he would take her to wine and dance at the Blue Peter Club, in Angmering on Sea. This club attracted the glitterati of the day – people with deep pockets who enjoyed socialising in the quasi-exotic surroundings of palm trees and views across the English Channel.

So what was going on inside Neville Heath's mind at this time? To attempt to answer this question we have to look deep – not just peer into the abyss, but climb over the edge and plunge in.

As we have already noted in this book, homicidal sado-sexual psychopaths are utterly devoid of any moral conscience, as we understand 'conscience'. Where there should be some remorse or pity or feelings toward others, these killers 'flatline'. Neville Heath is another blue-chip example of such a person, let's make no bones about it. These social misfits generate human suffering on a scale that no Stephen King nightmare story could come up with – all totally beyond the comprehension of the likes of you and me. To kill as they do and cause such unimaginable and immeasurable suffering is, to these monsters, as easy as swatting a fly. Indeed, do you feel any compassion when you swat an annoying fly . . . do you get any sexual satisfaction from doing so? Do you become overwhelmed with remorse? Of course you don't. But here is the awful godforsaken truth – all serial killers feel exactly the same way when they take innocent human lives. Indeed, many go even further: they commit necrophiliac acts on the corpses, they use the dead and often rotting corpses for sex, often revisiting the decomposing remains several times over.

It doesn't get any more twisted and perverted than that!

Therefore, simply put in totally non-professional terms, these monsters don't give a fuck! And, if any of my readers can find a law-enforcement officer, or a grieving next-of-kin, a half-wired-up psychologist or a psychiatrist who actually resides on Planet Earth who thinks otherwise, please tell them to ring my bell.

So, back to the question: where is Neville Heath's mind right now, as he's about to unload his lies onto Yvonne Symonds?

Without troubling you by suggesting that you research the criminal narratives of any other serial murderers, I can confirm that all of the killers I have interviewed never have, and never will, show an inkling of remorse and for a very good reason. As outlined in a previous chapter, these psychopaths are not wired up to outwardly exhibit, or psychologically feel, any remorse at all –which is why

I included Peter Kürten in this book as being an extreme example. In a nutshell – discounting the atrocity of his crimes – Kürten's underlying homicidal psychopathology is all but the same as all the serial killers I have interviewed. They are as emotionally cold as wintery days. Once you fully understand this, hopefully one will begin to understand what makes these killers tick.

Because these monsters feel the way they do, they are mentally programmed to shift the blame for their heinous offences onto others: in doing so they are able to confidently dissociate themselves from their crimes and portray themselves as 'normal' human beings.

As an example, one might look at Harvey Louis 'The Hammer' Carignan, whom I have interviewed in prison and who features in my book *Talking with Serial Killers*. 'Harv', who has probably raped and murdered some fifty young women, always maintains that it was his victims' fault that he beat them to death. He has told me numerous times '. . . and the women initiated the subject of sex. I went for it but I was forced to kill them after they demanded money from me or they'd report me for rape to the police.' And now we can see the same psychopathic dissociation with a homicide in Heath. What follows is Yvonne Symonds's recollection of Heath's story as she later gave it to police:

The murder took place in the same room that we had stayed in. I knew the girl. She was with some man called Jack who had nowhere to stay so I gave them the key to my room and went and slept somewhere else. The police, an inspector, got on to me and took me round to the room. I saw the body. It was a pretty gruesome sight.

Initially, Yvonne did not doubt Heath's account. He was, after all, the man she was falling deeply in love with. The dashing, courteous Neville was an ideal catch.

'How did the girl die?' Yvonne quietly whispered.

'A poker was stuck up her,' he remarked casually, picking slowly through his meal. 'I think that's what killed her.' Then, as an afterthought, Heath looked up and said, 'The police seem to believe she might have been suffocated.'

It simply didn't occur to our war hero that Yvonne would be horrified by what he had just told her. He may have just been talking about the dessert so unperturbed was he. But Yvonne was appalled. 'What sort of person could commit a brutal crime like that?' she asked, pushing her plate away.

'A sex maniac, I suppose,' came the indifferent answer.

If anything could kill a romantic date, Health's shocking revelations certainly did. So, let's get real here. Specifically for my female readers: can you imagine, for one instant, sitting down for a nice dinner and your dashing date starts talking about a poker being stuck up a woman's vagina being a gruesome sight – and, that's even before you start on the crème brûlée? Yvonne brought the meal to an abrupt end, with the chivalrous Heath taking her home –a peck on her cheek – before scuttling back to his hotel in Worthing.

The following morning when Yvonne and her parents read the reports of the murder in the newspapers there was a photo of Neville Heath staring straight back at them. She nervously telephoned Heath, 'My parents are very worried about the story in the papers,' she told him. He coolly explained to her that this was all a 'misunderstanding'. 'Actually, I thought your parents would be concerned,' he said, adding, 'I've now got a car and I'm driving back to London to sort things out. I'll probably give you a ring this evening.'

Yvonne never spoke to Heath again.

But now Neville had a problem, for he realised that if the Symondses decided to contact the police, the law would know of his whereabouts, so he penned a ridiculous letter to Detective Superintendent Tom Barratt in a pathetic attempt to get himself off of the hook; and it is a letter that might show us more about Heath's psychopathology than he would wish:

Sir, I feel it to be my duty to inform you of certain facts in connection with the death of Mrs Gardner at Notting Hill Gate. I booked into the hotel last Sunday, but not with Mrs Gardner, whom I met for the first time during the week. I had drinks with her on the Friday evening, and whilst I was with her she met an acquaintance with whom she was obliged to sleep. The reasons, as I understand them, were mainly financial. It was then that Mrs Gardner asked if she could use my hotel room until two o'clock and intimated that if I returned after that, I might spend the remainder of the night with her. I gave her my keys and told her to leave the hotel door open. It must have been almost 3 a.m. when I returned to the hotel and found her in the condition of which you are aware. I realised that I was in an invidious position, and rather than notify the police, I packed my belongings and left. Since then I have been in several minds whether to come forward or not, but in view of the circumstances I have been afraid to ... I should like to come forward and help, but

I cannot face the music of a fraud charge which will obviously be preferred against me if I should do so.

The personal column of the Daily Telegraph will find me, but at the moment I have assumed another name.

I have the instrument [whip] with which Mrs Gardner was beaten and am forwarding this to you today. You will find my fingerprints on it but you should also find others as well.

I can give you a description of the man. He was aged approximately 30, dark hair (black), with a small moustache. Height about 5ft. 9ins., slim build. His name was Jack and I gathered that he was a friend of Mrs. Gardner's of some long standing.

Heath's letter, signed 'N. G. C. Heath', with no promised parcel or 'instrument' enclosed, arrived on Detective-Superintendent Barratt's desk the next day – which was the 24th. It was dated Saturday, 22 June and postmarked 'Worthing 5.45 p.m.. Sunday, 23 June'. Detectives now had a solid lead. They sped down to the south coast to liaise with the local police who had already received a telephone call from Yvonne's parents who knew of his brief stay at the Ocean Hotel, on Beech Road. A search of his room yielded little except a military uniform and some medals.

As for Heath – he was gone.

The Tollard Royal Hotel, 141 West Hill, Bournemouth, began its life as a three-storey hotel on the cliff top, between West Hill Road and St Michael's Road. In the 1930s, two more floors were added, making it a place reeking of 'old money' and, where only the affluent could afford to stay. The hotel's brochure at the time boasted:

A Cliff Lift within a few yards – perfect freedom from traffic and noise. Veranda and Beautiful Gardens overlooking the Bay. 100 bedrooms with Private Bath of Hot and Cold Water – Gas Fires – No North Rooms – Solarium during dull days and every evening – Vita-Glass Sun Lounge.

New restaurant now open – Lounge accommodation doubled – Ballroom – Billiard Room – Two Passenger Lifts.

Beach Hut for Bathing – Efficient Night Porter.

Now booked into Room 81 of the Tollard Royal Hotel, Neville George Clevely Heath, aka Captain Selway, MC, Argyll and Sutherland Highlanders, aka Captain James Cadogan Armstrong, South African Air Force, aka Lieutenant-Colonel Neville Heath, aka Lord Dudley, aka Bruce Lockhart, Heath now purloined the name of Rupert Brooke – the English poet known for his idealistic war sonnets penned during the First World War. And, it has to be said that Heath did bear a passing resemblance to the real Rupert Brooke, whom the Irish poet W. B. Yeats described as 'the handsomest young man in England'.

And, it is here, in sunny Bournemouth with its seven miles of glorious beaches nestled beneath magnificent cliffs, blending in with the crowds, we can see rakish Heath strolling now: pipe in his mouth, demob grey flannel trousers, a mustard-coloured sports jacket and checked shirt, smiling blue-eyes; yes there he is in the lush lower park apparently without a care in the world.

What a piece of work.

Back in the hotel's lounge the 'Group Captain' regaled fellow guests with his derring-do adventures as wartime pilot in South Africa. He boasted of his links with the famous families – the de Beers and the Oppenheimers – conveniently omitting the fact that at one time he had married into the Rivers family, or that he was actually an emerging sado-sexual serial killer, come to that.

That his drinking companions and the staff noticed that he always wore the same clothes, never had any cash, was putting all his meals and booze on the bill, raised no concerns. 'Hey, chaps, Group Captain Rupert Brooke is an officer and a gentleman, after all!' Indeed, even the hotel manager, Ivor Relf, was entirely taken in by Heath's aristocratic performance. 'He was just like a normal holidaymaker,' he later recalled.

After six years of war, English holidaymakers were intent on enjoying themselves. Young women were wearing the first of the post-war fashions. Mixed bathing was now allowed. There were tea dances in all the better-class hotels. Now Heath needed a companion. However, although it is not entirely clear how Heath and Doreen Marshall first met, one might suppose that Heath's later account to police has a ring of the truth about it:

On Wednesday, July 3, during the morning, I was seated on the promenade on West Cliff when I saw two young ladies. One of these was a casual acquaintance whom I had met at a dance at the Pavilion during the latter half of the preceding week. Her name was Peggy but I was unaware of her surname. Although I was not formally introduced to the other I gathered that her name was 'Doo' or something similar. The girl Peggy left after about half an hour and I walked along the front with the other girl whom I now know to be Miss Marshall. I invited her to have tea with me in the afternoon and she accepted.

Born in 1925, shy and retiring Doreen Margaret Marshall was twenty-one, a pert and pretty ex-Wren, who, after she'd been demobilised had succumbed to a severe attack of flu and measles. Once she had recovered, her father Charles Marshall, a company director from Pinner in Middlesex, sent her to Bournemouth to convalesce. He had booked a room for her at the Edwardian-built Norfolk Royale Hotel, on Richmond Hill, and was paying all of her bills.

In the course of tea at the Tollard Royal Hotel that afternoon, Heath asked Doreen if she would you care to join him for dinner that night? She graciously agreed.

It was now about 8.15 p.m. and, initially, over the meal the yarn-spinning, flattering 'Group Captain Rupert Brooke' was sweeping Doreen off her feet, but then his mood darkened. Other diners would later tell police that he was getting drunk. She suddenly looked tired, drawn and pale and wanted to leave and get back to her own hotel for much-needed sleep. She explained to Heath that she was considering cutting short her holiday and returning home on Friday instead of the following Monday.

I got into conversation with Miss Marshall and my husband joined the party after putting the car away. I thought the defendant [Heath] had a little too much to drink and he asked me to have a drink. I did not accept. Miss Marshall looked very tired and very pale and absolutely sober. Just before midnight Miss Marshall asked my husband if he was going to bed and she caught hold of my husband's arm very pleadingly and said, 'Would you order me a taxi?' I think the defendant heard. On the way upstairs to bed – we had left the defendant and Miss Marshall alone in the writing room – my husband ordered a taxi from the night porter.

MRS GLADYS PHILLIPS, GIVING
HER EVIDENCE DURING HEATH'S
TRIAL IN SEPTEMBER 1946

By about 10 p.m., with Doreen not feeling up to scratch, still recuperating from her flu and measles, Heath had piled on the charm. He convinced her to stay a little longer, so they went into a smaller writing room to be joined by a Miss Parfitt and Mr and Mrs Phillips. Later, Doreen clutched at Mr Phillips's hand and asked him to order a taxi for her. It seems to me that the drunken Heath had asked her, somewhat crudely, for sex, and she was very upset.

Now in the hotel lobby, with Heath arguing with Doreen, he snapped at the night porter: 'Cancel the taxi, my guest has decided to walk home. I'll be back in half-an-hour.' With that, Doreen turned around abruptly saying to the porter: 'He'll be back in quarter of an hour!'

Then the couple left. It was about fifteen minutes after midnight and Doreen Marshall was never seen alive again.

At about 4 a.m. that morning, the night porter noted that 'Group Captain Rupert Brooke' had not returned. Concerned that the obviously highly intoxicated guest had come to some harm, the porter went to room 81 and tapped on the door. As there was no answer, he opened it to find the Group Captain apparently sleeping soundly in bed.

Over breakfast that morning, Heath explained to the

manager how he had played a 'joke' on the porter. He'd placed a ladder against the outside wall of the hotel the previous day . . . that realising that the porter would be waiting up for him to return, he'd climbed up the ladder and entered his third-floor room via the window. Ever the deferential manager, and despite whatever doubts he may have had, manager Ivor Relf took his blue-blooded guest at his word and nothing more was said.

Over tea the following day, Friday, 5 July, the strikingly attractive and well-heeled Gladys Phillips asked Heath 'How is your little girlfriend?' to which he blandly replied: 'All right as far as I know. I believe she is out with another friend today.' By now Mrs Phillips's suspicions had been aroused. He seemed 'oily' to her. Sneaky and glib. So, like Agatha Christie's Miss Marple, she remarked on the silk scarf he was now wearing when before he had always worn an open-necked shirt. She politely asked to take a closer look and when Heath removed it she noticed that his neck was covered in deep scratches.

But, Mrs Phillips was not the only person who had concerns about Doreen Marshall that day. The manager of the Norfolk Royale Hotel had realised that one of his guests had gone missing. The chambermaid had reported that all of Doreen's possessions were still in her room and her bed had not been slept in for two days. He telephoned Ivor Relf, expressing his concerns about the sudden disappearance of the young lady from Pinner.

Now it was Ivor Relf's turn to get concerned. He recalled that the 'Group Captain' had played a 'joke' on the night porter who had in turn told Relf that he had seen a young woman arguing with Heath in the foyer before they had left together. Then Mrs Phillips threw in her five eggs by recalling that the young woman had been very upset. She further mentioned the red wheals she'd seen on Heath's neck. This was becoming a real-life whatdunit, whodunit and whodunwhat, all being played out in the prestigious top-drawer, upper-crust Tollard Royal Hotel.

Questions and eyebrows were being raised in sync. 'Why does the Group Captain always wear the same clothes?' 'He's run up a huge tab . . . never has any cash to hand...a bit of a rake if you ask my opinion,' sort-of hushed conversations, which prompted hotel manager Relf to have a word in Heath's ear.

'Sir, there has been a report that a young lady staying at the Norfolk Royale has gone, um, missing, sir . . . might this be the lady you were dining with here the other evening? I believe she came from Pinner . . . and sir, there is the delicate matter of your outstanding bill.'

Heath shrugged the question off: 'Oh, no. I have known that lady for a long while and she certainly does not come from Pinner,' he said airily. 'I'll settle up with you shortly.'

Relf smelt a rat and suggested that the Group Captain might wish to get in contact with the police and, somewhat surprisingly, he did just that.

Heath's account with the Tollard Royal Hotel remains outstanding to this very day.

Immediately after his talk with Relf, Heath realised that he was between a rock and a hard place: that if he didn't contact the police, Relf and the manager of the Norfolk hotel certainly would, so he retired to his room where he wrote another letter to Detective Superintendent Barratt. Then he telephoned the local police asking if they had a photograph of the now missing woman.

The officer in charge of the investigation was not available, so Heath was asked to call back, which he did at 3.30 p.m. and, upon learning that Detective Constable George Suter did have a photo of Miss Marshall, he offered to walk up to the police station and see if he could be of any assistance. He arrived at 5.30 p.m. that evening.

Ever the true psychopath and arch-bullshitter, Heath was entirely at ease with himself when, after looking at Doreen's photograph, he identified her as the girl he'd had dinner with. He appeared upset and put on a great act of surprise and sorrow. He told the detective that he had walked her part the way back to her hotel but had seen her again the following morning entering a shop. When asked if he knew of her present whereabouts, Heath coolly supplied the name of a fictitious American officer called 'Wisecarver', whom he claimed had been one of her friends. 'Oh, and there was another American,' he volunteered, 'who'd offered to take her to Exeter.'

To Heath's warped psychopathology this seemed to be a perfectly plausible explanation. Knowing there were scores of American servicemen on furlough in the town, and with him calling himself 'Group Captain Rupert Brooke', he expected that his bluff would work – that the lowly county detective would buy his story hook, line and sinker and that would be the end of it.

Heath was wrong.

Detective Constable Suter was no bumpkin copper, far from it. Balding, tall, muscular, with steely eyes and a strong jaw, he carried himself upright and proud. He was every inch the dedicated police officer and he'd measured up Heath as soon he met him, for he instantly spotted the strong similarity between Heath and the man pictured in the 'Wanted for Murder' notice sent to every law-enforcement agency in the country. Yet Suter had to hedge his bets. He didn't have the authority to detain Heath until an inspector arrived; for while on the surface the so-called group captain seemed plausible enough, the detective now had to play a waiting game until his senior colleague could verify whether or not a 'Group Captain Rupert Brooke' existed. But time was running out. Despite his own gut feelings that Heath was the suspect wanted for the murder of Margery Gardner, Suter had no lawful reason to hold the man – then pure fate intervened.

Just as Heath was about to leave the police station, two people – Doreen's father, Charles Marshall, who had come to assist in the search for his missing daughter, accompanied by a Mrs Cruikshank, also his daughter, who bore an uncanny resemblance to her sister Doreen – walked past him, almost brushing shoulders. Suter saw Heath that instant break into a cold sweat and shiver. And this momentary lapse was all that Suter needed to detain him a little longer.

Heath's fate was sealed on the gut feeling of a dedicated copper's streetwise instinct.

Suter could contain himself no longer and showed Heath the photo on the wanted notice: 'Brooke . . . is your real name Heath?'

'Good Lord, no!' Heath replied. 'But I agree he does looks like me.'

When Detective Inspector George Gates arrived his first thoughts were not to immediately contact the elite Metropolitan Police. There had been enough numerous alleged sightings of Detective Superintendent Barratt's quarry already. False reports of Heath being in London, Hampshire,

Wiltshire, Berkshire and Dublin, amongst other locations, had already wasted much of the Met's time, so Gates needed to make further enquiries off of his own bat, and, considering everything, we can understand why. Up until this point it had all been hearsay with the suspicions of the two hotel managers, the night porter at the Tollard Royal Hotel and the quick-witted Mrs Phillips – along with the fact that 'Group Captain Rupert Brooke' had volunteered to help the police, counted for something. Yet, there was not even enough lawful suspicion to get a search warrant to enter Heath's hotel room to look for anything incriminating – until Heath opened his mouth once again.

Heath's bravado, his ego, had assumed that in going to the police station he wouldn't be staying there long. Thus, in anticipation of this brief visit he'd left the hotel without his sports jacket. Now feeling a bit chilly, he asked the police if his jacket could be brought to him and they willingly obliged, and what meagre belongings they found in Room No. 81 were brought to the police station and examined in front of the nonplussed man.

In Heath's sports jacket was found a cloakroom ticket issued at Bournemouth West railway station on the Sunday Heath had arrived in the town from Sussex. This ticket led police to a suitcase, which upon being opened was found to contain a neckerchief and a blue scarf both stained with blood and bearing hairs later proved to come from Doreen Marshall's head, and a leather riding whip with a plaited thong. The tip had been worn away, exposing the metal underneath.

In Heath's jacket pocket the detectives found the return half of a London–Bournemouth rail ticket, subsequently found to have been issued to Doreen Marshall, and an artificial pearl.

In a drawer in Heath's hotel room, police discovered a soiled, blood stained handkerchief, tightly knotted, with human hairs adhering to it.

Heath must have now realised that he was in a bit of a fix, for how could he explain that just thirty-six hours earlier, in order to raise funds he had pawned a ring belonging to Doreen for £5.00 and her fob watch for £3.00 (today's equivalent of what he received would be in the region of £400). Nevertheless, still insisting that he was 'Group Captain Rupert Brooke', he gave a written statement, which hinted that she had 'probably left town'.

In brief, he claimed that after walking out of the hotel together in the early hours of Thursday morning they had 'sat on a seat near the hotel overlooking the sea.' He added: 'We must have talked for at least an hour, probably longer, and then we walked down the slope towards the Pavilion.'

Embellishing this false account even more, Heath recounted that:

Miss Marshall did not wish me to accompany her but I insisted on doing so – at least some of the way. I left her at the pier and watched her cross the road and enter the gardens. Before leaving her I asked her if she would come round the following day, but she said she would be busy for the next few days, but would telephone me on Sunday if she could manage it. I have not seen her since although I thought I saw her entering Bobby's department store on Thursday morning.[Bobby & Co. was a chain of department stores later subsumed by Debenhams.]

At 9.45 p.m. that evening, Detective Inspector George Gates confronted Heath and informed him: 'I am now satisfied that you are Neville George Clevely Heath. I am going to detain you pending the arrival of officers of the Metropolitan Police,' to which Heath murmured, 'Oh, all right.'

Early the following day, Metropolitan Police Detective Inspector Reginald Spooner arrived in Bournemouth. On Monday, 8 July 1946, Heath was charged with the murder of Margery Gardner and taken back to London.

Branksome Dene Chine consists of about sixteen acres of steep wooded valleys, heathland and ridges adjacent to the beach just west, and a short stroll from Bournemouth. The day before Heath was charged with murder, a young woman called Kathleen Evans was walking her dog through the area during the evening when it started sniffing around rhododendron bushes, disturbing a cloud of flies. The following evening the same thing happened and she mentioned it to her father. The two of them returned to the spot and found a camel-hair 'swagger' coat; a type of woman's coat first fashionable in the 1930s, three-quarter length and flaring out loosely from the shoulders. Three was also a black frock and some branches of fir trees. Underneath was the decomposing body of a woman. She was naked except for a left shoe.

The smell of death was dreadful.

Police were quickly on the scene and they found a broken string of twenty-seven artificial pearls. A powder compact and stockings were some distance away and an empty handbag was found at the bottom of the chine close to the beach. Branksome Dene Chine had given up the body of Doreen

Marshall. The artificial pearls on broken string would match exactly the one discovered in Heath's jack pocket.

All of this clearly shows how incompetent so many serial killers can be. Heath had committed the two most dreadful disorganised murders one can imagine. He had concocted what he imagined to be plausible accounts of his innocence yet both stories would take him straight to the gallows.

At autopsy, pathologist Dr Crichten McGaffey's report stated that Doreen's throat had been cut. In places the cut was three-quarters of an inch deep, and this proved to be the cause of her death. There were bruises on the back of head and the left temple. These had been caused while she was still alive and desperately fighting for her life because there were defensive knife wounds on her hands before she had been subdued and her wrists pinioned behind her back. However, the injuries inflicted by Heath after death were even more horrific. Her right nipple had been bitten off and there were jagged cuts the length of the torso in the form of a 'Y' and an 'A'.

Heath showed a complete indifference to his fate. Wearing a grey chalk-stripe suit, he was sitting calmly in the condemned cell when Albert Pierrepoint, the public executioner who hanged Christie, arrived. The execution log records that Heath stoically remarked, 'Come on, boys, let's get on with it.' He accepted the traditional offer of a glass of whisky to steady his nerves, adding, 'While you're about it, you might make that a double.'

At least he met his death like a man.

So what made Neville Heath go off the rails is an interesting question to find the answer to. While we can understand that killers such as Christie, Kürten and hundreds of others, suffered abusive childhoods, the same cannot be said for the likes of Heath, who was raised in a healthy, middle-class home, by decent, hardworking parents. In this respect I think that Heath mirrors John David Guise Cannan and Joanne Dennehy – the latter whose life and crimes I extensively covered in my book *Love of Blood* (2015). Cannan, like Heath, was a sexual sadist, while Joanne killed simply because she hated men and had a love of blood. Nevertheless, these three individuals started to exhibit antisocial behaviour in their very early teens, and while we can attribute juvenile drug and alcohol abuse as a trigger for Dennehy's downfall, the same cannot be said of Heath or Cannan, where there was little to no evidence of substance abuse of any kind during their adolescent years.

Perhaps the best place to start with Neville Heath is during his adolescence; the noun being derived from the Latin word *adolescere*, meaning 'to grow up', and it is a critical period in all of our lives. During adolescence, major psychological as well as biological changes take place; furthermore, development of sexuality is an important bio-psycho-social development, during which an individual's thoughts, perceptions as well as responses, get coloured sexually. The many that occur during puberty can put adolescents under a great deal of stress, which may have all manner of physical and psychological consequences, some of them adverse.

During adolescence, physical growth peaks, while cognitive development reaches maturity. Biological factors, psychological factors, as well as social factors, including environmental factors, all determine how sexuality develops in adolescents. The important social factors include the attitude of an adolescent's parents towards sexuality, parenting style, peer relationship, cultural influences, all of which contribute to sexual learning and decide the sexual attitude of the adolescent. It is sexual learning/sexual attitude – psychological imprinting, if you will

In a nutshell, we might say that this could be one of a 'Nature v. Nurture' issue; one where no matter how good the parenting, and how healthy the environment in which the child is raised, we all enter into adolescence in a completely emotionally different way even to our siblings. And, this may also account for the fact that so many serial killers – indeed, quite a few that I have interviewed at length – had siblings brought up in exactly the same way who yet went on to live normal, decent and productive lives. In other words, child 'A' turns out to be the only rotten apple in a basket of otherwise good fruit all grown on the same tree. Indeed, we see this rotten apple analogy being played out in millions of families around the world today. There may be two or more children in a family and, while the majority of them turn out just fine there is often one of the kids, who, for whatever reason, goes wayward, and the parents are at loss to understand why.

We recall that Heath started to become sadistic while he was at school. He stamped on a girl's fingers when she tried to pick up a dropped pencil. On another occasion a teacher caught him spanking a screaming girl very hard with a ruler and the subsequent admonishment meant nothing to him. So, it is at this point I see the early signs of a developing deviant psychopathy, but there is more. Much more.

While it is true to say that many emerging and fully

emerged serial killers – obviously not all of them – have criminal histories which include causing pain and suffering, even the deaths of birds and helpless animals, it is a form of sadistic bullying. Jeffery Dahmer, Arthur Shawcross and Peter Kürten are three such individuals that spring to mind. Animal abuse can also be an indicator and a predictor of the commission of other violent acts in the future. This has been well documented in numerous research studies and has led to animal abuse being listed as one of the criteria for a diagnosis of conduct disorder in childhood. It is also well known that this type of animal abuse is often cyclical and that the only way to stop the cycle is intervention; the earlier the intervention the higher rate of success, but this cannot happen when a youngster has a developing psychopathy, as I suggest was the case with Neville Heath.

But what about the stamping on a little girl's hand, or the sadistic spanking with a ruler of another schoolgirl? Isn't this form of ill-treatment, the causing of pain to a child, echoing the behaviour of those kids who hurt animals? Several of Heath's teachers and peers at school thought of him as arrogant and a bully, and bullies often have trouble relating to their peers. Because they can be violent, manipulative, cruel, without empathy and generally unpleasant, they may not have many friends, and Heath could count his friends on one hand, that's how unpopular he was.

Another issue to factor in is that a common reason we find teens presenting to others with larger-than-life egos is due to a not so private sense of low self-worth. A low self-worth usually comes from having a sense of low competency in the world. As human beings we are hard-wired to be social creatures, and a significant milestone with any teenager is an expressed desire to be, and follow-through in becoming, of service to others. It is human nature for teens to want to aspire to certain skills or professions that serve the community, for which in return they experience a sense of belonging and recognition, but in Heath's case he would become one of those empty bottles that make the loudest noise.

And, it is this low sense of self-worth that compels such individuals to dress themselves up to be something they aren't. So, it is in this way many budding homicidal psychopaths go on to present themselves as they enter adulthood and why they learn to develop masks of normality, presenting themselves in a manner that their peers will accept, to even admire them for something that are patently not.

It is further ordered that on such scheduled date that you will be put to death by a current of electricity, sufficient to cause your immediate death and that current of electricity shall continue to be passed through your body until you are dead.

Take care of yourself, young man. I say that to you sincerely; take care of yourself, please. It is an utter tragedy for this court to see such a total waste of humanity as I've experienced in this courtroom.

You're a bright young man. You would have made a good lawyer and I would have loved to have you practice in front of me, but you went another way, partner. Take care of yourself. I don't feel any animosity toward you. I want you to know that. Once again, take care of yourself.

JUDGE EDWARD COWART SENTENCING
BUNDY TO DEATH IN 1979

An excellent example of this fake 'presenting' can be found in the chapter on Kenneth Alessio Bianchi in my book *Talking with Serial Killers*. Indeed, Theodore 'Ted' Robert Bundy often 'presented well' to many of his peers, in fact even, as may be seen above, to Judge Edward Cowart at Bundy's trial in 1979 for multiple homicide. Bundy had many faces and names which he used to conceal the evil person living within: Chris Hagen, Kenneth Misner, Police Officer Roseland, Fire Officer Richard Burton and Rolf Miller. Yet, using the apple analogy again – here we find a perfectly shaped shiny red apple, but upon peeling it we see that it is rotten through and through, and this sums Heath up precisely for he used multiple names and identities too.

As we have also noted throughout Heath's narrative, he had an incredible pathological elasticity enabling him to change his 'presentation' at the drop of a hat. I say 'incredible' because I have never come across a serial killer who has had this amazing degree of chameleon-like versatility before – another reason for his inclusion in this book.

Undoubtedly, Neville Heath was, in a perverse sort of way, the consummate method actor; one who possesses the skills, the ability and the art of experiencing – to which he contrasts the 'art of representation via presentation', thus mobilising his conscious thought and will in order to activate other, less controllable psychological processes, such as emotional experience and subconscious behaviour sympathetically and indirectly. This is what actors do, and it is a fact that many actors become so psychologically programmed to believe that they are so 'famous' – with their false personas bringing them worldwide acclaim – that when the limelight dims then extinguishes, their overfed egos pop like a Hollywood, all-glitzy, star-spangled over-inflated balloon. To compensate, they resort to drugs and alcohol abuse, become unmanageable by their producers and agents and often violent towards their partners. Some even commit suicide as the result.

Heath's service history, no matter how true or not, became rehearsals for the roles he intended to play. Like a method actor, Heath searched for inner narratives and motives to justify his actions and what he intended to seek to achieve at any given moment, place or time. He could don any uniform, any mask, any guise, and have his 'audience' totally believe in him. This was perfectly illustrated by his bullshit behaviour while staying at the Tollard Royal Hotel, and that was just one example. Another instance was when he conned the Fleet Street journalist out of a wad of money on the assurance that he would fly the guy overseas in his private airplane – and hard-nosed journos are never the easiest people to dupe! This homicidal maniac could walk off stage; change his clothes, and return to the boards with a totally different persona, within a heartbeat.

That Heath initially fooled almost everyone he came into contact is understandable because he also cunningly presented himself at a time in history when military officers were thought of as beyond reproach – the higher the rank the better soldier, sailor or airman they were. No non-commissioned officer rank would charlatan Heath adopt in his scams: 'Corporal Neville Heath' just wouldn't have cut the ice within the social circles in which he subconsciously believed he was entitled to be and to hold court over all and sundry.

But, how and why was he so plausible? That question is easily answered because he was a pilot; he had been in the war and he could, off-the-cuff, embellish and richly embroider all of his lies and utter deceits with large helpings of the truth. In other words, 'I've got the wings and the T-shirt to prove it.'

Nevertheless, like real method actors there comes a time when finally they have to take their bows and leave the stage to reveal who they truly are. Indeed, another analogy might be this. We often become star struck by a handsome and hunky or mega sexy actor/actress; in some cases we even form huge fan clubs and are prepared to literally kiss the ground they walk on, then one day they are revealed to be a woman beater or a diva who has been treating her staff like dirt for years, or worse, and are being sued for millions of bucks, and suddenly they fall from grace to become disenfranchised altogether.

We can apply that same analogy to Heath. With genuine actors, we love and admire their performances and the characters they play – but do we know the *real* person, of course not! Furthermore, many famous actors actually start to believe that they are the character they are playing. They egotistically massage themselves with all of the fur-stroking and adoration they get – until their careers are on the wane and they start becoming depressed, then into hard drugs and alcohol abuse, which often leads to death.

To make my point here, and I do speak from experience; I have met quite a number of 'famous' actors, usually in Hollywood or while appearing on TV shows. I had dinner with one of the world's most adored actors: his dirty fingernails were bitten down to the quick, his unwashed hair lank unkempt, and his face wan. He was shy, too, and I would not have recognised him in an elevator. As for actresses, our silver-screen sex bombs, the divas – suffice to say that they all wear masks in their roles of actors. Serial killers act in more-or-less the same way.

One of the most famous sayings attributed to Abraham Lincoln is about this deceptive element: 'You can fool all the people some of the time and some of the people all the time, but you cannot fool all the people all the time.' Neville Heath's presentation, his character acting was simply that – a show put on to please his audience at the time of his choosing and to suit his own, deeply flawed psychopathology . . . all of which brings me to murder most foul, for Heath was undoubtedly a reprehensible monster on and off stage.

Although by today's standards we might judge Neville Heath as not being a 'major player' in the homicide league, because he was, after all, an *emerging* serial killer, a novice with only two killings under his belt – in comparison with Dr Harold Shipman (200-plus murders) or Ted Bundy, Harvey Carignan, Henry Lee Lucas, or Peter Kürten or even Christie, all exceeding Heath by far – Heath was a mere lightweight. Nevertheless, in placing Heath's criminal mindset under the magnifying glass we can focus in on his basic non-homicidal motives as being the same as those of most confidence tricksters and cheap crooks, who give at least some thought to planning a crime most often for meagre short-term gains without even considering their post-crime actions to avoid being caught.

As we have seen with Heath, he was such a criminal because he was always being arrested and charged; sometimes locked up yet ever the recidivist, ,he never learned from his mistakes or even attempted to mend the error of his ways.

I suggest, therefore, that the financially and morally bankrupt Heath, while at once tricking people out of their money, treated his murderous activity in all but the same way.

He gave some thought to zeroing in on a victim, inflicting upon them an almost unimaginable degree of sexual brutality, but no forethought as to how, in God's name, he might get away scot free. It was if he were acting upon a variety of dark, uncontrollable sexually sadistic impulses, so perhaps, a quick review of my earlier chapter, 'The Homicidal Brain', might help us again. It was this 'I WANT it NOW, so FUCK the consequences' scenario being played over and over again throughout Heath's criminal narrative, and this seeking-out of instant gratification is repeated during his terrible murders.

I would like to be able to confirm that with all of the criminalistic state-of-the-art forensic-science techniques available to law enforcement today, police might have apprehended Neville Heath a lot faster, but I cannot say this at all. Indeed, I will go a step further by suggesting that back in the forties, the Metropolitan Police; although cottoning on to the killer of Margery Gardner within hours of her murder, were helped in spades by the pre-crime and post-crime behaviour of the murderer himself. Back then the police wouldn't have needed CCTV, a *Crimewatch* programme, or mobile telephone locational tracking systems to catch their man, for Heath might as well have given the law a gratis, no-expense-spared highly illuminated plan of his whereabouts – all allowing the cops to arrest and charge him quite quickly ... not bad at all when everything, including the era, is taken into consideration! In fact, given the facts, I doubt that modern police could have caught him even faster.

However, what I do find further fascinating about Heath's psychopathology is, that in the full knowledge that he was being hunted by every police force in the country for murder, his description and his face plastered over the front page of every national newspaper in the land, exacerbated him having no funds at his disposal, he had the front to wheedle his way into staying at the prestigious, blue-chip, blue-rinse-brigade Tollard Royal Hotel in genteel Bournemouth.

If, and only *if*, I were to give Heath even a smidgen of credit, I would say that this chappie had some balls. But I won't! For then Heath goes on to murder sweet Doreen Marshall; shortly thereafter ambling up to the local police station to offer detectives his 'assistance' in their enquiries.

Okay, I am being a tad facetious here, yet it still leaves us asking ourselves why he resorted to committing sado-sexual homicide in the first place.

I think, that like so many other murderers of this type, Heath was already becoming hooked on extreme sexual practices, because wherever he was stationed he frequented brothels and nightclubs and mixed with loose women whom he could use and abuse and treat like dirt as he wished. I further support this by confirming that once he had married the beautiful, somewhat naïvely besotted Elizabeth Rivers in South Africa, after she gave birth he hardly had sex with her again. He merely married into the Rivers family for one reason, and one reason – to line his own pockets, to feather his own nest. And he didn't give two hoots about Elizabeth or his son when her father offered him a large sum of money to piss off and never return.

So let's come down to earth here. Imagine, for a moment, that you are the stiff-upper-lipped, walrus-moustached, ramrod-straight, dyed-in-tweed, millionaire patriarch. It's time for breakfast and your innocent daughter drags in a sponging charlatan whom you can see through like a recently cleaned plate-glass window.

So how would you respond to this forthcoming (fictionalised) scenario?

Dear Papa. I want you to meet my beau. I think his name is Bruce . . . Bruce Lockhart. He is a war hero, a pilot and a captain. Can you get Belligerence the lower stairs black housemaid to run a bath for him and give him a few thousand pounds cos he is presently without funds on account of him being shot down somewhere. He was going back to England to recuperate but when the ship docked at Durban he limped ashore for medical treatment and the ship left without him. Papa, I love him. Hey, guess what, I only met Bruce yesterday and we're going to have a baby . . . Oh, what's that loud noise . . . goodness me it's the Johannesburg Police rushing by. Papa, I wonder who they are looking for?

Of course I just made that up, but just like every writer, novelist or otherwise, we start a chapter with a blank page and as we research and pen our words we go through a learning process too, and this chapter about Neville George Clevely Heath has been such an exercise for me. It is all too easy for us to go hysterical about how one views this depraved man, but now is the moment for me to take my foot off of the loud pedal and slow down a bit, for in Heath's case I have thought about his sado-sexual behaviour linked to alcohol as highly contributory factors in his two killings.

Taking sadomasochism (S&M) first of all. This is an interaction, especially during sexual activity, in which one person enjoys inflicting physical and mental suffering on another person who reciprocates by deriving pleasure from experiencing pain. As I have said before, each to his or her own, and we live in enlightened times so I will leave it at that and move on to heavy drinking.

It goes without saying that sexual assault can take place in a number of different instances and can happen to many different people. However, it is far more likely to take place when alcohol abuse is involved, reducing a person's inhibitions as it does, making things, such as sexual assault, even rape, seem more acceptable – and what a controversial thing this is to say, but it is widely recognised anyway. Even those who normally would not force sex on a woman may do so when under the influence of alcohol. Generally, women are most commonly victims of sexual assault, although men, most often homosexuals, have been known to have been sexually assaulted as well. In extreme cases, I would refer the reader to the US serial killer, Randy Kraft, indeed even the bisexual John Wayne Gacy, as two prime examples of homosexual sado-sexual/alcohol abuse. Of course intoxication in the victim may prevent them from avoiding risky situations or stopping their attacker once the assault starts . . . so the woman at the Strand Palace Hotel was placing herself in grave danger because she and Heath were well in drink when they first hit it off, and she escaped with her life thanks only to the hotel electrician who heard her screams and called the manager to investigate. The same thing happened to Margery the day she was killed. Both participants were very drunk, so she willingly placed herself in an incredibly risky situation with a man she barely knew.

From the moment Heath crossed the threshold and killed, there was no place for him to hide. Having got off relatively lightly for his past crimes, this was now an altogether different ball game. He soon learned that the police were on his trail. He would have also been aware that it was only a matter of time before he was caught, brought to court, convicted then hanged.

It was quite natural for Heath to travel to one of the most prestigious seaside resorts. Extremely easy for him to book into a posh hotel under the guise of being a phony, highly-decorated 'Group Captain Rupert Brooke'; even easier for him to run up a huge tab while staying there; all the while knowing that at any moment he could be recognised as nationally wanted man and have the police arrest him. Therefore, there can be no doubt in my mind that Neville Heath knew that his days were numbered.

When he picked up the former Wren, Doreen Marshall, I am convinced that he had no intention of killing her. Indeed, stepping back momentarily, I don't think that he had planned to murder Margery Gardner, either. I say this because even if we take into consideration all of the events leading up to both homicides, he didn't just spot them, jump out of the dark and attack them – quite the opposite, in fact. He dated them, socialised with them; took both young women to places, including hotels, where everybody and anybody could see them together as a couple – and this behaviour is extremely unusual for any type of serial killer. This is why I think that he is unique in a grotesquely morbid sort of way.

And, to me, there is another facet of Heath's psychopathology worth considering. We will remember Miss Yvonne Symonds as the being the young woman Heath met at the WRNS dance in Chelsea. That he swept her off her feet. He wined and dined her, too. They slept together the second night with no sexual impropriety or even the thought of harming her entering his mind before she returned to her parents' home on the south coast the following day. And, we know that immediately after killing Margery Gardner he whisked himself down to Worthing and started courting Yvonne again.

Why?

For my part I believe that Heath was using all of his devious skills skills not only to distance himself from the Margery Gardner crime scene, but also to resume a normality of sorts, to post-kill camouflage himself, with Yvonne as yet another tool in his box of tricks, just as he did when mixing with the well-heeled clients at the Tollard Royal Hotel.

During the research for this book, trying to get inside the 'killer brain' of Neville Heath to understand what made him tick, I discovered that Yvonne Symonds had been in the Women's Royal Naval Service, too, which is why she was at that Chelsea dance in the first place.

The manner in which he treated Yvonne almost mirrors how he initially treated Doreen Marshall. He flattered her, wined and dined her, and at first he treated her with the greatest of, perhaps phony, respect. To my mind he would have subconsciously wished to have continued to develop this relationship without harming her in any physical way – Doreen, had after all been a Wren, as had Yvonne Symonds, both young women, like his former wife, very decent individuals indeed. But he killed Doreen, so Yvonne could have gone the same way.

Remember that Doreen was ill with flu and measles and at her father's instigation was in Bournemouth to recuperate, relax and take in the fresh sea air. During their dinner at the Tollard Royal Hotel, Doreen was tired – as witnessed by 'Miss

Marple', the keen-eyed Mrs Gladys Phillips, her husband and the hotel staff. Doreen, therefore, needed to get back to her own hotel for a good night's sleep – and this is something the ego-driven and thoughtless Heath failed to appreciate because he was, once again, infused with alcohol.

If we had had the luxury of being a fly on the wall, we would have seen this dread scenario being played out before our very eyes, for after her first request to leave the hotel fell on Heath's deaf ears, the impressionable woman in good faith felt more or less obliged to accede to the alleged group captain's suggestion (he was a very senior officer in her eyes) that they spend a short while together in the quiet writing room before, being the gentleman he put himself forth to be, he escorted her back to the Norfolk Royale Hotel. But, that period in the writing room ended, I think, when Heath suggested that Doreen spend the night with him – again a replay of how he suggested the same thing to Yvonne Symonds, who politely refused. This would have been the moment when Doreen put her foot down and when she asked Mr Phillips to order a taxi for her and an argument ensued.

We know that the ever-manipulating Heath ordered the night porter to cancel the taxicab; then followed Doreen out into the night. It was past midnight. The area was deserted. His state of mind negatively influenced by too much drink, the pressures of being without funds, a demand for his hotel tab, with no more places to hide and the certainty that the police were closing in caused him to snap.

Maybe at first he tried to again convince her that she should spend the night with him. She refused. Then he would have said, 'All right, let me walk you back to your hotel.' She refused. She'd had enough of the man, and that was when

Heath, an extremely fit man, grabbed her. Now she was powerless. He would have cupped his hand over the mouth of the now terrified Doreen and marched her the short distance to Branksome Dene Chine where he carried out one of the most horrific killings England had ever witnessed at the time.

Had Heath remained at large, would he have killed again? Undoubtedly so, in my opinion, for sooner or later this alcohol-fuelled sado-sexual beast would have risen again for he was a sadistic sexual predator and there was, for him, no escaping from the monster living within.

Finally, I have also taken into account many of the statements made by Heath, either verbally or throughout his writings, the most important of which I headed this chapter with. In my work it is often not what an offender says or writes that is of import, it is what he doesn't say, omits to say, refuses to answer to, or forgets to say that becomes more important. So, when trying to get into the head of a highly dangerous offender all of these factors have to be taken into consideration.

Heath's statement on women: 'They're weak and stupid. Basically crooked. That's why they're always attracted to rascals like me. They have the morals of alley cats and minds like sewers. They respond to flattery like a duck responds to water,' I take with a pinch of salt as being Heath mouthing off. However, I do believe that when he said: 'I honestly don't give a damn what happens to me. I've faced death too often in the last six years to worry about it. Anyway, I've nothing left to live for since I lost my wife and child,' he meant part of it, with a measure of self-pity thrown in.

Heath's letters to Detective Superintendent Barratt, and his statement to the Bournemouth detectives, are, from a criminologist's, indeed a forensic psychiatrist's or a forensic psychologist's, point of view, absolutely fascinating. So, I will let you, the reader, pick through them, and with all that you have read in this chapter, indeed thus far in this book, see if you can understand Heath's psychopathology better than he ever could have. It is not rocket science, after all.

Then there is the statement of a woman who had an almost fatal encounter to consider. She came from Cambridge and gave this statement during Heath's trial. Her name is still protected but she had this to say:

> I'll never forget his face − that horrible, sadistic look
> which twisted and contorted it grotesquely ... then I got
> it ... two vicious smacks across the face.

This would have been the same face that the terrified-out-of-mind Doreen Marshall saw when she was being dragged to the most terrible of deaths.

Doreen Margaret Marshall is buried in Pinner Cemetery, London Borough of Harrow.

Margery Aimee Brownell Gardner is buried in the All Saints Churchyard, Ecclesall, Sheffield, South Yorkshire.

If you ever feel inclined after reading this book it might be a good thing to − yes, visit those girls in their final resting place and put a few flowers on their graves.

Neville George Clevely Heath is buried in the Pentonville Prison Cemetery, Islington, London.

And now we move on to two equally fascinating cases; contemporary examples of thoroughly complex, off-the-wall monsters − one of them an ultra-mega-respected male, the other an entirely drop-dead gorgeous woman – and their sickening crimes, which, I insist, must afford you sleepless nights.

6

Colonel David Russell Williams

And all the carnall *beauty* of my wife
Is but skin-deep . . .
THE PHRASE 'BEAUTY IS SKIN-DEEP' IS BELIEVED
TO HAVE BEEN COINED BY SIR THOMAS OVERBURY
IN HIS POEM 'A WIFE' (1613)

People like violence because it feels good.
ALAN TURING

There cannot be anything much scarier for a single woman than to arrive home from work after dark and get the rising hairs on the nape of the neck sense that someone has been in her property. A neat lass, one being absolutely positive that she had closed her underwear drawer – she always does – but now it's partly open and two of her bras have been arranged in crucifix fashion on her bed. Her knickers have been rummaged through. Some are missing. There are damp stains on the duvet cover and on the carpet. She calls for her cat and hears it mewing in the basement. Cautiously, descending the stairs she finds the cat hiding behind the humming boiler.

Then a homicidal killer emerges and she is doomed.

As the Canadian journalist Greg McArthur wrote in the Canadian newspaper the *Globe and Mail* in 2010, 'If there was ever a childhood to prepare someone for the transient existence of an Air Force colonel, Russell Williams lived it – a meandering journey that saw him twice change his last name, and took him from England to barren north-eastern Ontario and to one of Canada's most prestigious boys' schools.'

> I spent my career doing things right and avoiding things that were wrong. But here, I can't figure out what went wrong.
>
> DR JERRY SOVKA, INTERVIEW WITH THE
> *GLOBE AND MAIL*, 11 FEBRUARY 2010

Williams was born Thursday, 7 March 1963 in the small town of Bromsgrove, Worcester, England, to Christine Nonie née Chivers and Cedric David Williams.

David Williams (he is commonly known as 'Russell' or 'Russ') is now serving a twenty-five-year-to-natural-life sentence in the Port-Cartier super-max prison, located to the north of Quebec and about 600 kilometres from the historic city itself.

Williams shares the institution, which houses about 237 inmates, with some of the most dangerous killers and rapists in Canada, among them Paul Bernado, the 'Scarborough Rapist' who, with his wife Karla Homolka, killed three teenage girls; Robert Pickton, a Port Coquitlam pig farmer convicted of multiple homicides; and Michael Wayne McGray who killed seven people including a mother and child.

Russell Williams appears to have enjoyed his early formative years but was uprooted from the UK aged about four when his father was hired as a metallurgist at Chalk River Laboratories – Canada's premier nuclear research facility in Deep River, an 800-resident village in Renfrew County, Ontario.

They moved to Scarborough, Ontario, and settled in a house near the Scarborough Bluffs. But, as the *Globe and Mail* tells us, the home was merely a base: Dr Sovka's nuclear expertise made him in demand around the globe and by 1979, Jerry Sovka and Nonie were in South Korea where he was overseeing another reactor project. The two boys, Russell and his brother Harvey, who had taken their stepfather's name, stayed in Canada to continue their education.

> He [Russell Sovka] was a very good musician and also a fairly quiet, diligent guy.
>
> INNES VAN NOSTRAND, FORMERLY AT UPPER
> CANADA COLLEGE WITH RUSSELL WILLIAMS,
> LATER THE SCHOOL'S VICE-PRINCIPAL

As a youngster, Russell did a paper round to earn pocket money delivering the *Globe and Mail*. He also learned to play the piano. He attended the Birchmount Park Collegiate Institute in Scarborough, and went on to finish his education at the Upper Canada College in Toronto, spending his last two years, 1980–82, as a boarder while his parents were in South Korea. In his final year, he was elected as co-prefect for his boarding house.

Russell's appetite for structure and rigidity did not apply to his musical tastes. He played trumpet in the school band, and in the 1982 UCC yearbook his graduation message was a Louis Armstrong quote: 'If you have to ask what Jazz is, you'll never know.' 'He stood out in the row of gold trumpets in the band; his was the only silver one,' said Tom Heintzman, a former class and band mate, adding, 'He was very musical. He was very quiet. He wasn't the type you would see out at parties.'

There were reports of scandals at the school involving teachers there during the 1980s and 1990s, and it later came to light that during the period Williams was at the school, a housemaster there, Douglas Brown, was sexually abusing young boys. (He was later convicted and jailed.) Although there is absolutely nothing to indicate that the two had ever even come into contact with each other the young Williams might well have at least been aware that something was going on; years later, when asked by reporters from *The Toronto Star* if he'd known Russell Sovka (as Williams then was), Brown replied that he had not.

After leaving school in 1982, Russell went on to study economics and political science at the University of Toronto Scarborough College (UTSC), graduating with a Bachelor of Arts in 1986, While he was there he started engaging in elaborate pranks against his peers and hiding in their empty rooms to give them a fright when they came in – more of this strange behaviour will emerge later as we work through Williams's life and his subsequent crimes.

In 1983, UTSC slightly changed its name to University of Toronto Scarborough Campus, and since 1996 it's been the University of Toronto at Scarborough. The 1980s had its darker side for the campus, with a spate of unsolved rapes. These were not much publicised other than by the campus newspaper, *The Underground*, which in January 1983 observed:

Last Tuesday, a student was attacked in the parking lot, dragged into the valley and raped. This is the first reported attack . . . Something will have to be done to alleviate fears, even if it does cost the College a lot of money.

There have been no suggestions from the Ontario Provincial Police (OPP) that Williams was linked in any way to those attacks, but they will keep those historic allegations in mind. Neither does it seem to be thought significant that a student who attended UTSC at the same time as Williams was Paul Bernado, later convicted of committing three homicides in the early 1990s. Bernardo has admitted to raping at least a dozen women in Scarborough at the time, but he has not admitted to attacking any girls on the UTSC campus.

So, what have we learned so far? There can be no doubt that Williams enjoyed a healthy formative period in his very early life. He was relocated from the UK to Canada as a kid, his parents divorced and he was adopted by a hardworking nuclear scientist who did all he could to ensure that Russell and his brother Harvey had a first-rate education even while he and their mother were overseas.

It is true that, as mentioned above, while at university Russell got a kick out of breaking into some of his peers' rooms, to rig up some practical joke, such as a booby trap, or to hide quietly and then give them a fright as they came in – perhaps uncharacteristically childish behaviour, but these pranks were both harmless and inventive. In carrying them out, however, he must have honed the art of picking locks . . . On the other hand, unlike Heath, for instance, he showed no sign of any inclination towards violence. Nevertheless, something must have gone wrong: to repeat Dr Sovka's words: 'I spent my career doing things right and avoiding things that were wrong. But here, I can't figure out what went wrong [with Russell].'

I myself wrote to Russell Williams to try to find the answer to that question. He failed to reply.

During his undergraduate years young Williams – like Heath - showed an avid interest in flying. He took lessons at Toronto's Buttonville airport and, after graduating, joined the armed forces in 1987, with his assessment showing that he had all the aptitude to make a first-rate pilot. One of his first jobs in the military was instructing student pilots at the Prairie Southport Airport, Portage la Prairie, a small city in the Central Plains Region of Manitoba, and, it was here that he met Mary Elizabeth Harriman, a keen golfer like himself. They married on Saturday, 1 June 1991. There was still no hint, to anyone, of the terrifying storm of sexually perverted violence he was later to unleash.

Throughout this book we have learned of the mask of normality that homicidal socio/psychopaths wear. In the prequel to this book, *Talking with Psychopaths and Savages*, I examined this psychopathological charade in detail. Now, in this book, we have already seen the masks worn by Christie, Kürten and Heath, so where did the British medical profession go wrong in not spotting that one of their own, Dr Harold Shipman, was serial killer; and how on earth did Russell Williams slip in under the radar? For here was a pilot who had ferried the Queen and Prince Philip around – yet he was an out-of-control sex maniac.

His degree under his belt, Williams decided he wanted to become a pilot and went on to enrol in the Canadian Forces; to do so he had to apply to the Regular Officer Training programme, which involved a screening process consisting of five character references: employment check, criminal record check, credit check and security clearance questionnaire; the Canadian Forces Aptitude Test (verbal reasoning, spatial ability and problem solving) and a thorough medical examination, but apparently no psychological evaluation (the latter not required by the Canadian Civil Airline Authorities either). All of this Williams passed with flying colours and he was given a 'SECRET' security clearance.

Williams went on to attend the Preparatory Year at Royal Military College (RMC) Saint-Jean, Quebec. This programme consists of three phases of highly intensive training before attending Basic Flying Training at the NATO Flight Training Centre in Moose Jaw, Saskatchewan. Get through that lot and you get your wings. In 1990, Williams was a pilot in the Canadian Armed Forces or Forces armées Canadiennes, and through his impressive twenty-three-year career continued to shoot up through the ranks.

He was promoted to captain; given 'top security' clearance on Tuesday, 1 January 1991; posted the following year to 434 Combat Support Squadron at CFB Shearwater, Nova Scotia, where he flew the CC-144 Challenger in the electronic warfare and coastal role.

In 1994, now aged thirty-one and destined for yet greater things, he was posted to the 412 Transport Squadron in Ottawa, where he transported VIPs, including high-ranking government officials and foreign dignitaries. He was promoted to major in November 1999 and posted, this time to Director General Military Careers, in Ottawa, where he served as the multi-engine pilot career manager.

In 2004, he earned a Master of Defence Studies degree from the Royal Military College of Canada with a 55-page thesis that supported pre-emptive war in Iraq; in June of that year he was promoted to lieutenant-colonel; in July he was appointed commanding officer of 437 Squadron at CFB Trenton.

The square-jawed, highly-decorated Williams had a service record that to date was exemplary; in May 2006, he also served as CO of Camp Mirage, a secretive logistics facility believed to be located at Al Minhad Air Base in Dubai, UAE, that provides support to Canadian Forces ops in Afghanistan. On Friday, 21 July 2006 he was posted to the Directorate of Air Requirements where he served as project director for the Airlift Capability Projects Strategic (C-17 Globemaster III) and the Tactical (CC-130J Super Hercules), and Fixed-Wing Search and Rescue (CC-127J Spartan). So impressed was his superior officer with him that in January 2009 he recommended that Williams be promoted to full colonel. On Wednesday, 15 July 2009 Williams was sworn in as Wing Commander at Canadian Forces Base Trenton.

Although much of this information is readily available elsewhere, I have included it in this book to highlight the fact that, unknown to every single person who knew Russell Williams, he was a sexual predator; for while at Trenton, and probably well beforehand, he would spend a good few of his evenings stalking women, scouting out their homes, entering when they were out, rifling through their underwear, masturbating into these items, often stealing them, taking the garments home to dress up in, take selfies and carefully fold them up and put them in his closet. Worse, he began to sexually abuse women, which escalated to rape and then murder.

With all of that being established, CFB Trenton is Canada's busiest military air transport base and locus of support for military operations. The base also functions as the point of arrival for the bodies of all Canadian Forces personnel killed in action abroad, and the starting point for processions along the 'Highway of Heroes' whence their corpses are brought to Toronto for autopsy.

Colonel Williams was described as an elite pilot and 'shining bright star' of the military. He had flown Queen Elizabeth II and the Duke of Edinburgh, the Governor-General of Canada, the Prime Minister of Canada, and many other dignitaries across the country and overseas in VIP aircraft, so we cannot take any of that away from him, yet he brought utter shame and disgrace down upon the entire Canadian military who subsequently stripped him of his rank and medals, later dismissed him in disgrace with a 'Dishonorable Discharge', his uniform was burned, his medals cut to pieces, his commission scroll was shredded and his Nissan 'Pathfinder' SUV was crushed and scrapped.

Welcome to Tweed, Ontario! We invite you to come experience our four-season backyard, broad in all its dimensions. It has unusual breadth & depth to its natural environment, vibrant variety in its business and economic life, many social flavours & accents, and deep cultural history & roots in the landscape.

Tweed is both a village and a municipality located halfway between Toronto and Ottawa, in the Central-Eastern part of Ontario, Canada, in the County of Hastings.

As the Gateway to the Land O' Lakes and the Bay of Quinte Region, the area has become known for its small-town friendliness, affordability, accessibility, beautiful environment, outdoor recreational experiences, and annual events.

MUNICIPALITY OF TWEED'S OFFICIAL WEBSITE

Around the time of assuming command of CFB Trenton, Colonel Williams purchased a grey-roofed white cottage at 62 Cosy Cove Lane on Stoco Lake; a sixty-minute drive north from the airbase. Now vacant, it is still the same as when he lived there although all of the other residents demand that it be razed to the ground. On the surface, it all appears absolutely postcard perfect: surrounded by tall pines, lush green front lawn, a prime waterfront lot with its own boat jetty and spectacular view, it seems like paradise:

Even the street sign is charming: 'Cosy Cove Lane'. But behind that front door, deep within, are the remnants of a repulsive predator – a stalker, rapist and sex-crazed killer; a man so notorious, that strangers still drive to tiny Tweed to see the property with their own eyes.

MACLEAN'S (CANADIAN NEWS MAGAZINE)

Williams subsequently sold the cottage for Canadian $165,000 (in today's money only about £97,000), which was less than he had bought it for, in order to try to settle some of the many multimillion-dollar lawsuits filed against him and his wife Mary – who has been an innocent party throughout.

Corporal Marie-France Comeau

Have a heart, please. I've been really good.
I want to live.
CORPORAL MARIE-FRANCE COMEAU,
BRANCHE DES SERVICES LOGISTIQUES, TO WILLIAMS
SHORTLY BEFORE HE KILLED HER

Born on Sunday, 19 March 1972, thirty-seven-year-old Corporal Marie-France Comeau, an attractive young woman with short dark hair streaked blonde, was a military flight attendant with 437 Squadron, CFB, Trenton – she had even flown once with Williams. She was found dead by her boyfriend in her spick and span bungalow home at 252 Raglan Street, Brighton, Ontario, on Wednesday, 25 November 2009, at around 1 p.m. Following a post-mortem examination at the office of the Chief Coroner's office in Toronto, the Northumberland OPP concluded two days later that her death was a homicide. She had suffered five blows to her head with the probable cause of death being suffocation.

As reported in the Canadian papers at the time, such as *Ottawa Citizen*, Williams had broken into Marie-France Comeau's home on 16 November, while she was away. While there, he had taken photos of her military uniform and underwear, of sex aids, and of himself wearing her underwear.

A week later he returned to attack and murder her. With his face masked, he broke in through a basement window, while she was at work. He knew her drive from work, about thirty-one/thirty-two kilometres, would take some thirty minutes and waited by the boiler for her to come home, and lingered there awaiting the right moment. She was wearing only a shawl when she came downstairs to look for her cat, and found Williams, who struck her several times with a torch. Once she was subdued, he tied her hands with rope and then tied her to a metal post in the basement. He then broke off her house key in the lock so that no one would be able to open the door, and covered her bedroom window with a blanket.

Marie-France put up a furious struggle, leaving her blood on a light switch and staircase handrail, before Williams overpowered her, taking photographs of her unconscious and naked on the stairs before dragging her to her bedroom. There he repeatedly raped her, all the while filming and photographing her on her bed over two hours. The young woman made a brave, but unsuccessful attempt to flee at one point when Williams briefly left the bedroom. After he had killed her, Williams took further photos and videos, covered her body with a duvet, washed the sheets with bleach, stole nine pieces of lingerie and left through a patio door.

The videotape recordings that Williams took of his evil enterprise make for sickening listening, with her at one point saying, 'I want to live so badly,' and Williams asking her, 'Did you expect to?' The terrified woman mumbles, 'Give me a chance. I'll be so good . . . please.'

Jessica Lloyd

I feel like my heart has been ripped right out of
my chest. No mother should ever have to go through
what this has put me through. Now I am a broken
woman. I can never, ever forgive him. I can honestly
say I hate Russell Williams.

I miss her every day. First it was Mother's Day,
then it was her birthday in May. So many dreams I had
for my daughter have been destroyed. I will never walk
her down the aisle; hear that she's expecting a baby.
He has not only taken away my precious daughter, but
dreams of her future children, my future grandchildren.

ROXANNE LLOYD, JESSICA'S MOTHER, VICTIM IMPACT
STATEMENT

According to his own account given to the police on 7
February, on Wednesday, 27 January 2010, Williams was
driving his Nissan SUV past the home of twenty-seven-
year-old Jessica Lloyd when he spotted her working out on
a treadmill in her front room. Whatever the case, he waited
until she had gone out to visit a friend then broke in and, as
they say in criminal parlance, 'cased the joint' before leaving.

Jessica's detached property, in a rural area north of Belleville,
was set well back from Highway 37 and about a fifteen-
minute drive north from CFB Trenton, so this account, that
he'd first seen her as he drove past the property is highly
suspicious. As the police agree, it was snowy and dark, the
roads were icy; and the highway was arrow-straight here, so
his account seems preposterous. It is more likely that Williams
had seen Jessica some time earlier and had been stalking her

for a while – as he had been doing with countless other women for weeks on end.

It was weird to see a vehicle in that location.

ONTARIO PROVINCIAL POLICE OFFICER

The following evening, the 28th, three witnesses noticed a Nissan SUV parked on Jessica's property. It was 153 metres from the house and up close to a perimeter hedgerow – an extremely strange place for someone to park a vehicle while visiting the young woman. For his part, Williams had taken up a position in nearby trees where he could secretly watch and wait for her to come home, during which time he saw several people knock on the door and leave. A hardworking, vivacious young woman with green eyes and long dark brown hair, Jessica was adored by everyone who knew her, so it would have come as no surprise that people would drop by hoping to see her.

Although Williams did not know it, one of the visitors was a female Ontario Provincial Police (OPP) officer. Because the cop had not seen this SUV on Jessica's land before she went to the front door and knocked. Receiving no reply, she left. Had she noted down the SUV's licence number, things might have turned out somewhat differently, with Williams being arrested much sooner.

As is so often in cases like this, the media were quick to pounce on what they alleged was a breach of conduct; with Detective Inspector Chris Nicholas, the OPP officer heading the investigation, telling the CTV news channel: 'Obviously, she [the officer] didn't know then what she knows now and if she did, I'm sure she would have taken further steps to find out what that vehicle was. And that's something she has to live with and she's dealing with and she feels very bad. We're supporting her 100 per cent.'

Not long after the police officer had left, Jessica returned home. We know that Jessica was still okay at 10.36 p.m. that night because she used her phone at that time to contact a friend. However, it was shortly thereafter that Williams broke in, found her in bed sleeping, woke her up and struck her with a torch. To further restrain Jessica, he tied her up and lay on her stomach, covering her eyes with duct tape. Bringing lamps in from other rooms to better light his images, he took photos and videos of her standing in the hallway wearing what she'd worn to bed – a black tank top and grey jogging pants, then, at about 2 a.m. he took a video of himself raping her, while giving his word that if she obeyed all of his instructions he would let her go.

Williams later told police that she co-operated in every way. After spending some three hours in the house with Jessica, he abducted her, leaving behind his boot prints and the SUV's tyre impressions in the snow. He drove her, bound and gagged in the front passenger seat, to 62 Cosy Cove Lane, where they arrived between 4.30 and 5 a.m. on 29 January.

Later that morning, at half past nine, Jessica, having, uncharacteristically, not shown up for work, her mother visited her house. She let herself in to find the place empty. Three hours later, Belleville police were on the scene and a search for her started; soon two sets of footwear impressions were found outside in the snow – one set large and very distinctive, the other set much smaller – leading to where the SUV had been parked. Meanwhile, back at Cosy Cove Lane, Williams had forced Jessica to have a shower with him before allowing her to sleep for a couple of hours. At some point she had a seizure, which was caused by the stress. She said that she needed go to hospital or she would die. 'Don't make it worse for yourself, Jessica,' he told her. 'Talk to me, Jessica,' adding that she should relax and not bite her tongue. He videotaped everything, as reported in the *Durham Region News* of Ontario.

> If I die, will you make sure that my mom knows that I love her?
>
> JESSICA TO WILLIAMS AS SHE CONTINUED TO CONVULSE, BEGGING HIM TO REMOVE THE ROPES

After Williams had raped Jessica yet again, he gave her some fruit, dressed her, removed the duct tape from her mouth, promising her that he was going to take her back home – until, that is, he opened the door and smashed her head with his torch. Once he judged her unconscious, he strangled her with a rope. He photographed the whole process. Leaving Jessica's body in his garage, at around 10 a.m. Williams drove back to his office at CFB Trenton, sleeping there that night because he had to catch an early flight to drop off troops in California, after which he stopped off in Ontario. Upon his return to Tweed on 2 February, he drove Jessica's body, still bound with duct tape, to the place where it was later found, in a field off Cary Road in Tweed.

As February advanced through its first week, police began to suspect that the dozens of previous serious sexual assaults and rapes and Marie-France Comeau's murder were possibly connected, therefore over Thursday, 4 February and Sunday the 7th, police conducted an extensive canvass covering 285 homes. A roadside check was established in front of Jessica Lloyd's house where police stopped all vehicles, including, on the 4th, Colonel Williams's Nissan Pathfinder SUV. Answering routine questions, Williams told the police he drove that route to and from the airbase at Trenton and his home in Tweed, and that no, he did not know Jessica Lloyd. The police allowed him to continue on his way – but they knew what they were doing.

It goes without saying that the meticulous gathering and preserving of any possible crime scene evidence is crucial in any homicide investigation, for it can eliminate a potential suspect or incriminate him. However, in the Lloyd investigation, Williams had driven his SUV onto his victim's property and parked it where it should not have been – and in the snow where the tyre tread impressions would freeze as hard as plaster cast, therefore, careful forensic scrutiny would rapidly reveal the wheelbase of the vehicle and the brand and type of treads moulded onto the tyres that had been fitted to the SUV, to boot!

Notwithstanding this, every single tyre on every motor vehicle around the world bears marks and damage unique to only that tyre – a vehicular fingerprint, as it were. Thus, it was a case of finding the vehicle that had made those track marks, the only one that could have made those tracks.

The OPP were well aware of this and the cops at the checkpoint on Highway 37 had been issued with a description and photograph of the tyre tracks made by the probable killer of Jessica Lloyd. Bingo! One of the officers noted the tread patterns instantly . . . so an undercover OPP surveillance unit followed Williams to a car wash where he cleaned and vacuumed his vehicle. After he had left, they seized the contents of the vacuums – all possibly good forensic evidence for the future.

If anything, Williams was not a stupid man by any stretch of the imagination. The vehicle check right outside Jessica's home could not have been a mere coincidence so this incident would have sent shock waves through his head. Of course he would never have thought, even for a millisecond, that investigators had found tyre tracks, or even his boot tread marks on her property – they were just dumb cops after all.

Can you see inside Williams's mind now, for it's racing? His blood pressure had risen and he was telling himself that he'd disposed of Jessica's body in a rural location . . . it had not been found by the law, otherwise the discovery would have been all over the media but, wait a minute – with him becoming somewhat neurotic, as do all offenders when the cops suddenly appear out of nowhere, his thinking went haywire. Jessica had been in his SUV so, to be on the safe side he'd better damn quickly clean it inside and out, so off to the carwash he went.

Colonel David Russell Williams's days of freedom, military power and high-flying respect were numbered, but for the moment, with your permission I need to take a rain check; to digress before we try to find out how, when and why did Russell Williams nosedive to destruction. More importantly, to even attempt to answer any of these questions we need to try to get inside of his head.

From my experience, and I think that this is a fair, if controversial statement to make, forensic psychiatry and psychology are inexact sciences, while seasoned police interrogators base their 'mind-probing' on the material facts of any given case and when they have physical evidence and their suspect in front of them.

My book *Talking with Psychopaths and Savages* firmly documents that for decades criminals have been all too well-versed in pulling the wool over the eyes of the medical professionals, but much less so when they are suddenly presented with irrefutable evidence, as was the case when Colonel Williams's vehicle's tyre impressions were discovered near Jessica's home. His boot treads were found there also. What a clown this man was, for he even wore the same footwear and drove his SUV when he later attended his police interview with the totally amiable 'good cop', Detective Sergeant Jim Smyth.

On Sunday, 7 February 2010, the CFB Trenton base commander was at his newly built home in Ottawa, where his he and his wife lived part-time, when he received a telephone from the OPP asking him to come in for a quick chat. The officer laced his request with apologies for having disturbed him, with 'we would very much appreciate it if you could come in for a short while. We just need to tidy up a few loose ends.'

By the end of the ten-hour interview that followed, which started off in a buddy-buddy sort of way, Williams had confessed to the numerous crimes for which he was later convicted. Early the next morning he led investigators to Jessica Lloyd's body in a secluded area on Cary Road, thirteen minutes' drive from where he lived. Williams was then charged in the death of Marie-France Comeau.

Under certain circumstances the 'good cop – bad cop'

interrogation technique has some value; one where the good cop is amicable and allegedly sympathetic, while his partner is not. The suspect finds the good cop 'pleasing' to communicate with while the bad cop is shouting at him. This mind manipulation, this mind control, can work miracles in solving homicides even when any physical evidence linking the offender to a crime is vague at best.

I used a similar method when I interviewed Connecticut serial killer Michael Ross. He was brought down from death row heavily shackled and flanked by guards. Because of his movements through the facility, the entire prison was under 'lock-down', that is, apart from cleaners who, when I passed them by, were ordered to push their noses against a wall and not even dare to glance sideways.

Pre-planned with the officials, although it was against all of the prison rules for him to be unchained, I insisted that Mike's (first names, of course) restraints be removed – under ostensible protests from the officers . . . if you catch my drift? Then I ordered a soft drink and candy for him, again under more apparent protests. This pleased Michael, for he was now talking to someone who was satisfying some of his emotional needs, at once boosting his ego. He perceived (wrongly) that I was controlling the guards, the very people who controlled his life day-after-day, year in year out, thus giving me a psychological advantage, which resulted in amazing confessions to several cold-case homicides.

At face value, the highly decorated, well-respected very senior Canadian military officer that was Williams appeared as normal as anyone could be. Yet, chilling as it is, this man stalked his victims, often from afar. Knowing these types of offenders as I do, I would say that Williams got almost as much sexual pleasure from this pre-crime activity as he did from actually committing them.

Williams carried out pre-attack recces around and in his proposed victims' homes as if planning a military mission. Dressed in black, he would creep in through a window during the hours of darkness when he was sure no one was in. Using a torch (which he also used to bludgeon his victims) he would scout out the places, looking through underwear drawers, going as far as to steal intimate items such as bras and knickers before leaving, which further served to heighten his sexual desires. These 'trophies' he would later dress up in and photograph himself posing in. He fondled them, sniffed the feminine scent and masturbated, after which he would fold each one up and place it with military precision on his wardrobe shelves along with scores more, to then stand back and admire himself even further for being the consummate military man he imagined himself to be.

When he was ready, he would return to commit some of the vilest sexual attacks in Canadian criminal history, immediately thereafter reverting to the upstanding Colonel Williams whom all of CFB Trenton admired. Little did his wife, family and colleagues know that the sexual deviant, the psychopathic Williams, had a hoard of pieces of female underwear – all of it stolen from his victims as trophies of his perverted crimes.

For the reader who holds a specific interest in the interview methods used by law enforcement then I heartily recommend that the reader studies how Detective Sergeant Jim Smyth subtly interrogates Russell Williams. It is easily found using on YouTube. The 'Reid Technique' used by this officer is a 'master class' example (now used as a teaching aid by law agencies worldwide) for it shows how an experienced FBI Behavioral Science Unit-trained law officer can unstitch a psychopath's mind at the seams.

Detective Sergeant Smyth had methodically planned his approach to the suspect before inviting him in for a 'chat'. Colonel Williams: a pilot with an impeccable service history was someone used to being in control and issuing orders that everyone obeyed without question, yet, after he had sat down with the cop, Williams's egotistical, sexually perverted persona, his bald-faced narcissism, were slowly stripped away revealing a moral degenerate who stalked women; one who had a fetish for dressing up in his victims' underwear while cheating on a devoted wife; to enter women's homes in the dead of night, rifle through their most intimate possessions, eventually going on to terrorise, rape, then torture and kill two of his victims in a manner that no one could ever invent.

Detective Sergeant Smyth drew up a chair very close to Williams, because sitting across and over the top of a table provides for a psychological barrier between interviewer and interviewee – this was to be a 'friendly' non-threatening approach to put Williams at ease. Furthermore, the suspect was further psychologically disarmed as the day was a Sunday; a Holy Day for the quasi-religious colonel – a day, he was told by the considerate cop that would cause no disruption to his on-base weekday duties or arouse suspicion at CFB Trenton. It was all about giving respect to this military high-flyer, although Smyth could not have really given two hoots what day it was. It was all psychologically crafted to catch Williams off-guard, and when you watch the interviews on YouTube, study William's body language, his overall demeanour and his facial expressions – and also how the detective works his suspect into a corner, to eventually gain a confession. As I have said, this is master class stuff so I hope you will enjoy it.

Furthermore, this was the detective's game. It was his show. This was his interview. This was his playground, not the parade ground where the colonel reigned supreme: Smyth began by addressing the colonel: 'May I call you Russell, if it doesn't offend you? Call me Jim if you like' – thus bringing his suspect down to Ground Zero from the get-go. It was no longer a scenario where a mere sergeant was taking a full colonel to task. It was now a non-salutes level pitch with Smyth holding the ball, and it started off with the smug and grinning rapist-killer, Williams, not seeing what was coming. The trap had been set with better than military precision and the shit would soon hit the proverbial fan.

Like peeling an onion, Colonel Williams's perverted homicidal psychopatholgy was slowly revealed, and these four-part videotaped, oft-times disturbing interviews between Detective Sergeant Smyth and Colonel Williams are a 'must watch'. Far better than any fictional TV crime programme ever screened. But how and why, you may ask, does someone like Williams turn into such a predatory beast? If a man like this, with such a rich and illustrious history, commander of Canada's largest military base, a man who can function so well in society and within the well-defined structures of the armed forces to hold down positions of great authority, to have been granted all the TOP SECRET security clearances that exist – you might rightly ask, How did he slip under the radar? One might have thought that regular evaluations having been mandatory, at least one doctor, or someone, would have spotted something amiss, but *no one did*.

One might compare this with Dr Harold Shipman; killer

of some 250 of his sleepy-town patients who positively worshipped the ground he walked on. A true Dr Jekyll and Mr Hyde if there ever was one, yet, again like Williams, not one of Shipman's colleagues, including psychiatrists and psychologists, his friends or his family, ever suspected a thing. If we cannot trust a family doctor, or a colonel who has the country's security at heart, who on God's earth can we trust these days?

Michael Ross, Cornell University graduate with his very high IQ was as 'non-threatening as can be', says his arresting officer Mike Malchik – a top-notch Connecticut State Police detective who still holds the record for solving the most homicides – many of them were stone-cold cases – in the state's history.

Blue-eyed, blond-haired Mike Malchik, whom I have had the pleasure to meet several times, explained that when he first knocked on Ross's front door the man who opened it looked like 'the All American boy' who wouldn't hurt a fly. The full account of Michael Ross, his life and crimes, is published in my book *Talking with Serial Killers*. It makes for disturbing reading, I can assure you of this!

Although I will not exhume Ted Bundy again, for his life and crimes have been the subject of discussion for decades, for the sole purpose of this book Ted is the archetypal serial killer with around twenty accredited kills and maybe a lot more.

Well-educated, handsome to a fault, and as many women say, glib, charming and with a good line in 'pick-up chat', Ted moved through society with comfortable, self-assured ease. An unusual mix of both 'organised' and 'disorganised' sex offender, he had women falling at his feet – speaking literally, he most certainly did. At face value he, like Ross, appeared to be the 'All-American boy', maybe the charming guy who once lived next door to you. And, although heavily criticised for his sentencing remarks, Judge Cowart had a succinct point when he sentenced Bundy to death. 'What a total waste of humanity,' was an insightful statement, not just because of the terrible inconsolable suffering this killer caused to his victims, their next-of-kin and friends, or the immense problems and cost caused to law enforcement and the decent taxpayer in bringing Bundy to justice, but for Ted also, for he chose another way, with him later saying, probably insincerely: 'Murder is not about lust and it's not about violence. It's about possession. That's the way it is.'

I think that the same applies to Russell Williams.

With every day, and from both sides of my intelligence, the moral and the intellectual, I thus drew nearer to the truth, by whose partial discovery I have been doomed to such a terrible shipwreck: that man is not truly one, but truly two.

ROBERT LOUIS STEVENSON, *THE STRANGE CASE OF DR JEKYLL AND MR HYDE* (1886)

What an incredible quote by Stevenson that is, because I can see it writ large throughout Williams's psychopathology as he sees himself being drawn inexorably into the depths of an abyss from which there can be no return. In fact, I vividly recall the now executed Michael Ross telling me that after every rape or murder he pledged to himself that he would never, ever commit such an awful crime again. That he would stop and get on and live a decent life. He said this:

'Christopher, I felt that I was like a spider trying to climb up a pane of glass to escape the sexual torment raging inside of me. But, just as I almost reached the top I fell down again.'

I am sure that Russell Williams felt exactly the same way as Michael Ross did and if one were to ask this question of Williams, I feel he would certainly agree.

Russell Williams was an 'organised' offender. Unlike Christie, Kürten and Heath, Colonel Russell Williams planned all his crimes to the nth degree with an almost pathological degree of military accuracy. But, even this methodical attention to detail would prove to be his undoing; simply because like all others of his ilk, his ego became over-confident. Like Heath and all other sexual predators, his sociopathic ways and days would eventually come to an end.

After Williams's arrest, a whole raft of attacks on other women and young children came to light. In one instance he broke into a neighbour's home only a few houses away from his own in Cosy Cove Lane. The lady – not named to protect her identity – told police that she awoke to someone hitting her over the head. Williams blindfolded her and at one point he left to get painkillers for her headache. A police dispatcher received her 911 call at 5 a.m. She was still blindfolded when they arrived. Police were unable to identify her attacker until the 7 of February during their interviews with Williams.

Williams said he did not know the woman prior to the assault. He told police he chose her because he knew she lived alone. He was in her home for more than two hours. He had three folders of photographs on his computer that graphically depicted everything; adding that after the two-and-a-half-hour sexual assault, he went home to bed and then to work the next day as usual. He had previously broken into the woman's home on two separate occasions. But this rape was just the tip of the iceberg. An agreed statement of facts later read out in court traced the chronology and escalation of Williams's offences, from the theft of women's and girls' underwear from their homes to the killings. The evidence against Williams included thousands of photographs Williams took of himself during and after the break-ins, which occurred at a total of forty-eight Ontario homes in or around Belleville, Tweed and Orleans. Yes, you have read it correctly – forty-eight homes and these are just the cases that were reported, for undoubtedly there were more.

This book is largely about distress – that of the offenders and of their many victims. With that in mind I'd like to quote from a letter sent to me years ago from the then Lord Chief Justice of England, the Lord Lane, who wrote concerning the emerging serial killer, John David Guise Cannan, with whom I had corresponded over several years and about whose life and crimes I published a book called *Ladykiller: Did This Man Kill Suzy Lamplugh*, revised and reissued as *Prime Suspect*.

> The prospect of a young man spending the rest of his life in prison is appalling. It is a pity that there seems to be no humane alternative. There is good in the worst of us. Oddly enough, prison sometimes serves to allow that fact to be proved.

This sentiment expressed by the nation's most senior criminal judge was echoed by one of Cannan's many female victims. Sharon Major (not her real name) suffered terribly at John's hands and the memory of Cannan's almost fatal rape will undoubtedly haunt her for the rest of her life. Yet, of Cannan who claimed he was let down by the people he knew and loved, she had to say to me at a meeting in Bristol: 'I know what John did to me was wicked but there is a good side to John which is desperately trying to get out. He almost killed me and I still live in terror of him today but one has to learn to forgive and that I have done.'

For my part, I confirm I find not a single speck of mitigation anywhere for Williams's awful crimes. He offers up to us a psychopathological enigma, and this is why I have awarded him a chapter in this book. So, placing his criminal history aside for a moment, let's try to understand his mind a little better?

It must seem almost incomprehensible to us that on the one hand we find a man who, militarily speaking, was absolutely at the top of his game, yet on the other hand we find a homicidal sex killer and multiple rapist. It just doesn't fit together, does it? Think of Stevenson's character Dr Jekyll who is also Mr Hyde: we find the same pathological mindsets in Williams. I say 'mindsets' because I suggest that Williams was 'two people': The professional Air Force officer with an incredibly heavy workload and mega responsibilities vying against the sex monster that slept underneath.

We must also appreciate – if we are to be impartial – that such was the overwhelming power of his sexual appetite he was prepared to take a gamble, with the risk of losing everything he had worked for and achieved throughout his life. This is the kind of mind that prompted me to include 'The Homicidal Brain' chapter in this book.

When discussing these types of human predators, we

often talk about a 'divided personality' and of the 'entity' or 'disordered self'; that part which was fascinated by sexual violence and worked in harmony with the other 'normal self'. With Williams, I therefore suggest that it was the 'entity' that actually committed the crimes and the 'normal self' that planned them.

I believe I can support this hypothesis by adding that despite all of the previous rapes and burglaries committed by Williams the police hadn't a clue as to who the offender might be. As I understand it, no attempt was made to 'offender profile' the crimes or look for any common MOs or trace evidence linking the offences until Williams eventually admitted it all. What the police should have picked up on, and there is no reason to argue against it, is that whoever the perpetrator or perpetrators might have been, there was a degree of 'forensic awareness' and 'organisational ability' throughout. Whoever was committing these pre-killing crimes knew his stuff; therefore, perhaps the OPP didn't attach to the crimes the importance they deserved. I suggest again, that the FBI and just about every cop on Planet Earth will agree that once a man embarks on rape, then multiple rape, with the offences becoming more violent every time, it will, more often than not, end in sexually related homicide.

With Williams, the abnormal entity took over with increasing frequency, forming a love-hate relationship with the normal self. This sounds very dramatic, to be sure, even over-dramatic, the reader might think, but the fact remains that we are not talking about two different minds, but two different behaviour patterns of the same mind – one with a moral compass the other, without.

There can also be no doubt that Williams became gripped

by feelings of excitement mixed with anticipation as he began seeking out his next victim, and when he zeroed in on a target he had already depersonalised them, for he cared nothing about them as decent, hardworking people; nothing at all about their lives or who loved and cared for them. Once control over the victim had been established, the rape would follow and then in two cases the killing. By the time the compulsive frenzy abated, he would have realised the danger he was in of being spotted, arrested and convicted, and his normal self would regain control and start the process of coming back to the real world. As Williams himself admitted, when this was achieved and the adrenalin rush over, exhaustion and sleep ensued − a type of behaviour I have found in so many of the serial sex killers I have interviewed over the years. Heightened adrenalin rushes gone, most always deep sleep follows − it's the way our brains work . . .

I contend that in the immediate aftermath of the rapes and murders, Williams would have resolved never to do it again. This would have been his contrition phase. Ordinary relationships were now possible, in which the normal self was back in control and opportunities to claim another victim could be avoided if he focused on his work. A feeling of having accomplished something resulted; a feeling of satisfaction that his urges were under control. Then the resolution 'never to do it again' would evaporate, to be overtaken by the resolve not to get caught. This desire would come into strong focus as the preceding event faded and the anticipation of the next event became all-consuming. He reasoned that the very nature of his crimes, with all his careful planning made them easy to commit and to get away with.

Like pretty much all the serial killers I have worked with,

corresponded with, and studied in literature, Williams would have imagined that he was always one step ahead of the police; virtually immune from detection. Success fed upon success and he would have become completely emboldened, and this part of his personality, needing the stimulation of violence, would increase in appetite.

In their attempts to explain the specific phenomenon of serial rape and sexual homicide, some commentators have used – as I do – the electronic vernacular, suggesting that such offenders are 'wrongly wired up'. Therefore, any explanations that reflect the desire to find physically related causes for the upsurge in violent behaviour might not be too wide of the mark, for where is an alternative? At the time of writing I cannot find one. Nor can anyone else, come to that! This being said, there is general agreement that the breakdown or malfunction of the brain's biochemical pathways, which trip the brain beyond what we can agree are normal social restraints, is an explanation deserving further study.

And, it is at this point we kind of hit a brick wall as far as Colonel Russell Williams is concerned, because if it were the case that he was wrongly 'wired up', how is it that he achieved the senior military position he undoubtedly did? I mean this guy was given the additional responsibility of procuring aircraft for the Canadian Air Force. He was an expert in electronic warfare and countermeasures, so how do we get our heads around what was going around in his head? It's an almost impossible task, most might say.

Experts acknowledge that serial rape and homicide considered as a form of mental illness is not a concept that falls into any accepted medical or legal classification. Yet, because it cannot be classified by traditional techniques does not mean it is lacking in validity. New ground is being broken and every success in applying profiling to apprehend these serial offenders provides fresh data for the researchers and, in doing so, opens up the eyes of you and me.

While we are groping our way towards root causes of episodic violence, possibly to a level of understanding sufficient to exercise prevention, as we have seen with the serial offender studies thus far in this book, there are few doubts about the effects once an individual is in its grip, and, so powerful was this stranglehold on Russell Williams there could be no escape.

Serial sexual psychopaths don't suddenly pop into existence; they don't abruptly spring up from somewhere, although this cannot be said of them in relation to their victims, who are unaware of anything until it's too late. The act of killing is only the advanced stage in a gradual build-up of offending and violent behaviour. The beginnings may lie in voyeurism, minor sexual offences, escalating through aggressive sexual relations to violent rape, serial rape, to cross that dread threshold into murder and multiple homicide, virtually taking a form of ritual. Joel Norris, psychological consultant and writer, admirably likens this to 'a portal between two realities' in which 'the individual is simply driven to satisfy lust'.

The next development is one where rapists and killers such as Williams begin to trawl for a victim. He – for this type are invariably men – will frequent areas where he is likely to find a suitable victim – car parks, shopping malls or dark, deserted streets, even homes in which a woman alone and vulnerable may be found. All such predators, and this applies perfectly to Williams, are directed by a keen sense of purpose, yet their outward appearance is, to all intents and purposes, normal.

Once the intended prey is identified, the organised predator may stalk from a distance just as Williams did. He would have sized up the situation in terms of the opportunities open to him. He looks for escape routes and a method of operation that will bring him quick and satisfying success. Can you hear Williams's brain ticking now? God forbid, I am not asking you to think like him, I am suggesting that you think about what he is thinking. and there is a big difference here.

In Williams's case, his next phase was capture – it is the moment when the snare closes, and this is well documented when the trap snapped shut on both Corporal Marie-France Comeau and Jessica Lloyd. It is the very instant that he enters their space – one he now effectively controls. Alone with his victims, the consummate military organiser can do as he wishes. With Marie-France and Jessica, he could play with them as a cat does with a mouse. This is his 'fun time' and 'I could not give a fuck time to how you feel, what you want, and your pleas to be spared are falling on my deaf ears' time.

Finally – as with so many other serial sex murderers and rapists, and Williams is not unique in this regard – comes the depression phase when he would have realised that his triumph is short-lived, that he has achieved more-or-less nothing. Every bit of pre-crime planning, the fun and sexual satisfaction he had achieved was so short-lived. Indeed, he has actually failed because his sense of sexual frustration, which the rapes and murders were supposed to have erased, is still there, only to rise again sometime later. The whole pattern is then repeated and another victim in another place is at risk. This time the suffering and pain he inflicts will have to be greater than the previous in an effort to satisfy the cravings that left him short of total satisfaction after the previous killing. It has to be this way and it will always be the same addiction pattern played out over and over again.

While Williams feels no guilt, nor ever will he genuinely experience any remorse for his terrible crimes at all, I can say that the only guilt he presently feels is that he fucked up *big time*. He screwed up by being so dumb as to leave his SUV's tyre tread marks and his distinctive boot prints in the snow on Jessica's property, in doing so at once flushing his life and his exemplary career down the toilet.

When, how and why did Russell Williams start to fall off the rails – the answers to these questions are, in all probability, to remain for ever a puzzle, and simply because he will not even know the true reasons himself. Nevertheless, as we have seen throughout his back narrative there were waypoints when he could have changed direction and taken another route, realising that his deviant pathology was going in an entirely different direction to his 'normal' professional, military self. As Jack Levin, professor of sociology and criminology, said of Williams, 'He is a rare specimen in a number of different ways. He doesn't fit neatly into the profiles of the typical serial killer.'

For my part, and this can only be supposition, we pinpointed much earlier in Williams's narrative that his education may have been tarnished by the presence of a sexual abuser, a teacher, at his school. We also remember the account of him later entering many of his fellow students' rooms at university, and hiding, to jump out and startle them or play some practical joke on them. Well, I want to turn this account upside down. Perhaps it was a throwback to a young, impressionable lad hiding from the sexual predations of this teacher? Of course I am sure that Russell Williams would never admit to this – if indeed he was sexually abused as a schoolboy – for he is too proud a man to do so. But the pattern of secretively entering someone else's place for a motive other than simple theft is significant in that, years later, that is precisely what he did when committing his scores of break-ins, two rapes and the two homicides. Coincidences, I think not.

In many of my previous books – not to mention elsewhere in this one – I have referred to 'Murder Road': the crossroads where two lives meet with one life ending forever and the other, the offender's, taking another direction, being irrevocably changed forever. With my hand on my heart, this dread scenario has always applied, that is until I came across Russell Williams, for he has managed to take two routes at the same time: the evil entity, the 'Mr Hyde' that sleeps within Williams took one road while 'Dr Jekyll', the normal Williams selected another.

Marie-France Comeau, 1972–2009, is buried at the Beechwood Cemetery, Ottawa, Canada.

Jessica Elizabeth Lloyd, 1982–2010, rests in peace in the Victoria Cemetery, Plainfield, Hastings, Canada.

11

Jodi Ann Arias

The fury of the demon instantly possessed me.
I knew myself no longer. My original soul seemed, at
once, to take its flight from my body; and a more than
fiendish malevolence, gin-nurtured, thrilled every
fibre of my frame.

EDGAR ALLAN POE (1809–1849) 'THE BLACK CAT'

Although five-plus years of incarceration in a women's supermax prison has washed away some of her former stunning good looks, Jodi still remains one of the most enigmatic, and attractive females serving a natural life sentence anywhere across the world, today.

Jodi Ann Arias was born Wednesday, 9 July 1980, in Salinas, California, to William Angelo and Sandra 'Sandy' née Allen, Arias, the third oldest of four siblings: an older sister, a younger sister and two brothers. According to the Arizona Department of Corrections, Arias stands a shade over five feet tall, presently weighs 126 pounds – just a little heavier than she was before her arrest for murder on Saturday, 5 July 2008 – and has brown hair and brown eyes. At the time of writing she is held in ASPC-PV Lumley Unit, Perryville, 2015 North Citrus Road, Goodyear, Arizona.

Now think *Psycho*, the 1960 psycho-thriller-wet-your pants-movie directed by Alfred Hitchcock, one of the great directors of the twentieth century, in which Phoenix secretary, Marion Crane (Janet Leigh) gets well and truly stabbed in the shower of the ramshackle Bates Motel by Norman Bates (Anthony Perkins) – a horrific murder scene and one that still shocks us when we watch it today.

Interestingly, Hitchcock became obsessive about guilt, punishment and sex, which played out in all his movies. He had declared himself celibate after once sleeping with his wife. He became possessed, trying to infiltrate the private lives of stars such as Grace Kelly, Vera Miles, Kim Novak, Janet Leigh and Tippi Hedren. Indeed, his schoolboy obsession with sex included telling nasty, vulgar stories and jokes – even whispering them in the ears of his actors before shooting a major scene. Yet, behind the mask of the Master of Suspense was a fat, utterly gross man who admitted that he hated his own body and had grown up as an isolated child in Limehouse, East London.

Now you may well ask why I am discussing this at all – well, I do so for a very good reason, because you see that Hitchcock's psychopathology, and the low esteem in which he held himself, demanded that he 'punish' these beautiful actresses for not falling for his charms, so 'obsession' plays an important part in what follows with regard to Jodi Arias, who did what Norman Bates did to Janet Leigh, but with a viciousness more than ten-fold.

I think that most crime buffs will have watched the 1987 psychological thriller *Fatal Attraction*. This is the movie in which the supposedly happily married Manhattan lawyer Dan Gallagher (Michael Douglas) has a fling with Alexandra Forrest (Glenn Close), who becomes infatuated with him; then, when he dumps her, she seeks revenge by putting his beloved family bunny rabbit, into a pot of boiling water while he was out of the house.

The phrase 'bunny boiler' to mean a dangerously obsessive and vengeful person (usually a woman) originated from that movie, and while Jodi has never – at least to my knowledge – ever boiled a Roger the Rabbit, she certainly is a real-life homicidal 'bunny boiler' in every other sense because she was an obsessive, lethally dangerous lover who stalked the young man who spurned her and shot and stabbed him to death. Her victim was the all-American boy-next-door type; a thirty-one-year-old, six-pack fit-as-can-be hunk called Travis Victor Alexander, who died on Wednesday, 4 June 2008, at his spacious upscale home in Mesa, Arizona.

So, forget the movie *Psycho* because the murder of Travis is as bad as any hands-on killing can get. This was not just a murder – it was overkill-times-ten, which truly puts the shower killing in *Psycho* into the shade.

Women who kill a friend, a former partner, or a family member are not uncommon, and I expect many of us have felt the familiar sting of jealousy. It is a human emotion that is often very hard to turn off. Many people end up having little to no control over their emotions; as is so perfectly illustrated by Glenn Close in *Fatal Attraction*, they become so envious they end up committing murder. The bottom line being that it boils down to self-control in overcoming one's own insecurities; sadly, some just can't do it.

With Jodi Arias, this jealousy started out small and grew with her every thought and action. Ultimately, she turned into a horrific green-eyed monster with a red mist suddenly overtaking her with the most terrible outcome for Travis, the upshot almost unimaginable to the likes of you and me.

My book *Talking with Female Serial Killers* provides many examples of the most heinous crimes committed by the 'fairer sex' from historic times to the present day, but, although she is a one-off killer, I think that trying to understand what finally made Jodi blow a fuse is worthy of study here.

As we work our way through Miss Arias's life – her back narrative – we really don't see any false mask of normality, and it seems to me that she didn't live a double life either, as do the others whose case histories we have examined within these pages. What, however, I do suggest is that she most certainly developed a narcissistic personality, one that turned into a warped psychopathology that totally overwhelmed her as Travis Alexander gradually, quite understandably, distanced himself from her, as her possessiveness went completely off the rails. He felt emotionally suffocated by her. She wouldn't leave him alone. She pestered him night and day. She tried to manipulate and control him. In this respect, Jodi's need to have Travis all to herself became over-possessive, and possessiveness is born from fear – in her case the fear of losing him. This cost him his life!

As Arias stands today, I'd say that she is an ice-cold psychopath: witness her flip-flopping behaviour, her sly and attempted controlling and manipulating demeanour during her 2013 trial in Maricopa County Superior Court, and the manner in which she currently holds herself behind bars showing a self-promoting and cocksure character, seeking sympathy while signally lacking any true remorse for the literal bloodbath she created. Therefore, it is important for the reader to understand that what she says one minute can change to something entirely different in a heartbeat so it is extremely difficult to sort the wheat from the chaff.

Although for most of the time Jodi Arias claimed and still does that she adored her parents and they had brought her up well, she has also said, flip-flopping as it suits her, that from the age of seven years she suffered child abuse; that her parents used to beat her with a belt and wooden spoons, an issue that was thrown in by her rather inexperienced and poorly briefed defence-appointed psychologist at trial as some form of mitigation, one that held no water at all. In fact, there is absolutely no evidence that Miss Arias suffered from any form of childhood abuse whatsoever, so we can take any of this stuff with a pinch of salt.

Jodi attended the Yreka Union High School in California, but she dropped out in the eleventh grade; however, she later earned a GED (General Education Development) or High School Equivalency Certificate, which is an internationally recognised test. So far so good.

At about the age of ten, she developed an interest in photography. This led her to pursue it as a profession. As a result she took up several part-time jobs as a self-alleged 'professional' photographer. Her ability to use an expensive camera featured in the actual killing of Travis Alexander when she enticed him into his shower on the pretext of photographing him naked under running water and when he was completely oblivious to her homicidal intentions. Indeed, it was the use of this camera that ultimately sealed her fate. She left it behind at the murder house and police were able to recover photos, some taken deliberately during sex acts, others snapped accidentally, which more or less captured on the memory card, the entire sequence of events all of which led to Travis's agonisingly slow death struggle.

And, there is a similarity here worth noting. We recall how calculating was Colonel Williams was in planning his crimes, his attention to minute detail as if doing one of his pre-flight checks on a plane? Yet he came unstuck by leaving his vehicle tyre tread marks and his boot prints at a murder scene. Jodi Arias also planned the killing of Travis Alexander in minute detail, yet left behind the camera, with its record of the slaughter.

> When Jodi applied for the job she was outstanding. She was on time, interviewed well and dressed appropriately. I hired her immediately.
>
> DARRYL BREWER, FOOD AND BEVERAGE
> MANAGER, VENTANA INN AND SPA

In autumn 2001, when she was twenty-one, Jodi took a waitress's job at the upmarket sixty-three-room Ventana Inn and Spa, in Carmel, California. Here she met the restaurant's food and beverage manager Darryl Brewer, forty years old, recently divorced, with a young son. Some time later, they began dating.

For Jodi this must have seemed a plum job at the time because her photography work hardly earned her a dollar, so this woodsy-chic 243-acre resort off the Pacific Coast Highway half a mile from Pfeiffer Big Sur State Park and thirty miles south of Monterey, was ideal and it paid reasonably well with food and accommodation thrown in for free. As Jodi's relationship with Darryl Brewer merely provides us with some of her back narrative, I will condense it as best I can.

The couple fell in love. They continued to live separately in onsite employee housing until 2003, and then moved to Monterey, thirty-two miles away. Initially, Jodi did not move in with Darryl yet they still saw each other two or three times a week before the decision was made to live together. In 2005, they purchased a three-bedroomed house in Palm Beach ... they had taken out the mortgage together, and to all intents and purposes this was developing into a stable and loving relationship. Indeed, looking at photos of how stunningly attractive Jodi was at the time, I'd say that Darryl must have thought he'd won first prize.

The mother of Darryl's son, although planning to remarry, wanted to move to Palm Beach, so the lad could live with both of his parents by way of shared custody. This suited Jodi who got on very well with the boy. According to Darryl her relationship with Jack was 'outstandingly close'.

Although the couple occasionally discussed wedlock, having recently come out of a marriage, Darryl wasn't quite ready to commit again so soon, but they hoped to stay in the house they had purchased for at least two years then maybe sell it to move up the property ladder, as so many couples strive to do.

The monthly mortgage payments were $1,700–$1,800 which Jodi and Darryl split between them, paying about $850.00 each, which is approximately UK£640.00 in today's money. When asked at Jodi's trial whether they could both afford that amount, Darryl answered with a categorical 'Yes!' But I wonder if this was actually the case. Jodi worked in a pizza restaurant and she also held down a second position at another eatery, called Quito, so we cannot say that she was work shy. From studying court documents it appears that Darryl finally found a job after two and a half months, and with everything else taken into consideration, such as his child-support payments having to be met, I would have assumed that as a couple they certainly were not flush. Nevertheless, he recalled that at no time, from the day they first became involved, had Jodi been bad-tempered about it; neither had he ever seen her jealous of other women. But a slight glitch was looming on the horizon.

Around March or April 2006, Darryl learned that Jodi, while still holding down two jobs, was going to a Las Vegas Pre-Paid Legal (PPL) convention where this pyramid outfit was recruiting commission-on-sales-only agents to sell their products. It was while attending this conference that she met Travis Alexander who was one of the firm's top salesmen and a motivational speaker.

That autumn, Darryl's son Jack started school and with the mother now living about ten hours' drive away, and having joint custody of the boy, it made sense for Darryl to move so as to be closer to his son. This would entail selling the house – and some friction set in. Jodi was now settled. She had two jobs, a reasonable income and a thoroughly decent partner. This issue of upping sticks caused their relationship to begin to deteriorate.

At the same time, while Jodi was becoming more immersed in Pre-Paid Legal, she was becoming less responsible with the household bills. Although she continued to pay the mortgage, all of her travelling around seeking out clients with few sales had put her in debt.

There is no doubt that at this time most people saw Jodi Arias as a decent, hardworking young woman and they later confirmed as much. She had come from a religious family so it was perhaps natural that she took an interest when the Mormons came on the scene. She became active in Mormon fundamentalism, and against Darryl's wishes Mormons started visiting their home for prayer sessions. Jodi's behaviour changed rapidly. She stopped all sex with Darryl, arguing that she would now save herself for a husband, and as he had not even proposed to her the rapport abruptly ended, although apparently on fairly amicable terms.

Because the mortgage payments were not being met, the house foreclosed in February 2007. Darryl moved to be closer to Jack, while Jodi was baptised into the Church of Jesus Christ of Latter-day Saints at a ceremony in southern California, on Sunday, 26 November 2006. She then relocated to Mesa, Arizona so she could be nearer to the much younger Travis Alexander, with whom she had become infatuated.

Travis Alexander was born in Riverside, California, on Thursday, 28 July 1977, to drug addicts Gary David Alexander and Pamela Elizabeth Morgan Alexander. Both parents are deceased with Gary passing away in 1997 and Mrs Alexander dying in 2005. He was one of eight children.

When he was eleven years old Travis ran away from home and was taken in by his paternal grandparents, Norma Jean Preston Alexander Sarvey and her husband James; the remainder of the siblings followed soon after their father's death. In turn the grandparents introduced Travis to the Church of Jesus Christ of Latter-day Saints.

It is at this point I refer back to my term 'Murder Road'; a road where fate dictates that two people from two entirely different backgrounds and circumstances are inextricably brought together at 'Murder Crossroads' – where one life ends and the other life is irrevocably changed for ever. Indeed, going by the US Population Census back then, the chances of Alexander and Jodi ever meeting were somewhere in the order of 327.7 million-to-one, but they were helped in no small part by Pre-Paid Legal.

While I am not suggesting that, after having met Travis, Jodi cheated on Darryl Brewer, we know that Travis and Jodi were dating intermittently in the February of 2007. In March, she left Mesa and moved back to Yreka, where she lived with her grandparents, her long-distance relationship with Travis maintained by their taking turns travelling between Arizona and California. Later, during her trial for Travis's murder, some of his friends who had met Jodi said that they had formed a negative opinion of her; that her and Travis's relationship was unusually tumultuous and her behaviour worrying – something that Jodi has always denied.

Nevertheless, according to authors Chris and Sky Hughes who have written the excellent book called *Our Friend Travis: The Travis Alexander Story*:

Travis was a good-looking, charismatic, entrepreneur and motivation speaker. He was in the prime of his life enjoying good health, financial success, world travel and a bustling social life. But things weren't always good for him. His life began in dismal circumstances, and tragically, it ended worse than it began. He was born to drug-addicted parents and suffered many of the worst privations of life. His family was poor and his parents were neglectful and abusive. He was teased and bullied as a small child and had few, if any, friends. After running away at the age of ten and going to live with his grandmother, he became active in his church.

I rather think that this sums up Travis Alexander perfectly, but let's return to Jodi Arias, for both were practising members of the Church of Jesus Christ of Latter-day Saints, and Mormons believe that sexual desires should only be satisfied within heterosexual marriage, though sex is not only for having children but also as an expression of a couple's unity. Sex outside of marriage is banned, and this includes any sexual relations before marriage and necking and petting. Sexual perversions are also banned because Mormons think that chastity should be a dominant virtue among young people, who are expected to maintain a very high standard of sexual ethics and restrict their physical relationships before marriage to gestures of affection, rather than lust. These restrictions on sexual activity are regarded as helping people appreciate the true value of marriage. However, as far as Travis and Jodi were concerned, none of this applied, for in this regard they stuck two fingers up to their faith and went for it like rabbits. Kinky sex often in the forefront of their minds, the Mormon Bible being heaved out of the window, we can hardly say that the couple was devout by any stretch of the imagination. In fact, it was not their faith keeping them together, it was hot, rampant sex that stuck them together like Superglue.

Having watched hours upon hours of the videotaped police

interviews and court hearings concerning Jodi Arias's trial – and you can do the same if you have a month to spare and hanker for a fast divorce – and having taken everything I can into consideration, I have now come to the conclusion that at this stage of their relationship they were an ill-matched couple – a relationship that would never have ended in marriage – almost from the get-go. But, I mustn't be over critical or old-fashioned. Hey, they were having fun, bless them!

Now, out of the staid, boring and restrictive relationship with the older Darrell Brewer – which had suited Jodi's emotional needs at the time – perhaps it is understandable that she should seek a bit of excitement. At this time she was only twenty-seven. She had found herself a successful all-American young man, clean as a policeman's whistle, complete with a six-pack; a handsome hunk, popular, great company, and with his own upmarket home, a decent car, good income and worldwide travelling prospects, he was the ideal catch for her. But Travis would soon think otherwise.

Travis Alexander was a free spirit; a young man of thirty, with his whole life ahead of him; by all accounts a chap who had no intentions of being tied down, fussed about or controlled and manipulated in any way. Having dragged himself up and out of a childhood, semi-raised by drug-addicted parents, he had, by sheer dint of hard work, now gotten himself ready to rock 'n' roll. The world was more or less his oyster. There was a pathetic attempt made during Jodi's trial to drag his name through the mud, with false allegations that he was some type of sexual deviant who had exploited the accused Jodi – suggested by her defence team as at least some form of mitigation for her losing the plot. But so what? Millions of couples, Mormons or not, enjoy seamy sex sessions. Whatever the case, the media gloated over it all. Why? Because it all sold newspapers and made for excellent prime time TV viewing figures, that's why!

Nothing like a sexy femme fatale, a handsome Chippendale-type young hunk, untold amounts of bonking with cuffs and leather restraints, a bloodbath, plus a large helping of 'Goodliness is next to Godliness' thrown in, to grab the headlines, you might agree?

Part way through their one-year relationship, friends of Travis noted that Jodi's mood was darkening. At social events he was always the life and soul of the party while she stood in the background suspiciously eyeing up other women and hardly ever joining in. On other occasions his friends saw the couple bickering, with Jodi criticising him and making big fusses over nothing at all. He only had to smile and chuckle with another girl and she was all over him in an instant. She was becoming jealous, very insecure and possessive, and he had had just about enough. Beautiful she might be, highly sexed with it too, but that would have been enough emotional and physical glue to keep him stuck to her, and he told Jodi that he needed some space. He was going overseas on vacation anyway. He told her that some time apart would be a good thing, but they could at least remain good friends.

Jodi Arias was now coming up to twenty-eight. She was still not married, had no domestic security and was still in debt. Her complexion was not as peachy as it had once been. Except for Travis, her expensive boob job had failed to attract any man she considered half-decent and she could see with her ever-increasingly green-with-envy-eyes that many much younger women than her viewed Travis as a man magnet. She knew, deep down, that she was going to lose him, and there was absolutely nothing she could do about it. So, taking the view that if she couldn't have Travis Alexander nobody would, Jodi decided to kill him. But first she'd have to set her trap.

There is no doubt that Jodi's killing of Travis was premeditated, and she imagined that she had planned the murder down to the nth degree but in doing so she unwittingly left a trail of clues that resulted in the police nabbing her shortly thereafter, which is all a bit slow by Lieutenant Columbo's standards. Our lovable scruffy cop always puts his prime suspects in cuffs within the hour, and this amount of time includes about twenty minutes of TV advertisements promoting essentials like creosote for the garden shed you don't have, or cream for haemorrhoids that you don't have, or want!

Now back to the murderous plot.

Before Travis had dumped her, in early 2008, he told his firm, Pre-Paid Legal, that Jodi would be joining him for a work-related trip to Cancún, Mexico. They were to fly there on Sunday, 15 June. During the interim, however, Jodi was becoming more paranoid by the day. Neighbours of Travis had seen her car parked close to his house as if she was spying on him. She had even hacked into his mobile phone system so she could spy on his text messages. At one time she prowled around the property in the very late evening and saw him through a window cuddled up to a pretty young lass while they watched the television. Jodi flipped. She phoned him and, as a result, he changed his mind about taking her to Cancún. He would take another woman. Jodi, as far as he was concerned, was history. He would let her down lightly, but in doing so he unwittingly started the countdown to his murder most foul.

On Wednesday, 28 May, a 'burglary' took place where Jodi was living at the home of her grandparents. Among the missing items was a .25-calibre automatic Colt pistol, which has never since the murder been recovered. However, this calibre of firearm became significant as crime scene technicians later found a shell casing from a .25-calibre round very close to the shower where Travis was shot in the head. Jodi Arias has always denied that she was the person who stole her grandparents' pistol, while law enforcement counter by saying that the burglary was a 'staged' event. Having reviewed the case file, I have to agree with the police on this 'staged' issue. However, the shell casing was not conclusive evidence in that it there was no pistol to match it to – only the grandparents' report that such a firearm had been stolen from them. On the other hand, this would have certainly played a part in making a case based on circumstantial evidence alone. All we can say is that during a staged burglary at a home where Jodi was living, a .25-calibre pistol was stolen, and a .25-calibre pistol was used to execute Travis Alexander.

Between 1 a.m. and 3 a.m. on Monday, 2 June, telephone records later showed that Jodi rang Travis no less than four times with no answer. Shortly after 3 a.m., Travis called her back twice. The first call lasted 18 minutes, the second time they talked for 41 minutes. We don't know the substance of these calls, but, at precisely 8.04 a.m. she rented a car at Budget Rental, Municipal Airport, in Redding. En route to Utah, Jodi Arias visited friends telling than that she was going to a PPL conference and to meet up with a co-worker, Ryan Burns. This was to give herself any alibis she might need later, a smokescreen.

By late evening, Tuesday, 2 June, she had set out for Salt Lake City. She had been careful not to use her own car for fear of it being seen parked near his property, and now she filled up two gasoline (petrol) cans – borrowed from Darryl a few days before – at a Shell station in Yreka before crossing the state line into Arizona, at which point she switched off her mobile phone. These moves were to ensure that if she ever came under suspicion there would be no paper or mobile phone signal trail to show that she had been in Arizona at the time Travis was murdered.

Just how Arias killed Travis Alexander would take a book to cover thoroughly, so I will abridge it here as best as I can, based on having watched videos of the entire trial and all of Jodi's interviews with detectives, along with reading reams and reams of trial transcripts.

During the morning of Wednesday, 4 June 2008, with ice running through her veins, Jodi knocked on Travis's front door at 114828 East Queensborough Avenue, Mesa, to receive no answer. Knowing that the garage door was always unlocked, she opened it enough to get in. She proceeded through a small utility room and surprised Travis, whose male lodger was away at the time. Her pretext for surprising Travis was to tell him that as she happened to be in the area, on her way to a meeting, she'd popped by just for old times' sake; the upshot being that they ended up naked on his bed for extremely hot sex, with her managing at the same time to take sexually explicit photos, according to the camera at around 1.40 p.m.

with his own expensive camera – after which he would take a shower.

Can you see her killer brain working now?

If anything, Travis was proud of his finely honed physique – as can be seen from the many photos Arias took – so she persuaded him that she ought to take professional shots of him under running water. At 5.29 p.m., from the expression of his face, and his hunk poses, we can determine that he certainly was enjoying the attention. These were the last photographs taken of Travis still alive, and you can easily find them online.

Then, in a flash, Arias produced a knife from behind her back and started the stabbing, which caught the vulnerable Travis by surprise, and he was given no chance of defending himself against this suddenly explosive homicidal female demon.

Jodi Arias gave various conflicting accounts of the killing during her trial – it was self-defence, she argued . . . it was because she suffered from domestic violence, which proved to be utter lies, for the now deceased Travis would, himself, talk from the grave and give forensic evidence against her in the form of the results of his autopsy, while crime-scene blood spatter and drag marks and a shell casing inadvertently left behind, along with Travis's camera, which, before she left his house, she threw into a washing machine – in the mistaken belief that the wash cycle would, if not destroy the camera, at least wipe the photos from its memory – all told the true story.

In brief, after the first stabs, Travis staggered from the shower to the washbasin as she kept stabbing into his back. Blood poured onto the floor, splashed all over the basin, the Formica top and the mirror, and in a desperate attempt to escape, now on his stomach Travis crawled towards his bedroom leaving a blood trail on the floor and skirting boards. At the point where he had almost reached the bedroom, Arias bent down and sliced his throat, killing him; thereafter, she dragged his body back into the shower and discharged the pistol – firing one shot into his head.

I think that it is fair of me to advise the reader that the actual sequence of events that unfolded during the murder are somewhat hotly debated even today. But murder the defenceless Travis she most certainly did. The autopsy photographs taken by the medical examiner, Kevin Horn, are easily found on the internet, as are photos of Travis dead in the shower and the blood-soaked crime scene. WARNING: If you have a sensitive constitution please DO NOT even look at them. It is sickening stuff: all-in-all Travis suffered some twenty-eight knife wounds, plus defensive gashes on his hands, a single gunshot to his head – and his jugular vein and trachea had been slashed.

Yet, cold as a wintry day, after the murder, Jodi Arias washed herself off and calmly drove away.

The following day, Arias met up with the aforementioned business associate called Ryan Burns in the Salt Lake neighbourhood of West Jordan. Burns would later testify at her trial that over a meal he had noticed that Jodi had cuts on her hands and that she had dyed her blonde hair back to its natural dark brown. On 6 June, she left Salt Lake City to drive back to her grandparents' home in California. En route, and now using her mobile phone, she called Travis's home several times – probably to make sure that he was dead or to give herself another 'I'm innocent' alibi if she was ever spoken to by the police.

On 9 June, Travis's friends and colleagues became

concerned that he was not answering their calls; which was highly unusual because he was always, without exception, quick to pick up the phone or respond to text messages. Then his lodger returned home to find that the master bedroom door was locked. He hammered on the door. He noticed a heavy blood reddish stain on the carpet. He found a key, then found Travis dead in the shower. He dialled 911.

Very soon afterwards, Jodi Ann Arias came under suspicion.

On Wednesday, 9 July 2008, Arias was indicted by a Maricopa grand jury for the first-degree murder of Travis Alexander. She was arrested on 15 July and extradited to Arizona. The result is now well-documented history.

So why is the case of Jodi Ann Arias – come to it, that of former colonel Russell Williams – important for the reader of this book? The answer, at least to me, is one of 'interaction'. Around a decade back we would have simply read a book, a magazine feature, or a series of newspapers articles covering such terrible cases to enlighten ourselves, or, for that matter, watched some half-assed, totally phony movie that advertised that it was the 'truth-all-based-on facts', just to get bums on seats. However, with so many of the most notorious US homicide cases, initial arrests, interviews, trials and convictions now being filmed and posted on YouTube, we can get more up front and personal with these offenders, to see precisely how they are brought to justice through their own flawed modi operandi and deeply flawed psychopathologies. For the reader who is truly 'into' these types of murder trials, YouTube provides for superb research material and riveting viewing if one can drag oneself away from the rubbish that is constantly pumped down our TV pipe every day.

This is why I use the term 'interaction'. By all means read this book and if you are triggered to look further, use YouTube and any other internet search engine to form your own opinions about how and why a particular crime was committed – look also deeply at the offenders while they are being interviewed by police and while they are on the stand at trial. In this simple way, you can become one of the jury members, albeit in a very distant sort of way.

As for the workings of Jodi Arias's mind – I have tried as best I can to work through her back narrative already in this chapter and I can find no mitigation at all for the awful crime that she committed. There have been times when one might try to understand her, but any of this is blown away as easily as a straw in a gale when it comes down to hard facts – perhaps even more so post crime and her 'fuck you' attitude during her trial. Here we can witness the attitude of a fully emerged narcissistic homicidal psychopath. No remorse. No true feelings of guilt. But what truly shocked me is this:

Having been presented with all the overwhelming evidence against Arias, and I suggest that there could have been no doubt in any juror's mind – nor your mind when you view the video recordings of the police interviews and her at trial – that she was as guilty as sin. For my part, if I had been Jodi's attorney, I would have told her in no uncertain terms to: 'Shut up! Admit your guilt, Jodi. Avoid a trial and the mega expense it will cost to the taxpayer who will have to pay the tab. DO NOT have the bereaved come to court and express their heartbreak. Please, I beg you not to make yourself look like an idiot and an evil killer in front of millions of people who'll be watching these televised proceedings. Jodi, throw yourself at the mercy of the court, and you may just come out of this with 1 per cent credibility instead of FUCK-all!'

Why this advice was not rammed down Jodi's throat I do not know. But I would put money on it that so deep is her flawed personality she would have disagreed anyway. From start to finish, Miss Arias loved the attention she was getting during and after the court proceedings and she'll continue to revel in her ill-deserved blood-drenched notoriety for the remainder of her days.

Travis Alexander, 1977–2008, is buried at the Olivewood Cemetery, 3300, Central Avenue, Riverside, Riverside County, California.

12

Douglas Daniel Clark and Carol Mary Bundy

No, man, I don't care who he is. Who would let a
half-blind bitch reach over, shoot at the head of a
hooker suckin' his cock and hope like hell she didn't
blow a hole in his knee or chest? I mean, what if the
hooker's jaw locked shut?

DOUGLAS CLARK REFERRING TO CAROL BUNDY.
INTERVIEW WITH THE AUTHOR, SAN QUENTIN STATE
PRISON, 1995

If there ever were a couple of serial homicidal misfits Bundy
and Clark must take the biscuit, but what if were one of them
were innocent – well, maybe innocent, I should add – and that
the 'innocent' one is Douglas Clark – as he vehemently claims
from death row? Therefore, for the purposes of this book, let's
try and get inside the heads of these two individuals to see
where they are at. However, I must first explain that Clark,
now seventy-one, is currently on death row at San Quentin
State Prison (SQ), California, and Carol Bundy died of a heart

attack aged sixty-one on Tuesday, 9 December 2003. We can posthumously examine Bundy's psychopathology anyway, because if you think that Jodi Arias is a bad egg you haven't seen anything yet, for Bundy was one of the dreaded 'Sunset Strip Killers'.

Perhaps another reason for me to include Clark and Bundy in this book is that I truly believe in giving some of these killers a fair crack of the whip, as I have done with Aileen 'Lee' Wuornos, for instance. I met 'Lee' before she was executed in Florida. My book, *Monster* (2004), accompanied the 2003 motion picture of the same name starring Charlize Theron. Nevertheless, many of the world's leading forensic psychologists – to include the eminent Professor David Wilson – and many of the more responsible TV documentary producers are inclined to agree with me that she only killed in self-defence, as hard as it may seem to be for the diehards who think otherwise. And, for the record: once again I do not think that she was a psychopath in the homicidal sense at all. Indeed, although she was a bisexual interstate hooker and went with some two hundred 'clients', she only shot seven of them to death because they started beating her up and treating her like dirt. To my mind Peter Sutcliffe the 'Yorkshire Ripper' and Steve Wright the 'Suffolk Strangler' and all the other cowardly serial-killer scum who beat up, torture and abuse any women deserve to have been shot by the gals too.

If ever a man looks how you might imagine a serial killer to look, and behaves as you might expect one to, then Doug fits the bill. He isn't smooth or charming – indeed, what you get when you meet him manacled hand and foot at SQ is the whole enchilada. Loud, mouthy, rotten teeth, and every sentence that he shouts out is laced with enough profanities to give one the jitters. He doesn't wear any pretending normality mask and his claim that he is innocent and that he has been fitted up by the police, at face value, holds some water . . . or does it?

For me at least, Doug Clark is an enigma, for when I study serial killers, I find the majority of them easy to understand, but Doug I cannot. This can be partly explained in that here, in the so-called Sunset Strip Killers or Sunset Slayers, we have a man and a woman apparently working as a 'tag team', much in the same way as did Ian Brady and Myra Hindley, and also Fred and Rose West. I explained the dynamics of this joint sado-sexual criminal enterprise behaviour in my book *Shared Madness: True Stories of Couples Who Kill*. However, thrown into the mix of the so-called Sunset Slayings is another perverted sex offender called John 'Jack' Murray. And if this were not enough, there is the very strong possibility of a police fit-up, lost or ignored evidence, added to which we are not just looking into the mind of one individual but into the minds of three individuals all at once.

So when it boils down to it, this really should be a simple case of whodunit, if-they dunit, and why? All grim stuff and fascinating, to say the least; however, there is nothing simple about the Sunset Slayers at all . . . and who was Carol Bundy?

At this point it would be redundant of me to go into too much depth except to say that she had allegedly had a troubled childhood. Both of her parents were abusive alcoholics. Her mother died when she was young. Her father, according to her, and only her, sexually abused her when she was around the age of eleven. After his wife's death, the patriarch remarried and because Carol was a troublesome child he placed her into a foster home.

With that in mind one might have thought that Carol would have grown up harbouring a deep pathological hatred towards men, but she didn't, for in 1959, aged seventeen, she married a fifty-six-year-old man. In fact, by the time she met Clark in 1979 she had been married no less than three times, and had two children who had, at one time, been placed into care, so it is a wonder that she ever became a vocational nurse, yet she did!

Nonetheless, to sum up Carol Bundy, I find without a shadow of a doubt, a short, dumpy, extremely shortsighted (in the optical sense and just about everything else sense), a nymphomaniac, a common slut, pathological liar, arch-manipulator, sexual abuser of very young girls, and a homicidal maniac – all which added up to the most unattractive piece of work; a person so riddled with pathological lack of self-esteem, devoid of any redeeming traits, one who would have cheap sex with any man who looked just the once at her. As one woman who knew Bundy succinctly described her: 'She walks like a duck and she is as ugly as sin!'

Clark, however, was a different kettle of fish altogether. A well-educated man, handsome to a fault with a superb physique, charming, cheeky, he was a lady magnet. But all that glitters is not gold. Doug was also a rat, a freeloader who sensed that if he hooked up with Bundy, or any woman with a few dollars, and gave her a 'good time', he could milk the relationship for all he could get. What goes around, comes around and with Doug it did, for he got more than he could ever have bargained for when he hooked up with Bundy. Indeed, when I spoke to Doug off-camera at SQ, I told him that he had been an idiot coupling up with Carol Bundy in the first place. Instead of going nuts, he looked down at his feet and said: 'To be honest, Chris, I was a fuckin' asshole. Nothing can change this now.' But, despite all his macho, alpha-male pretence, Clark had a fondness for wearing women's underwear. He was a paedophile. He was a sexual deviant of the highest order. He was convicted of committing necrophiliac acts on his very dead mutilated victims, and he hacked off a girl's head, applied makeup to it like a Barbie doll, and used the mouth for oral sex. Now, you don't read about that every day, do you?

So, here we already find two almost polar opposites: on the one hand a sex-starved female nutball with an extremely low sense of self-esteem meeting up with another like-minded piece of work, yet he was a guy who had women craving his attentions. Everywhere he went, young lasses threw themselves at him. Apparently, back in his earlier days he had 'come-to-bed-eyes' and was a bit of a Romeo, there can be no denying that. So Carol Bundy must have thought she'd won the 'Love Lottery' meeting up with Doug Clark – but first she had to rid herself of another lover in the form of the fairly handsome John 'Jack' Robert Murray, married with two children, himself a sexual pervert, thief and freeloader who would, given half a chance, fleece anyone and everyone at the drop of a hat. What went around for him came around too!

Carol Bundy had just come out of a third disastrous marriage and had moved into an apartment complex managed by Murray, and he soon got wind that she had received half of the proceeds of the sale of the matrimonial home – a sizeable amount now nestling snugly in her bank account, into which were also paid her disability supplements (for her extreme short sight). Sniffing this out, forty-one-year-old Murray had honed in like a heat-seeking missile, twigging at the same time that she was into rough sado-sexual sex, just like he was. Great bedfellows they were indeed!

Completely infatuated with Murray and so obsessed was she with his sexual performances, that Bundy started paying him for sex and, by the end of 1979, he had wheedled some $18,000 out of her on the grounds that he needed the money for his wife's non-existent cancer operation. In reality, he had used half of the cash to pay off the outstanding finance on his Chevrolet van, a vehicle that he frequently used as his mobile sex den. The remainder of the money he splashed out refurbishing the interior, which was soon to become splashed with copious amounts of his blood and particles of skull along with brain matter.

Predictably, the dim-witted Bundy with her two kids, aged five and nine, soon got low on funds. Murray realised that her financial sponsorship sell-by-date had expired. He had no further regular use for her; but, as he was the block's manager he did later arrange for her to move into an apartment on Lemona Avenue, Van Nuys, LA, and a comfortable three miles from his own home, and he got her a job at the Valley Medical Center in Van Nuys. However, Bundy would not leave Murray alone. She tried to bribe his wife to leave him, and when that failed she threatened Mrs Murray. The besotted Bundy was certain that Jack loved her no matter what he told her; and she started going to the Country and Western bar where he sang. In actuality she was stalking him and he made things even worse for himself by still having sex with her.

Then, in May 1980, we find another aspect to Bundy's sick character.

She befriended a young girl, the daughter of a neighbour, whom she found rather attractive. She was not deterred when she learnt that the 'Shannon O' was only eleven years old. The girl was mentally and physically well developed, as well as sexually precocious, and the pair established a relationship by trading filthy jokes. Bundy was slowly grooming Shannon for other things and succeeded when she encouraged the minor to move on from gentle petting and cuddling to full-blown lesbianism. In the meantime, despite the split, Bundy and randy Murray continued their sordid affair, though in a less evident manner. Progressively, the sex turned increasingly deviant, and the couple tried to encourage young girls to indulge in three-way sex with them. Fortunately, the youngsters were all put off by the thought.

Therefore, at this point we can see a little deeper into Bundy's psychopathology. She liked sado-sexual sex, the rougher the better. She was also into lesbianism and had a 'fondness' for younger girls, with whom she wanted to have three-way sex with the perverted Murray. In this respect we see echoes of the same modus operandi used by Fred and Rose West; one that Bundy would very soon develop with Clark, one to be polished into a familiar and extremely murderous pattern in the months to come. But, it is the three-way sex angle that will interest us a little later.

Just after the Christmas of 1979, Bundy, then thirty-seven years old, met Doug Clark at the Little Nashville Bar on Barbara Ann Street, where Murray sang Tom Jones hits. Aged thirty-one, Clark was a handsome man with a soft, slightly European voice – a gift that enabled him to have the pick of any woman he so chose. He was also a leech, and a sexual hedonist, who enjoyed nothing more than a varied choice of eager girlfriends who were willing to share their homes with him. That being said, he did hold down a job as boiler engineer at the nearby Jergens soap factory; all of which made him an attractive proposition to the degree that he was much in demand, and he was sleeping with so many girls at their homes, he would often even forget where he was actually living himself.

One might have thought that with all these female admirers making themselves available around the clock, Doug would have been more than satisfied in the bonking department, but apparently not. As we will see, when he wasn't working or banging one of his many girlfriends, he was trawling the red-light districts of Hollywood and partying with prostitutes.

Knowing both Bundy and Clark as we now do, it will come as no surprise to learn that on the evening of their first meeting they spent the night together. Doug Clark was as gifted as Murray in sniffing out money, so he came up with a yarn and told Bundy that he was having rent problems with his landlord and was about to be evicted from an apartment he shared with a girlfriend called Bretta 'Joey' Jo Lamphier, on West Verdugo Avenue, in Burbank. Bundy promptly told him that he could move in with her when he was ready. No rent would be needed. It would be a simple arrangement whereby he would screw her brains out in exchange for a roof over his head.

Carol Bundy may have been dim-witted but at least we can award her a Gold Star for manipulation. She had been taken for a ride – in every sense – by Murray more times that she could count so now it would soon be payback time, not only for Jack Murray, but, a little later on, Clark, too.

DOUGLAS DANIEL CLARK AND CAROL MARY BUNDY

The tempting proximity of a sexually advanced youngster in the shape of Shannon, and Bundy's coaxing talk of three-way sex, proved irresistible to Clark, and Bundy photographed him simulating sex with the heavily made-up child; pictures which later proved to be some of his undoing. During my interview with Doug at San Quentin State Prison, he ranted on about this particular subject, saying:

'I had sex with Bundy about three times in all our relationship, although Carol will say otherwise. Murray was her intense S&M lover. She and Jack had three-way sex with Shannon. He tried to orally and vaginally rape the kid. They repeatedly tried to engage my roommate, Nancy, in three-way-sex. Carol even tried to get Nancy to join her and Shannon in three-way female sex. She told Nancy and Shannon not to let me know she was busy with Jack, trying to have sex with them, since I would not like her and her fuckin' around with one of my girlfriends.'

In isolation, on the face of Doug's heated rant we can either believe him or not. However, with that being said, the sordid photographs taken by Carol Bundy – incriminating evidence of illegal activity – were later to become swords of Damocles hanging over the heads of Clark and Murray.

Hereafter, I will try to break down the events leading up to Murray's murder, and Bundy's and Clark's arrests in chronological order – no easy task either.

To start with, having reviewed most of the police documents concerning the 'Sunset Slayings' and having interviewed some of the principle detectives, visited the crime scenes, having interviewed Clark at SQ, and then reviewed scores of court transcripts, I am obliged to state that the dates, the timings and the witnesses' accounts are all over the place. Even the Californian Court of Appeals transcript is undoubtedly flawed at times. Added to which is my filmed interview with Doug Clark, where, in no uncertain terms, he protests his total innocence. The reader can easily find this uncut interview on the internet and it makes for uneasy watching. Sadly, however, there are a few minutes missing from the end of the interview, but you will catch my drift, if, or when, you watch Clark fly off the handle, and by gosh he certainly did!

As an aside, my film crew and I had driven all the way to SQ to interview Clark; then, the night before our scheduled meeting, we were informed by the PR officer that the interview with him was off. Clark was insisting that he wear a baseball cap while the authorities insisted otherwise. Not to be completely outdone, we drove to SQ and parked up, again to be told that it was a 'No Deal'. We had wasted our time and a lot of dollars too. My long-time dear friend and producer, Frazer Ashford, who had forked out serious money to get us to SQ, wanted me lynched from the nearest hanging tree, but then the angels smiled upon me. Just as we started to drive away in our two Mitsubishi Shoguns, a guard came running down the ramp to flag us down. 'Hey, guys, it's back on, fellas. But we gotta tell ya that Clark is well pissed off. He's going freakin' nuts in there.' Indeed, if you watch the YouTube video you will see just how freaked out he was!

I have added that anecdote because, as I indicated at the outset of this book, getting to interview serial killers is not an easy business. Several times in my career, despite all of the permits and worth 'Jack Shit' promises, the moment one gets to the prison gates it can suddenly become a no-no, as in

FULL STOP . . . MONEY DOWN THE DRAIN . . . END OF STORY!

It happened when I went to meet Melanie Lyn McGuire (see: my books *Dead Men Talking* and *Talking with Female Serial Killers.*)

It happened again with the serial killer, James Allen Paul. Despite his promises, once the crew got to New Jersey's State Prison, Trenton, and before we unloaded our kit, he summoned me in to talk to him alone. The obnoxious little creep gave me 30 seconds of his time before giving me the finger. That truly pissed me off so we went ahead and made the programme without him. You can find it on YouTube under 'James Allen Paul: The Executioner'.

Harvey 'The Hammer' Carignan did much the same thing. We get all the way to the Minnesota Correction Facility (MCF), Stillwater, and 'Harv' suddenly refuses on-camera time. I went ahead to interview him using audio only. He has a very soft voice. You can find this programme: *Harvey Carignan Harv the Hammer: Serial Killer* documentary, on YouTube, too, and you'll love the opener from Detective Russell 'Russ' Krueger. He is a cop that doesn't do diplomacy. You can find my chapter on Harvey in my book *Talking with Serial Killers*.

But, then, it's a case of 'win some' and 'lose some'.

The late William George Heirens gave me his first ever on-camera interview at the Vienna Correctional Center in southern Illinois, while I was en route to meet John Wayne Gacy who was then on death row at Menard CF. I have always maintained that Heirens is innocent. My chapter on 'Bill' covers his case in my book, *Talking with Serial Killers II*.

Ronald 'Butch' DeFeo agreed to go on TV camera with me, as did Michael Bruce Ross, as have other serial killers such as Cathy May Wood and Gwendoline Graham, Kenneth Allen McDuff and Good ole boy Henry Lee Lucas.

But I have digressed again. With apologies for the promos, let's get back to Messrs Clark and Bundy: Clark whom I have interviewed, the latter who is probably in Hell.

Charlene A.

Hey, mister, that's blood. You're hurting me.
CHARLENE A, AS SHE WAS BEING STABBED
BY DOUGLAS CLARK

At around 10 p.m. on Sunday, 27 April 1980, 'Charlene A.' (name changed to protect her identity) was touting for business in a bar close to Sunset Boulevard when Doug Clark approached her and asked, straight off, for a blowjob. After she entered his car (it was Bundy's Buick) Charlene gave him the oral service he'd requested after which Clark took a knife from behind the sun visor and started stabbing her repeatedly in the back, neck, arms, chest and stomach. At one point she said, 'Hey, mister, that's blood. You're hurting me.' He laughed and said, 'I know.' At this point a bouncer called Nick came out of the bar, pulled open the door of the Buick, and attacked Clark with a 'blade'. Using his knife Clark fought back. In the ensuing struggle for her life, Charlene grabbed the knife only to sever tendons in her hand. She was finally able to escape. When Doug finally got back to Bundy's apartment he was covered in blood. He told Bundy that he'd tried to pick up a hooker and kill her but she had escaped, adding that he had killed Nick, which he hadn't! When I interviewed Doug, he denied that this incident happened as portrayed, although Charlene would later identify him at two separate police line-ups as being her assailant.

But, here I have some difficulty, for I find it extremely unlikely that Clark, or any man for that matter, would hook up with a hooker in a busy bar in front of scores of witnesses, take the woman outside and within a few feet of the door and right in the bouncer's line of sight, start attacking her with a knife. Indeed, having looked at some of the 'unused material' in this case, I would say that Clark did pick up Charlene A. in the bar and they did go outside for sex in Bundy's station wagon, that there was an argument at which point the bouncer intervened and produced a knife. Clark tried to defend himself and at this point the woman scrambled from the car and escaped with some injuries, as did Clark. That said, neither Charlene nor the bouncer – a man known by the police to be in the 'murder business' – can make for credible witnesses.

Gina Marano and Cynthia Chandler

According to the LAPD homicide detectives I have interviewed, the first confirmed murders committed by the Sunset Slayers were the double killing of fifteen-year-old blonde-haired Gina Marano and sixteen-year-old dark-haired Cynthia ('Cindy') Chandler.

The almost naked bodies of the two attractive teenagers were found at about 1.30 p.m. on Thursday, 12 June 1980, by a Caltrans street cleaner working off a freeway ramp near the Forest Lawn Cemetery. Cynthia was found with a pink jumpsuit wrapped around her legs. One leg of the jumpsuit was slit to the crotch. There was blood and a spot of grease or oil on the outfit. Chandler's stepsister, Gina, was clothed only in a red tube-top pulled down around her waist. No underwear was found on, or anywhere near, the bodies. In addition, police found no IDs in the vicinity.

The medical examiner determined that the girls had died late on 11 June or up to 4 a.m. on the 12th. The signs of lividity on the bodies were consistent with them having been moved from one location to another after death: the absence of blood where the bodies were found, and post-mortem scratches and abrasions (drag marks) on the bodies also indicated that the victims had been murdered someplace else and subsequently moved to where they were discovered.

Police criminalists discovered that '. . . microscopic examination of vaginal material from Cynthia Chandler contained spermatozoa.' Samples from her mouth were negative for semen. No evidence of sexual assault on Gina Marano could be detected, but neither could sexual activity be ruled out because no bruising would have occurred as a result of post-mortem activity.

Cynthia had been killed by a single .25-calibre gunshot wound to the back of her head, which had left the bullet lodged in her brain. The second shot had penetrated her lung bursting open her heart. It was also determined that both shots had been discharged at point-blank range (contact wounds). Gina had also been shot twice. One round entered behind her left ear, exiting near her right eyebrow, and the second bullet blasted through the back of her head, also exiting behind the left ear. But let's backtrack a bit because the girl's movements over the preceding week will illustrate all too clearly Bundy and Clark's, if not also Murray's, MO.

On Sunday, 1 June 1980 Cynthia and Gina had attended a party given by attorney Mark Gottesman at his Hollywood home. Many people were present there, including a number of Gottesman's clients. A mixed bag indeed! Gottesman would later tell police that he was unsure whether his business card was handed out, but a Mindy Cohen chatted to the two girls – who were obviously prostitutes – and gave Gina Marano her telephone number. Marano wrote the number in an address book that she always carried with her. How and why Gina and Cynthia managed to get an invitation to this party is a matter of delicate supposition and as Mr Gottesman is a lawyer I had best leave it at that.

Nevertheless, during the afternoon of Tuesday, 10 June, one Henry Brigges was driving a truck and he picked up the two girls who were hitchhiking. Brigges gave Gina his business card bearing both his own telephone number and the number of his brother George, and his sister-in-law, Laurie Brigges. This was the second time in nine days that telephone numbers and contact details had been passed around. In the event, Brigges dropped the girls off, alive and well, at the entrance to a freeway onramp.

Angelo Marana, the father of Gina and the stepfather of Cynthia, later told homicide cops that he had last seen the girls alive in early June. He affirmed that Gina always carried her address book containing business cards and other information because it was very important to her.

Having looked at all of the evidence concerning these

double-shooting deaths, it is patently clear that the two girls had been forced to strip naked, or had done so at a 'client's' request, were then shot dead and their bodies taken to the Ventura Freeway where they were unceremonious dumped like so much trash.

But where had they been murdered? Clark says that it was Jack Murray and Bundy who had done the killing and he knew nothing about it. We shall come to this piece of the puzzle later, but now events took an even more ominous twist.

At about 1 p.m., Saturday, 14 June, a woman called the LAPD Northeast Division at Van Nuys. She told a detective that she thought that her lover was a murderer. 'What I'm trying to do,' she said, while the officer recorded the call, 'is to ascertain whether or not the individual I know, who happens to be my lover, did in fact do this . . . he said he did . . . my name is Betsy.' Later in the conversation she changed her name to Claudia. Her real name was Carol Bundy.

The police were very anxious to learn the full name and address of the alleged killer, but the caller refused to give out this vital information, though when pressed she did give a brief description. 'He has curly brown hair and blue eyes. His Christian name is John, and he's forty-one years old,' she said. 'I've found a duffel bag in his car, full of bloody blankets, paper towels, and his clothes.'

This description matched Jack Murray perfectly – not Doug Clark, who was thirty-seven at the time. Warming to her theme, the garrulous informant added, 'He tells me he fired four shots. Two in the girl's head and virtually blew her head away. One shot in the head and one shot in the chest of the other girl. He used a .25-calibre pistol. Does that jibe with what you've got?' When the woman hung up, a detective wrote on the tape cassette: 'Either the killer, or one who knows the killer!'

Immediately after the call from this informant, police compiled a list of people who had purchased .25-calibre pistols in recent months. Carol Bundy's name came up as she had purchased two Raven automatics in Van Nuys on Friday, 25 April. In fact, she was the only female on the firearm register at that time. The gun shop provided the police with Bundy's address, vehicle registration and social security numbers. However, for reasons only known to them, the police chose to ignore this crucial information, despite the telephone call from Betsy/Claudia, which indicated a connection with the murders of Cynthia Chandler and Gina Marano. Quite why the cops chose to act this way will always remain a mystery because when I pressed detectives about this lapse I couldn't get a straight answer. In fact I could get no answer at all!

Telephone records show that at precisely 2.36 p.m. on Monday, 16 June 1980, Ms Laurie Brigges received a brief telephone call at home from a man asking for her brother-in-law, Henry Brigges. The caller identified himself as a police officer in the Hollywood Division who was investigating the murder of two girls whose bodies were dumped near the freeway on 12 June. The 'officer' said that one of the girls had her brother-in-law's business card. The 'policeman' assured Laurie that her brother-in-law was not a suspect in the killings, and that it was not necessary for him to contact the police. Laurie recalled that the man gave his name as Detective Clark. She thought the call was unusual because as the conversation proceeded, the caller became more casual and less police-like. For instance, he commented that the girls had been '... doing what they shouldn't', meaning they were prostitutes. Doug Clark maintains that this so-called cop was Jack Murray despite the fact that telephone records later showed that the call had been made from Doug's girlfriend Joey Lamphier's place on West Verdugo Avenue. Doug for his part alleges that the call could have been made by Murray, who, it is true, often visited that apartment; anyway, whatever the truth, just after that call, at precisely 2.40 p.m., a man called the office of Mark Gottesman and, when his call was answered, immediately hung up. Records showed that that call came from the same number.

On Tuesday 22 June, Bundy moved from Joey Lamphier's place on Verdugo to Lemona Avenue, in Burbank. Clark, among others, helped her by taking furniture and other possessions across town to her new home, which was a stone's throw from Clark's place of employment at the Jergens soap factory.

That same day, at 11.30 a.m., Mindy Cohen – the woman who had been at Gottesman's party – received a telephone call from a man identifying himself as a detective with the LAPD. He told Mindy that he was enquiring into the murders of Chandler and Marano. He said that Gina had been shot in the head, and Cindy in the heart. When Mindy enquired how the police had got her phone number, the man said it was found on the bodies, which it wasn't.

Of course the 'real police' had found no ID or notebook or telephone numbers on, or by the bodies at all, so the man who phoned Mindy Cohen was lying, for Mindy's phone number had, indeed, been found in Gina's possession – by her killer after she had been shot to death – and removed.

Karen Jones and Exxie Wilson

Between 2 and 2.30 a.m. on Monday, 23 June 1980, Burbank police officer Greg Guzzetta was patrolling Sunset Boulevard when he met a prostitute named Karen Jones. 'Sunset' is always well frequented by streetwalkers and the police regularly carry out sweeps to get these women off the streets. This night was to be no exception. Officer Guzzetta told Jones not to loiter around the area or he would book her, so she sullenly walked off into the night.

Between 2.24 a.m. and 2.40 a.m., a local resident heard a scream outside his home. At 3.15 a.m., police attended a residential street near the NBC studios in Hollywood, and found Karen's body lying by the kerb, a pool of blood surrounding her face and hair. There were indications that she had been dumped from a moving vehicle. The cause of death was obvious – a gunshot to the head. A .25-calibre jacketed ACP bullet was retrieved from the skull. The firearm had been held approximately six to twelve inches from the head when it was fired. At autopsy, the medical examiner estimated that Karen had died between midnight and 2 a.m., but he could not find any evidence that she had engaged in sexual activity shortly before her death.

The same morning, at 7.15 a.m., another body was found in the car park of a Sizzler diner. It was here that I interviewed one of the lead detectives, Leroy Orozco – a solidly built, experienced homicide investigator who has worked many of LA's most notorious killings, including a number of those committed by the 'Hillside Stranglers' – Kenneth Bianchi and Angelo 'Tony' Buono. Although the body had been decapitated with the head now missing, she was quickly identified as a known prostitute called Exxie Wilson. A red dress with a sash was recovered from a dumpster next to the body. The sash was cut into pieces and no other articles of her clothing found. Moreover, Detective Orozco told me that both Jones and Wilson shared the same pimp who told police that he had last seen his two girls working together around Sunset Boulevard shortly before midnight.

> I thought I'd found some treasure!
>
> JONATHAN CARAVELLO, WHO FOUND
> EXXIE'S HEAD IN A BOX

Four days later, at around 1 a.m., on Friday, 27 June, Jonathan Caravello was about to park his car in an alley by his home in Studio City, when he found an ornate wooden box dumped there. At first, he thought it looked like a 'treasure chest'. It was a crudely made, stained pine box, measuring 10 inches wide by 12 inches high and 8 inches deep. It had a brass clasp on the front, brass ring decorations and a metal border. Upon opening it, Caravello received the shock of his life. Inside, was the severed head of a young woman wrapped in a pair of blue jeans turned inside out with the crotch area removed, and a pink T-shirt with the inscription 'Daddy's Girl'. (These items of clothing were later identified as belonging to another victim, Marnette Comer.) The head had been frozen. It appeared to have been scrubbed, or scoured, and bore the remnants of crudely slapped on makeup – resembling that of an ugly Barbie doll. For the reader with more than a particular fascination for the macabre, there are photos of Exxie's head on the internet. For decency's sake her lower body has been covered by a sheet; however, for some bizarre reason, police initially took a photo of the head on what resembles a silver platter.

The medical examiner determined that Exxie, like Karen, had died some time between midnight and 2 a.m. on 23 June. The head had most likely have been cut off after death and not where the remainder of the body had been found by the dumpster, although there was a proviso: Exxie might have been dying or unconscious. It would have taken fifteen to twenty cuts to sever the head in which was found a .25-calibre lead-jacketed bullet. Three spermatozoa samples were taken from the remains – one from the rectum, the other from the vagina and one from her mouth. Ballistic tests on the bullets used to shoot Exxie, Karen, Gina and Cynthia proved that all the rounds had been fired from the same pistol.

Marnette Comer

On Monday, 30 June, the part-naked corpse of a reddish-blonde prostitute called Marnette Comer, aka, Annette Anne Davis, from Sacramento, was found by snake hunters in a ravine off Foothill Boulevard in Sylmar, not far from the freeway. Partially covered by scrub and an old mattress, the body was lying on its stomach.

Sabra Comer, the sister of five-foot-seven-inch tall seventeen-year-old Marnette, had last seen her on Wednesday, 21 May 1980. She had been wearing a pink T-shirt with the logo 'Daddy's Girl' printed on it. This was the same T-shirt found with Exxie Wilson's head. Therefore, it was estimated that she had been dead for some time – 'from 20–90 days' according to the medical examiner's estimate because the skin had become dried and mummified. Her belly had been slit open. She had died as the result of three gunshot wounds to the chest; two .25-calibre ACP bullets were recovered from the body. These centre rimfire bullets matched, in every respect, the rounds that had killed all of the other previous victims.

By now the police had traced the ornate chest that had contained Exxie's head to a J. J. Newberry 'Five and Dime' store at 18215 Sherman Way, in Reseda. Here, a clerk remembered the customer being an overweight woman who wore glasses with thick lenses and black gloves. The sales assistant especially recalled the gloves because it had been a very hot day. 'She was dumpy, and kinda ugly,' the clerk told police describing Carol Bundy to a fault.

The clues floating around as to the identity of the mystery informant Claudia/Betsy were adding up. Five prostitutes had been shot with the same .25-calibre pistol using the same ammunition, and the description of the buyer of the chest matched that of Carol Bundy, the only woman in the whole of 'The Golden State' who had recently purchased two all but identical 'Saturday Night Special' Raven six-shot semi-automatic pistols. Yet, still the might of California law enforcement couldn't match up any of these leads. It makes one want to weep!

To muddy the waters further, at 7.11 a.m. on Thursday, 24 July, Mindy Cohen was awakened by a telephone call. She immediately recognised the man's voice as the one she'd heard on 22 June, nearly a month earlier. The caller enquired, 'Is this Mindy?' and she answered, 'Yes.' He went on to ask if she remembered that he had previously called her about the double homicide, and said, to her horror, 'Well, I killed them and now I want you.' The man then added that he had shot Gina in the head and had to shoot Cindy in the heart. He explained that they were prostitutes and that he'd paid Cindy $30 to 'suck him off.' 'I shot them and then I made love to them and it felt so good. It felt so good,' he said. 'Now I want you, Mindy and you're next.'

Mindy Cohen noticed that the caller's breathing changed during the course of his call. That, coupled with the hesitation in his voice, led Mindy to believe that he was masturbating and was reaching a sexual climax. She got very scared and hung up the phone before asking her father to call the police.

Telephone records show that although Clark denies ever phoning Mindy Cohen the call was traced back to the Verdugo Street address, which was just a three-minute drive from where he worked at the Jergens soap factory at the end of Verdugo Avenue and close to the railroad tracks, where he clocked on at 7.28 a.m. that morning. The call remains something of a mystery.

On Tuesday, 29 July, there were indications that Carol Bundy was cracking up. At one point she asked Clark to shoot her, which would not have been a bad move in any event. When he refused, she attempted suicide. She sat in her other car, a blue two-door Datsun, and injected herself with insulin and Librium. Then she swallowed a handful of sleeping pills. Despite her knowledge of drugs, gained from her nursing experience, the suicide attempt failed. She was found and taken to hospital.

The next day, Bundy's first action was to telephone Jack

Murray from her hospital bed. The needy, neurotic woman wanted to be taken home so could he come and pick her up in his van? When he arrived, he was, she saw, accompanied by a much younger, slimmer and far more attractive girl, called Nancy Smith. Bundy became so furious she refused to get into Murray's Chevy van, and, seething with rage, she walked home. None of this prevented her and Murray from having three-in-a-bed sex with young Shannon four days later.

John 'Jack' Murray

On Sunday, 3 August 1980, Bundy made arrangements to meet Murray in the car park of the Little Nashville bar on Barbara Ann Street. Her timing let her down, for when she turned up at the rendezvous as planned, she found the priapic Murray was already in his van and about to have sex with a woman called Avril Roy-Smith. Carol banged on the door and Avril left.

It would seem that this chance encounter with yet another woman was to be the straw that finally broke the camel's back. Bundy and Murray drove several blocks and parked where they prepared for sex. Now undressed, Murray lay on his stomach while, crouching behind him, Bundy parted his buttocks and pushed her tongue into his anus. She would later describe the act as 'anal linctus'. As Murray groaned with delight, and with Bundy apparently savouring the moment, she reached into her over-extended waistband and drew out a Raven pistol. With her tongue still in situ, she touched the muzzle of the firearm to the back of Murray's head. He would have felt the cold steel and frozen for an instant before she discharged a single bullet into his brain. But the man wasn't yet dead, so she fired again.

Still his heart kept on beating.

Throwing the gun to one side, Bundy pulled out a heavy boning knife from her bag, which she repeatedly drove into his back. After nine stabs he finally died.

We remember how Jodi Arias stabbed and then shot Travis Alexander. That was not just a killing for killing's sake, for the murder was carried out in a lust-for-blood-inspired homicidal rage. Jodi had grown to hate her former lover with a passion and the seeking of 'revenge' was required. I suggest this 'revenge' factor played a part in the murder of Murray. I have seen this explosion of violence again and again with killers such as Ted Bundy, Harvey Carignan, Arthur Shawcross, Kenneth McDuff, the British serial killer, Joanne Dennehy and Peter Sutcliffe, to name but a few.

So Carol Bundy hadn't finished with Murray quite yet. Like a scene from a grotesque snuff movie, she then sliced open her victim's buttocks and mutilated his anus before hacking off his head. After rummaging through the van's cupboards, she scattered pornographic videotapes and magazines around the blood-drenched corpse. Emptying his briefcase, she removed several Polaroid sex snapshots, and took his keys and his gun, before placing his head in a plastic bag. I have seen all of the crime scene photographs, so, as my publishers will not allow them to be published in this book, how best can I describe it all? The only way I can think of is to imagine a hand grenade going off in an abattoir. The rest I leave to your imagination. Nevertheless, after committing one of the most awful homicides in US criminal history, this duck-like Bundy, covered with blood, then calmly waddled to her own car still parked in the club's car park. Now, in the early hours of Monday, 4 August, she drove to a call box and telephoned her apartment where Clark was sleeping.

At this point let's review the killing of Murray, and do we not see an MO being repeated again and again and again; one almost identical to the murders of the previous victims, especially the removal of Exxie Wilson's head? Although not unique post-killing behaviour exhibited by serial killers; that a woman could hack off a man's shows that she can do the same to a woman.

Once again, we see a Raven firearm being used and we know that Bundy had not long previously purchased two of these pistols – one nickel-plated, the other chrome-plated – that two of the girls had been shot in the back of their heads, as was Murray, can be no mere coincidence either.

We also know that on 14 June a woman calling herself Claudia or Betsy – who had to be Bundy – telephoned the LAPD and gave a detective information that only the killer (or someone who had intimate knowledge of the killer of Gina and Cynthia) would have known. During this call Bundy gave a description of the man – a description that matched Jack Murray precisely, and she referred to the man being her boyfriend, which Murray certainly was, to a degree. The thinking behind the call, characteristically, remains unclear. As did her reasons for killing Murray, some six weeks after the call.

Bundy herself admitted to police that she shot Murray and that she had acted alone and out of a homicidal jealous rage, all of which seems to fit with the 'overkill' element – for instance, the terrible wounds she inflicted upon him post mortem. When asked to account for the reason why she hacked off the man's head, she would give no sensible answers – the varying four accounts would leave the police wishing they hadn't asked her in the first place.

Clark, on the other hand, maintains that Bundy killed Jack Murray because Jack was her accomplice and she was trying to stop him from implicating her in the murders that they had committed if they ever came under suspicion by the police.

In trying to better understand Bundy's and Clark's warped psychopathologies, I think that the answer to both accounts sits somewhat conveniently in between.

Day after day, Carol Bundy's state of mind was rapidly deteriorating. She was mentally falling apart at the seams, as evidenced by her knee-jerk reaction to the Marano and Chandler homicides, in which she was clearly implicated, and when she telephoned the police calling herself 'Claudia/Betsy' – and giving a description of the killer that fitted Jack Murray's. In doing this she was, of course, trying to throw any possible suspicion elsewhere, or was she? In other words: tell the cops that the killer was someone other than Clark if he ever came into the frame and might fit her up into the bargain – call it 'self-protection'.

At the same time, there can be no doubt that Bundy was becoming pathologically jealous of losing Jack Murray to a much younger woman, and he, like Clark, had plenty of young women at his beck and call. However, Murray's murder was a callously premeditated act, thus, in my opinion, the mouthy Bundy had previously boasted about the killings she and Clark had committed, and then she belatedly decided to rid herself of Murray just in case he went and told the cops.

As for hacking off Murray's head? Once again we need to

look a little closer because killing someone and leaving the corpse as a whole is one thing, but taking away the head and disposing of it is entirely another matter. It almost beggars belief – yet, maybe not if one is thinking like the totally psychopathic Carol Mary Bundy, which brings me to Exxie Wilson's head.

There is no doubt at all that both Bundy and Clark – possibly Murray to some degree – worked as a 'tag team' to lure young women into their murderous clutches – in much the same way as did Fred and Rose West, or Ian Brady and Myra Hindley did with young kiddies. In fact the black annals of criminal history are littered with similar cases, where the presence of a female most often allays any suspicion a potential victim might have when, say, invited to get into a man's motor vehicle. For another excellent example, the reader might find the case of Gerald Gallego and his wife Charlene of interest. They murdered ten women, mostly teenagers, between 1978 and 1980, using more or less the same MO as Clark and Bundy – with the female accomplice being utilised as a tool, the innocent-looking bait.

Therefore, one can safely say, using all of the evidence given at Clark's trial and his subsequent appeal, taken together with his own flip-flopping confessions to police, his rants to me on camera, supported by statements made by Bundy and documents and other material not used for legal reasons, that she was present when Karen Jones and Exxie Wilson were, with no time lost, enticed into Bundy's motor car and that Bundy was present when Exxie's head was cut off and made up like a grotesque Barbie doll for Clark's oral satisfaction. Going a little further, although forensic tests did not prove substantive, the remnants of cheap makeup applied to Exxie's face were of the same brand later found by police in Bundy's cosmetics bag.

To conclude – and this will take some getting our own heads around – we must remember that both Clark and Bundy were possibly into necrophilia – although Clark denied this when I put it to him at interview.

Of course, Clark would deny it. However, correspondence he'd sent to woman (like himself incarcerated) while he was on remand for his trial proves how sick this man's mind is. His letters to Veronica 'VerLyn' Wallace Compton (whom I have also interviewed) suggested that if he was freed they should open up a mortuary and have sex with the corpses – all of which somewhat shoots his self-professed 'apple pie' view of himself in the foot!

So, Bundy cut off Jack Murray's head. But, as stark, raving bonkers as she undoubtedly was, she did it for a very crafty reason: she'd get Clark to help her dispose of the head –which she could have easily done on her own – thus implicating him as the Sunset Slayer, if needs be. But now we must return to the early hours of Monday, 4 August with Bundy telephoning Clark and ordering him to get out of bed. She had given Murray his comeuppance and now it was Doug's turn to feel her ire.

Doug was sleeping with Nancy Smith when the shrill ring dragged him out of a heavy sleep. 'Carol was whispering and giggling on the phone,' Clark told me, and as the call continued, Nancy, who suffered from epilepsy, had a seizure. Clark told Bundy to shut up and get back home. Then he called for paramedics to attend to Nancy, which they did. Indeed, when Bundy arrived very shortly thereafter, the medics were already on scene.

After the ambulance left, Bundy took Clark to her car where, in the footwell of the front passenger seat, she showed him Murray's head inside a plastic bag. The ragged and bloody stump was exposed and Clark threw up. What with Nancy's fit and now this, it was all too much, but when Bundy coolly asked him if he would help her dispose of the mess, like a complete idiot he agreed, despite the fact that he was due to start his shift at the Jergens soap factory within the hour. Nevertheless, they drove off in the direction of the factory, with Bundy cradling the plastic-wrapped head in her lap. As they passed a pile of trash, she wound down the window and tossed the grisly article out. Murray's head was never seen again.

What about *my* fuckin' head?

DOUGLAS CLARK TO THE AUTHOR
AT INTERVIEW, 1995

On Thursday, 7 August, the sexually insatiable Bundy invited Tammy Spangler, yet another one of Clark's former girlfriends, over for dinner. Clark knew from the get-go that Bundy was trying to initiate another three-way sex session and says that he declined to take part. In any case, he fancied Tammy for himself. He also feared for Bundy's state of mind. 'If she could do that to Jack,' he told me, 'what the fuck could she do to someone else? What about *my* fuckin' head?'

After the meal, Tammy had to leave to go to work. Bundy and Clark were now alone. Her sexual expectations for a threesome with the pretty Tammy had been thwarted, so she convinced Doug that they should drive into Hollywood and find another girl, one who would treat him to a hooker's blowjob.

Clark told me that this would be his birthday present from Bundy, but this just doesn't stack up. His birthday had been way back on 10 March. But it could have been construed as an early gift from Carol-to-Carol as her birthday was sixteen days away on 26 August: as fate would decree, precisely the day another dead body would be found.

According to Clark, they drove to North Highland Avenue, between Sunset and Santa Monica Boulevards. Here they spotted a prostitute whom they called over, and a 'birthday gift' deal was agreed. The girl's name was 'Cathy', but before she took payment she said, 'I don't do nothing with no woman.' With her concerns allayed, she climbed into the back seat followed by Clark, who tilted the driver's seat forward against the steering wheel. This enabled Carol Bundy, sitting in the front passenger seat, to have a grandstand view. She revelled in the unedifying sight through her bottle-bottom-thick spectacles.

Clark described to me his version of what happened next, and this time I say that he is correct.

Chris, I was on the left an' Cathy was on my right, and twisted around with only her left buttock on the edge of the seat. She was working me up with her mouth, and stuff like that. Then I noticed Carol fidgeting in her seat. She began heaving herself up and down, craning her neck to view the area around the car, like she was looking to see if there was anyone around. I saw Carol's hand reach around the seat, like she was gonna grope Cathy. Then I saw the fuckin' gun. For an instant, I thought she was going to shoot me, like she did Murray. But Carol placed the pistol to the back of the hooker's head and pulled the trigger.

Fired as a contact shot, the bullet passed clean through Cathy's head and struck Clark in the lower side of his stomach. This was only a flesh wound but the blood flowed onto his work shirt. 'I was shocked and freaking out,' he explained. 'Carol told me to drive the fuckin' car while she climbed in the back, tore the clothes off the dead girl and sexually assaulted her, all the while ranting that she was sure the dead girl would have liked it.'

When the body had been dumped, they drove back to Bundy's apartment where he changed his soiled clothes. He wouldn't see them again until the police arrested him.

On Saturday, 9 August, the Van Nuys police received a complaint from an unknown woman about a Chevrolet van that had been left unattended on Barbara Ann Street. The anonymous caller also mentioned a foul smell emanating from the van. Within minutes a squad car arrived and a police officer, looking through one of the windows, saw a blistered, blackened decomposing body in the rear. As the scene was being cordoned off, Detective Roger Pida climbed in to conduct a preliminary investigation and, among the documents scattered about, he found a wallet identifying the headless victim as John Robert Murray. Checking through their computer, the police learned that Murray's wife had reported him missing several days earlier, and the cops were able to ascertain that he spent a lot of time with a woman called Carol Bundy.

During the morning of Sunday, 10 August, LAPD homicide cops knocked on the door of Carol Bundy's Lemona Avenue apartment. She invited them in and they were introduced to Clark and Tammy Spangler. After a few preliminary questions,

Clark and Bundy were taken downtown for a grilling while Spangler followed in her car to bring them home after the interviews had finished.

At the police station, the couple offered different alibis for the time of Murray's murder. Clark told the truth; saying that Bundy had come home late that night which she indeed had. In a separate interview room Carol Bundy lied by claiming to have also been at home all evening. She was adamant that she had not ventured out. When asked if she owned any firearms, she said that she had recently sold a pair of pistols to a tall guy with red hair and a scar. To the amusement of the cops, the only name she could conjure up on the spur of the moment was 'Mike Hammer' – the fictional hard-boiled detective central to the American author Mickey Spillane's long series of detective stories that began with *I, the Jury* (1947). Then Tammy Spangler piped up and told the detectives that she had seen Murray with a woman called Avril Roy-Smith on the night of the murder. 'Perhaps you'd better go talk to her,' she suggested.

Well done, you, Tammy, because you had just fashioned the noose about to be hung around Carol Bundy's neck; however, having no solid evidence with which to detain Bundy, the police allowed her to leave while they went in search of Avril, who gave a verifiable alibi to account for the time encompassing Murray's dreadful demise. She said that she had been with Murray in his Chevy van and Carol Bundy had hammered on the driver's door When she left, Murray was still very much alive. Avril had gone back into the club where she stayed for three hours drinking with friends who all supported her alibi. Nevertheless, she had seen Bundy get into the van, which blew Bundy's fabricated alibi of being at home all night out of the water.

Now armed with this fresh information, the following day police prepared a warrant for Bundy's arrest. While they were completing the paperwork, she walked off her job at the hospital after confessing to colleagues that she was responsible for murdering and decapitating her lover. She told them that she was going back to her apartment to 'clean out the evidence before Doug gets home from work'. As soon as she left, a senior official at the hospital reported Bundy's bizarre allegation in a frantic call to the LAPD.

On her way home, Bundy called in at the Jergens soap factory and asked the gatehouse security officer to summon Clark. When he came out, she told him that she was about to tell the police everything. Clark was livid. 'You crazy cunt!' he raved. '*Get the fuck away from me.*'

Once Bundy had moved off the premises, Doug stormed back into the factory where he tried repeatedly to phone Detective Pida who was not in his office. 'Bundy was trying to fit me up with murder,' he has since said many times, protesting his innocence for the Sunset Slayings, 'an' who the fuck is gonna believe a woman is doing all this murder stuff? An' she had incriminating photos of me and Shannon hidden away. Blackmail. Yeah. That's what it is,' he railed on at me during our interview.

Just after 11 a.m. that morning there was a telephone call to the Northeast Division of the LAPD, and a woman asked to speak to homicide police. When Officer James Kilgore picked up the call on his extension, the woman said, 'Sometime, way back, you were having a string of murders involving prostitutes in Hollywood.'

'We still are,' replied Kilgore, totally unaware that the caller was recording their conversation.

'Do you still have a code name on the girl by the name of Betsy/Claudia?'

Kilgore said that he wasn't sure.

'All right, never mind,' said the caller. 'Would you like your man today?'

She talked about the murders, and said that the weapon was a .25-calibre semi-automatic. She said her man had told her he had 'hit over fifty people'. Then she said that she had killed a man named Jack Murray, and added that she had been involved with several of the homicides. 'The one he cut the head off. Well, I played around with that one . . . and the fat girl [Karen Jones] that he dumped off near the NBC studios, I was involved with that, too.'

Realising that the game was almost up anyway, the cunning Bundy was hopefully setting herself up to try for a plea bargain deal with the law. To her mind, she could become a prosecution witness and thus circumvent a murder conviction and avoid any chance of being given a death sentence, which was now very much on the cards.

Kilgore asked how many murders there had been. 'Probably twelve or fourteen,' came the reply. 'But I can't verify all of them. I can only verify eight or nine.'

'And you helped him on some of them?'

'Yes, I did,' said the caller. 'Specifically how I got involved with it was a case of being scared to death because I knew that he had done these things. I felt I had to get involved. If I was involved he'd have no reason to kill me,' came the weak excuse.

She then said she was calling to give herself in, and that her real name was Carol Bundy. Finally, referring to the killer, she blurted out, 'He's my boyfriend and his name is Douglas

Daniel Clark.' A cunning move by Bundy; with Murray now dead by her own hand, she was shifting the blame onto Clark, who was very much alive.

'Doesn't it make you feel bad that you killed somebody?' asked the detective. Bundy replied, amazingly, 'The honest truth is, it's fun to kill people, and I was allowed to run loose, I'd probably do it again. I have to say, I know it's going to sound sick . . . it's like, going to sound psycho, and I don't really think I'm psycho, but it's kinda fun. It's like riding a roller-coaster. Not the killing, not the action that somebody died, because we didn't kill them in any way they'd suffer. It was just killing them straight out.'

After making her telephone call, the devious Bundy, who was hell-bent on doing everything she could to incriminate Clark, started rearranging her apartment in the misguided belief that she had at least a few hours to get things in order. She had miscalculated, however, and within minutes detectives arrived on her doorstep and arrested her.

Almost immediately, Bundy held up a cardboard box. It contained a pair of panties and assorted clothing. These items later proved to belong to an as yet undiscovered murder victim who would be toe-tagged 'Jane Doe 28'. The same box also contained a purse belonging to another unidentified victim, 'Jane Doe 18'.

'This box belongs to Clark,' she said, 'and, do you want to see what kind of guy Doug Clark is?' she asked, as she reached for her handbag on a table. An officer stopped, suspecting that the bag might contain a gun, but, inside, was Bundy's key ring. She selected a key and offered it to one of the detectives to open the cabinet in Clark's bedroom. The cupboard contained a photo album of Clark with his numerous lovers, including his poses with eleven-year-old Shannon. Also, hidden among various papers was a firearm sales receipt made out to a Juan Gomez, which was later found to be fake.

While Bundy was doing all she could to lay most of the blame for the murders onto Doug Clark, detectives Pida and Orozco had arrested Clark at his place of work and taken him to Van Nuys Police Station for questioning.

For his part, Clark was unmoved. He was not too concerned because he believed that the questioning would all be about Bundy's admission that she'd killed Jack Murray, for which he had a solid alibi, so he told the cops all he knew, while totally unaware that Bundy was presently grassing him up for the Sunset Slayings.

Detective Orozco began by asking Clark about his activities in the Hollywood area, and he admitted he went there 'pretty much' on regular basis, primarily to 'troll for prostitutes' and to go to clubs. When pressed further, Clark explained that sometimes he would go out on his own and other times with Carol Bundy to visit Sunset Boulevard and other locations. When asked for something more specific, Doug said that one night he and Bundy 'cruised' Anaheim after reading news stories of the Sunset killings because they wanted to see other areas where prostitutes hung out. Then he admitted that Bundy sometimes went with him and that she paid 'hookers for threesomes'.

Detective Leroy is an unassuming guy with an easygoing demeanour. Polite, stocky and always immaculately suited and booted, he, with Detective Pida, gently worked on Clark who suddenly told them that his mother had known that he'd 'been a little weird for a long time,' adding, 'She caught me dressed in her and my sister's underwear when I was nine years old.' By the time he was in the ninth grade in Switzerland, he went on, 'I had started into damn near everything. And since then I've never been able to look at sex just straight on. It has to be kinky or at least good communication.'

Orozco and Pida allowed Clark to ramble on. 'And, so with hookers, if the girl was a human being first and a hooker second, instead of visa versa, then it was great. It – it was a challenge because picking up hookers is too easy. So, I started going to dancer bars because it was an ego trip . . . to be the one man of all those in the bar who walked out with a dancer. Ya know, it was also the kind of woman I wanted – tough enough to stand up there and say "You can look; don't touch!"'

With still no mention of the Sunset slayings, Clark's ego now got the better of him, and on he boasted, 'I've known about a hundred whores since I've been living in LA. Ya know, it's important to have conversations with prostitutes . . . I kinda shine on them when they just say "how much" and gets down to it.'

'Have you ever had any interest in necrophilia?' asked Pida out of the blue.

'Nope. Never have,' replied Clark.

'When you learned that Carol had killed Jack Murray, why didn't you report this to the police?'

Clark thought for a moment before saying, 'Well, Bundy has lots of incriminating photos of me with a girl called Shannon. She told me that if I ever reported her for killing Jack, she'd expose me as a so-called paedophile. It was like blackmail.'

Clark was then booked in on a holding charge of child molestation. For the police this was a stop-gap measure, for they had wider ambitions as far as Clark was concerned.

With that, Pida produced photographs of the then five known victims and Doug immediately recognised Cynthia Chandler as that of a part-time prostitute he had met at the Malibu pier, some twenty-eight miles south-west of his home in Burbank. Detective Orozco thought that this seemed rather odd because prostitutes are not known to frequent the pier at all. Then Clark added, 'I think her name was Cynthy or Cindy. I've got her phone number in my wallet. We'd partied about half a dozen times. I was really upset when I read about her death in the newspaper. It scared the fuck outta me because she had my phone number too. I exchange phone numbers with all the girls I like . . . hey, someone's tryin' to lynch my ass, and I have a hunch I know who it is.'

Clark denied all knowledge about the murders of the five girls. He said that he had read of the name 'Exxie' in a paper but 'must have missed' any reference about a head in a wooden box connected to the crime. He explained that he read the newspaper 'religiously every day', and had been specifically interested in stories about the Sunset killings because they involved prostitutes.

Over the next few days, Clark was moved from police station to police station. He would later complain that the law had never read him the Miranda warning, had denied him food and water and the services of legal representation. When an attorney did turn up at Van Nuys Police Station, Clark was no longer there and no one seemed to know to where he had been transferred.

Eventually the detectives decided to turn the screw tighter. They asked Clark whether he was familiar with the two .25-calibre Raven semi-automatic pistols registered to Carol

Bundy. He admitted that he had handled both guns and test-fired them into a telephone book, 'but I believe that Carol has gotten rid of them or sold them,' he added.

'We'd like to have those guns,' Detective Orozco quipped.

'I bet you would,' Clark responded. 'I can understand that. I have no idea where they are. They are not in my area . . . but to be honest with you, I have often carried a .25-cal. auto in a clip-on holster in my boot. Yeah, and I know it's against the law.'

Clark was also questioned about owning a knife. He admitted having a folding knife, which he thought he'd left at work. He also had a buck knife, which he had given to his brother.

When asked if he had a car, Clark said no, adding, 'I drive Carol Bundy's Datsun sometimes, but I do have a motorcycle. I also drove her Buick station wagon off and on until she recently sold it.'

It was now the moment for the detectives to lay their cards on the table – actually it was Clark's wallet, and in it was a piece of paper with words on one side: 'Mindy C [telephone number]. B. Hills not working. Friend of Cindi's. Pretty.' The opposite side contained the notation: 'Cindy [telephone number]. Blonde hooker 30. Cathy too.'

The telephone number given for 'Mindy C' was Mindy Cohen's actual telephone number. The number listed for 'Cindy' was that of the Palm Motel on Sunset Boulevard, in an area frequented by prostitutes.

At the conclusion of the interrogation, Detectives Orozco, Pida and Stallcup took Clark to his former address on Verdugo Avenue, where he pointed to his bedroom. Inside a filing cabinet Orozco found a newspaper article describing the recovery of the box containing Exxie Wilson's head, and numerous pornographic books and magazines, some depicting necrophiliac activities.

During his interrogation, Clark had let slip that he had once rented a small storage garage in Burbank from January through to May 1980. However, it was later established that he had rented the same place through June and had abandoned it in July. When criminalists examined the floor they found several dark stains that appeared to be blood. One was a smear approximately two and a half feet wide and eight feet long, as if something bloody had been dragged across the floor. Presumptive, though not conclusive, testing of the stains proved positive for human blood. One of the stains was a partial print of a sole of a boot. The boot print itself also showed a positive reaction to a presumptive test for blood. The police later seized the pair of black boots Clark was wearing. The sole of these boots matched precisely the bloody boot print, and it was the same boot in which Clark had admitted carrying a .25-calibre semi-automatic pistol.

Clark would always say, and he still does argue, that the police were 'uncooperative', while he was quite the opposite. He says that he gave them permission to search his apartment and his place of work and his motorcycle (when actually they didn't need his permission because they had a search warrant).

'I gave them everything,' Clark complained during my interview with him. 'I gave them my fuckin' boots, my fuckin' saliva, my fuckin' blood. I offered to take a polygraph, but changed my fuckin' mind cos I ain't never trusted the cops. I could see a fit-up coming from a mile off.'

While the noose tightened even tighter around Doug Clark's neck, police were interviewing people who knew their prime suspect.

Eleanor 'Cissy' Buster had first met Clark in May 1980. He had moved in with her shortly after Memorial Day, the 27th. She told the cops that he habitually carried two small Raven semi-automatic pistols, one in his boot and the other in his jacket. That he never went out without taking the guns with him. When she had asked him where he'd got the pistols from, he told her from a pawnshop on Van Nuys Boulevard.

Frances Huys was Clark's high-school sweetheart. They had lost contact in 1968, but in 1980, Clark invited her to visit him over the Memorial Day weekend. He took her to an apartment that he told her he had formerly shared with Carol Bundy (the Lemona Avenue apartment). Frances told police that while at the apartment he picked up a chrome-plated pistol and ammunition; explaining that as he had a federal conviction and could not buy a gun for himself, Bundy had bought it for him.

Perhaps most damning of all was the information provided to police by Carlos Ramos, who, like Clark, was a licensed steam boiler operator at the Jergens soap factory. Ramos had seen Clark cleaning three firearms while at work. 'There were two smaller guns and a large gun like a .44,' he told the cops.

Then on 15 August 1980, another Jergens employee told Ramos that police were going to search the plant. However, before they arrived, a now suspicious Ramos found two Raven pistols inside a cosmetics bag hidden in a remote area near the top of the boiler room. Detective Stallcup took possession of the bag and pistols the same day.

A Jergens watchman told police that at 2.06 a.m., on the

night of 10 August, Clark came to the plant after hours saying that he wasn't feeling well and wanted to get something out of the building. He signed out at 2.15 a.m. Although the watchman did not see Clark carrying any guns, he was wearing a jacket that could have easily concealed two small pistols like Raven semi-automatics. Police determined that the round trip from the watchman's station to the place where the guns were found would take approximately five minutes.

After completing ballistic tests, the examiner established that all of the bullets recovered from all of the victims had been fired from the nickel-plated Raven – one of the two Ravens found hidden by Clark at his place of work. The evidence against him was now pretty much overwhelming, but the police had also turned their attention to the cars owned by Carol Bundy and driven by Clark.

During the time covering all the Sunset slayings, Bundy owned a blue Buick station wagon. She sold it on Thursday, 17 July 1980. She had also purchased a small Datsun car, and throughout this time Clark had regular access to both vehicles. In fact, even when he was not living with Bundy he frequently drove the Buick.

Cissy Buster said that Clark had the use of the station wagon virtually every day from the time he moved in with her on Tuesday, 3 June to the day he left on Sunday, 22 June.

Frances Huys told police that he had picked her up from the airport in May 1980. He was driving the Buick and, on 7 June, they met up with a woman called Elaine Forrestall, who also confirmed that Clark was driving the Buick.

Joey Lamphier told detectives that she often saw Clark driving around in a small blue car, 'like a Datsun or a Toyota.'

After the arrests of Bundy and Clark, the police recovered the Buick and the Datsun and thoroughly searched through both vehicles. In the station wagon were found .25-calibre bullets and casings matching both the nickel- and the chrome-plated Raven semi-automatics. Crucially a bullet from the nickel Raven was embedded in the passenger door of the Datsun. Evidence of blood was found inside both vehicles, as well.

While searching the Verdugo Avenue apartment, police saw a large painting of a ski scene. It was soon established through other trace evidence that it had been kept for some time in the garage rented by Clark. Several spots of blood were found on the reverse side of the canvas indicating that it had been propped up face against a wall. Analysis of these blood spots identified a number of different blood types and enzyme characteristics matching blood from the body of Gina Marano. A blood-typing expert later testified that only one out of two hundred people would share all of these characteristics. Another examiner testified that a blood sample taken from Bundy's blue Buick station wagon shared seven identifiable characteristics matching the blood of Karen Jones. Only one person in 125 would share all seven characteristics. Other blood samples found in the Buick also matched four blood-type characteristics of Exxie Wilson: only one out of five persons would share those four characteristics.

With Doug Clark, who still to this very day is protesting his total innocence in all of the Sunset slayings, and with Carol Bundy being the liar she was through-and-through, and with confusion as to who lived where, and who did what, rife throughout the case, can one really get to the truth from either of these two psychopaths? I think that we can try, so let's return once again to Carol Bundy and try to fit a few more pieces of the Sunset Slaying puzzle together.

While homicide detectives were putting Clark through the mill, Bundy was unloading her story onto the cops. She corroborated Clark's denial of guilt for Murray's murder, saying that while she had shot Murray, another man, 'a psycho', had hacked the head off to remove the evidence of traceable bullets. Questioned as to why she had left the cartridge casings in the Chevy van, she gave conflicting answers, which only goes to prove that she was never going to be the sharpest tool in the box. At first, she stated that she didn't realise that the weapon automatically ejected the cases. When it was pointed out to her by a cop that, 'It's a fuckin' automatic pistol, for Christ's sake, Carol', she changed her story to one of her forgetting to pick them up.

But I sense something quite wrong here because having reviewed all of the police evidence regarding the murder of Jack Murray, I see that that despite an extensive search of the interior of the Chevy when its grisly contents were discovered – and I mean a 'very extensive initial search' as the police say – there is no record of a single shell casing being found, let alone a casing fired from Bundy's nickel-plated semi-automatic pistol. Some time later, however, a detective said that he had found a single shell casing, and that ballistic evidence proved that it had come from Bundy's chrome-plated Raven. This would have been impossible as at the time Murray was shot dead the chrome-plated Raven was in Clark's possession and he was in bed with Nancy Smith. Moreover, this issue took on a more sinister aspect when it transpired that a police evidence envelope, once sealed and marked '2 x shell casings found at unspecified sources' had been torn open and one of the shell cases was missing.

Nevertheless, when Bundy was asked why she had shot Murray, she gave four vague reasons in rapid succession. The first was that Murray had stolen money from her – which he hadn't as she'd freely given cash to him. The second reason was equally pie-in-the-sky – that he had jilted her and she was furious with him for doing so. Then it was a case of her shooting him because he had planned to rape and kill Shannon; and finally, that Murray was going to report Doug to the police and accuse him of being the deadly Sunset Slayer.

None of this made any sense whatsoever to the police but, incredibly, they seemed inclined to believe her. Regarding which of the four stories to believe, they didn't know back then and still don't today!

Moving on to the action – with an attentive audience of good-looking, well groomed, sharp-suited, legally pistol-packing policemen surrounding her, Bundy was in her boggle-eyed element. Almost flirting with the cops she went on to admit that she had been involved with the 7 August, 'Cathy birthday gift', murder. She said that the prostitute had been shot while sitting in her blue Datsun. When the police initially told her there was no evidence of a shooting found in the Datsun, let alone a homicide, she flip-flopped, saying that the crime had taken place in her Buick, which she had loaned to Clark. For his part, and I am inclined to believe him, Doug says that it was most certainly the Datsun because the car had two doors, and he had to push the driver's seat forward to let Cathy in. And we will recall that crucially a bullet from the nickel Raven was later discovered embedded in the passenger door of the Datsun. This was the bullet that went through Cathy's head before hitting Clark, causing a flesh wound, to end up where it was found.

Bundy then went on to say that she'd paid the hooker to give Clark a blow-job as a birthday present, which didn't wash either. She said that it was agreed that he would give her a signal as to when to shoot Cathy in the head. Clark vehemently denies this, arguing, 'No, man, I don't care who he is. Who would let a half-blind bitch reach over, shoot at the head of a hooker suckin' his cock and hope like hell she didn't blow a hole in his knee or chest? I mean, what if the hooker's jaw locked shut?'

Although I somewhat doubt that any of my male readers have been in a similar situation, perhaps Doug does have a valid point.

When questioned about the Marano and Chandler homicides, Bundy claimed that she had not been involved. 'I only learned about the two murdered girls when Doug told me,' she sniggered, adding with the most improbable flourish, 'He said that he shot them while they were both giving him oral sex.'

During his interview with me at San Quentin State Prison, I asked Clark to comment Bundy's claim, and he didn't mince his words.

'You are pulling my pecker,' he declared. 'Do you think I'm fuckin' crazy, man? Some broad is blowin' me off and' I stick a gun to her head and blast away. What about the fuckin' blood, man? What about my dick, man? I'd have been covered with the shit and it would have been painted all over the inside of the fuckin' car.' Once again, I think that Doug Clark has a valid point here, too!

When pressed further on the murders of Gina Marano and Cynthia Chandler, Bundy explained that 'Doug had dragged the bodies out of the Buick and into his lock-up garage where he had sex with them'. She added, 'And it was because of this bloody mess in the car that Doug put it through a car wash.' Clark has never denied washing the Buick and, indeed, he says that he even volunteered this information to the detectives who then confirmed that he had been to the car wash on 21 June, about a week after Bundy made her Betsy/Claudia telephone call to the police.

At this point, the reader may wish to sit down, pour a stiff drink and take a few moments to collect their thoughts, because what follows would be no easy task even for our lovable LA cop, Lieutenant Columbo. However, it does illustrate how difficult it is to get any semblance of the truth from a pair of homicidal psychopaths.

Clark has always asserted, 'Everyone who saw or rode in the Buick from 14 June to 21 June – and there will be many who testify to this – will say that the car was dry, and right after the car wash on 21 June it was soaked and damp with steamy air for a full week. The point is, what fucking vehicle was Bundy washing out, just before the taped phone call to the police? The Datsun was broken down, the Buick was dry, and only Murray and his van fit the details of the killer she made in that call.' Indeed, although never previously disclosed by police, it was a fact that the Datsun had been off-road at the time. And the police also established that Murray's van had been washed out after the first three murders. Yet, this also raises the question as to why the police chose to ignore this evidence – evidence that would prove beyond doubt that

Bundy was lying through her back teeth once again. And we might ask ourselves if Clark is telling the truth when we know that he is a pathological liar more often than not?

Well, the answer might rest in supporting evidence falling in his favour. This was given by people who confirmed to police that he was telling the truth – yet the police dismissed these people out-of-hand.

During the evening of 20 June, Clark had called upon Joey Lamphier, one of his many girlfriends – and a woman who had always been upfront and totally honest with the detectives. She confirmed that when Doug left her apartment, he accidentally reversed over an alley cat, crushing its hindquarters. He lifted the critically injured animal into the Buick where she saw it crawl under the front passenger seat. For all his sins, Clark is known for his love of animals, and, in the past, had taken in several strays. He has rescued more from animal pounds and found new homes for them. Sadly, the cat died en route to the vet's so he disposed of the animal, as Lamphier testified, by placing it in a cardboard box and – somewhat unfeelingly some will say – placed it in a rubbish skip.

After work on 21 June, Clark to the car wash in the Buick with one of Bundy's sons. She was pressing for the return of the car in preparation for her move to Burbank. Doug hosed the cat's blood, urine and excrement from under the front seat and vacuumed the excess water away. Later, the boy told police that the 'small amount of blood' was still wet when he got into the car, which totally contradicted Bundy's claim that the blood had been there for some ten days. As Clark explained to me, 'If this car wash had a sinister motive, why would I have taken a mouthy kid along?' He makes a valid point here once again.

Yes, it is true that police technicians did find blood in the Buick that was consistent with having come from both Karen Wilson and Exxie Wilson, or so we are asked to believe, yet in no way was the back seat contaminated in the manner which would have been consistent with Bundy's claim that three brutal and bloody murders had already been committed in this vehicle.

Around mid–1991, Carol Bundy changed her story yet again. This time for the benefit of a journalist who was writing a book about the Sunset Slayings. She now said that the car wash on 21 June followed the murder of Cathy (Jane Doe 28), which had been committed the night before. Now, according to her latest claim, the blood was no longer of Chandler and Marano, neither was the Cathy murder committed in the Datsun. This time it was someone else, but, once again, the police seemed to ignore these contradictions.

When previously questioned about the murders of Karen Jones and Exxie Wilson, Bundy denied any involvement in these crimes, and said that she was merely relating an account given to her by Clark (despite admitting at another time that she had been with him when he cut Exxie's head off). 'There were three hookers working together,' she said. 'Clark picked up Exxie and shot her in the head before decapitating her behind the Sizzler Diner.' (Witnesses heard a vehicle racing away from this precise location at about 1.15 a.m.) Bundy went on the say that Doug returned to pick up Karen Jones and he shot her while she was giving him oral sex in the car. 'He killed her and dumped the body,' she said. Witnesses heard a scream around 2.40 a.m., and Karen's corpse was discovered at this location less than an hour later.

Following these two murders, Bundy alleged that Clark

brought Exxie's head back to her new apartment, in Burbank, where he placed it in the freezer before phoning her at her digs at Lemona. Telephone calls show that this call was made at precisely 3.08 a.m. But is Bundy's story true?

Bundy claims that it was Clark who called her to explain what he had done. Doug says that it was Bundy phoning him – which she would later do after decapitating Jack Murray. The difference is that his account can be verified, for he had a solid alibi that night.

Tammy Spangler confirmed that Bundy had called Clark at around 3 a.m. at the Lemona address where they were sleeping on an old mattress. 'Doug was in a lot of pain because he had hurt his back while moving Carol's stuff,' she said. 'He was in agony and pretty wild that Carol had got him out of bed.' Once again, the detectives ignored Clark's story and that of his alibi, Tammy Spangler, and chose to believe Bundy, who, at best, was a pathological liar . . . and one who had already admitted shooting a man and cutting his head off. But was there any other evidence to support Clark and Spangler's claim, that they had spent the night at Bundy's apartment? There was.

Clark had been in an argument with Cissy Buster on the Sunday. She said, 'Leave me if you don't want to live with me.' Clark responded with, 'Fuck it,' and lugged his stuff down to the Buick. 'Carol had been complaining about the dampness and lingering smell of the cat faeces from the previous day's car wash,' he explained, adding, 'I had offered to dry it out cos I needed the car. I promised to dry it out and return it on time for Carol's move to Burbank. I then drove to Lemona, at about 1.30 p.m., to 2.30 p.m. The movers came about 3 p.m. to 4 p.m. and moved Bundy into her Burbank place in two

U-Haul trailer-loads. I rode with them and Carol had a slew of kids to help her put the kitchen shit in the Buick.'

The interesting part of all of this is that Clark told the police all of this from the get-go and he has not changed this account one jot since. He has also maintained: 'At the other end, the movers moved it all up. I helped and strained my back and ended up nearly unable to move. I left early and rode my bike to Van Nuys. I called Al Joines, my assistant at Jergens, around 6 p.m. I told him that I'd hurt my back, and asked him if he could start up the boiler the following morning. I then drank several beers. Then Tammy came over and we crashed on a mattress in the now empty Lemona apartment. I was woken from my sleep by a call from Carol at a time I know to be 3.08 a.m., because the police confirmed that such a call was made.'

Every detail of Doug's statement was later shown to be true; yet, the police opted to ignore it.

Most prostitutes are reluctant to trick alone, preferring to work in pairs for safety, with one girl jotting down a vehicle's registration number if they have their wits about them. Contrary to this practice, Bundy claims that Exxie Wilson allowed herself to be picked up by Clark, who killed her and then returned to the red-light district on his own with the intention of enticing the now dead girl's colleague into the Buick. One wonders what Karen Jones would have thought when the same punter returned without Exxie . . . something here doesn't seem at all right to me.

Furthermore, as was later shown at autopsy, Exxie Wilson was still very much alive during her decapitation, and that it would have been impossible to accomplish this act of mutilation without Clark being sprayed with arterial blood, which was not the case. Even more startling was the medical examiner's statement, which maintained that Murray's head, which Bundy had admitted cutting off, and that of Exxie Wilson had been cut off by the same hand, using knives, or a knife which were later found in Bundy's apartment.

The time interval which elapsed between the murders of Exxie Wilson and Karen Jones is also of interest, for it has the Bundy/Murray modi operandi written all over it. Bundy revealed her MO when the birthday gift homicide came into it. That Exxie had been decapitated by the same hand that had cut off Murray's head, and that it had been Murray's Chevy van that had been washed out several times just after the murders, all point to Murray and Bundy as being the real murderers of Exxie and Karen.

Then there is the Claudia/Betsy telephone call to the police when Bundy described the killer as a man called 'John' and gave a description that matched John 'Jack' Murray down to his correct age.

During her tape-recorded interrogation, on Monday, 11 August 1980, one hears Bundy making a categorical reference to Clark murdering another prostitute (later to become known as Jane Doe 18) 'two weekends ago'. She was adamant about that date. Somewhat curiously, she was allowed to change this all-important date when police ascertained that Clark was 380-miles away, attending his brother's wedding, on the weekend pinpointed by Bundy. Eventually, and with police prompting her, she could only say 'sometime in July'. But if this serial killer was allowed – indeed encouraged by police – to change a specific date to any one of her and the cop's choosing in a given month, it paled into insignificance when she added, on tape to the police, that date had been 'Doug's last murder', adding, 'He told me nothing about it. Absolutely nothing at all, and if he wouldn't tell me, then he won't tell you, so you might as well forget it.'

Now this may take some swallowing, but within minutes, she changed her tune again by giving a full description of the crime, including the nickname Clark had supposedly given to the victim – 'Water Tower' – and then she offered up the exact location of the body.

Jane Doe 18

On Tuesday, 26 August 1980, a body was discovered near the Sierra Highway in Antelope Valley. A worker inspecting nearby water towers came across human bones, scattered in a 10-foot radius in an 'oily spot' smelling of decomposing flesh. A clump of blonde hair was found nearby, and it was determined that the unknown young female victim had died about one to two months earlier. The cause of death was a single gunshot wound to the back of the head. A .25-calibre jacketed bullet was removed from the temporal area of the skull. During his interview with me Clark referred to Jane Doe 18 as 'Water Tower'.

Jane Doe 99

On Thursday, 28 August 1980, the mummified remains of Jane Doe 99 were found 30 feet down an embankment in a remote area known as Tina Canyon near Malibu. The victim was wearing a black tank top and skirt, both wrapped around her waist. Sheriff's deputies also found a clump of blonde hair near where the body was found, as with Jane Doe 18. It appeared to belong to the victim.

The coroner's examination showed that Jane Doe 99 was approximately twenty years old, and 5 foot 3 inches tall. She had been killed a by gunshot wound to the left forehead. Ballistics examination of the bullet fragments taken from the skull revealed that they came from a .25-calibre ACP bullet jacket. The characteristics of these bullet fragments 'matched generally' the characteristics of the bullets found in all of the Sunset Slayings.

As might be expected, yet again Clark has denied all knowledge of this murder, claiming that it was Bundy and Jack Murray who'd committed the crime. However, Bundy later testified that some time in July 1980, possibly before 20 July, she and Doug had driven along the Pacific Coast Highway to Oxnard. Along the route, Clark had pointed out a mountainous region near Malibu and told her that he had dropped off a 'package' – his special name for a dead body – there, and that he had had sex with the dead body. But, here again it could be Bundy shifting the blame from Murray onto Clark.

Jane Doe 28 (Cathy)

The skeletal remains of Jane Doe 28, a woman in the region of seventeen to twenty-three years of age, were found on a creek bed in the Saugus-Newhall area of LA in early March 1981. Various bone fragments were discovered: part of a femur bone, some ribs, vertebrae, a lower jawbone and a skull. There was a bullet hole in the skull behind the right ear. The medical examiner's examination showed that all the bones belonged to one individual. She had sustained a fatal bullet wound about two inches from her right ear. No bullet was found, but the size of the entry wound and the wound pattern were similar to the wounds inflicted on Exxie Wilson, Karen Jones and Jane Doe 18.

Once again, Clark told me, and the many others with him he corresponds, that he knows nothing about the murder of Jane Doe 28. However, amongst the documents seized in a search of Joey Lamphier's residence was a letter in Clark's handwriting in which he – along with Bundy – boasted of killing a young, blonde prostitute called 'Cathy' and had disposed of her body near Saugus.

Without any doubt, Carol Bundy was a sexual psychopath and a serial killer. As for Douglas Clark; well, he was most likely a serial murderer too. But what of Murray? For I think that he played a part in several of these gruesome homicides as well. Bundy blew his brains out and, therefore, is unable to tell his side of the story; likewise with Bundy, for she is stone dead too. The only one of this deviant trio remaining alive is Doug Clark, so please make of his story as you will. Like so many of his sort, he pathologically lies while at once richly embroidering his accounts with much of what is proven fact. That is the homicidal brain – and this is a fact too.

Conclusions

There was nothing they could have said or done.
They were dead as soon as I saw them. Yes, I used them,
abused them, killed them and dumped their bodies like
so much trash. What more can I say?
THE NOW EXECUTED MICHAEL BRUCE ROSS TO THE
AUTHOR, DEATH ROW, SOMERS PRISON, CONNECTICUT.
26 NOVEMBER 1994

There is this dread place, as I have mentioned before, that I call 'Murder Crossroads'. It is a location where two lives meet with one of them coming to a brutal and terminal end, while the other person's life changes for ever, as do the lives of those grieving next-of-kin who are left to pick up the pieces.

Whether you are female, male, elderly, young or even a child, your chances against ever becoming a victim of such evil men and women are literally many millions-to-one.

You are more likely to be killed in a car or even plane crash then ever having the misfortune of meeting a Carol Bundy, a Jodi Arias, a Joanne Dennehy, a Michael Ross, a John David Guise Cannan, a Colonel Russell Williams, a Jack Murray, a Douglas Clark, a John Christie, a Peter Kürten, perhaps a Neville Heath, a Ted Bundy or the likes of any of the others referred to in this book. But, let's make no bones about this: they are out there and one could be zeroing in on you right now. This being the case, you are up Shit Creek and you will not know anything about it until it is far too late!

There may be some of you who will criticise me for being a tad over-dramatic here. Nevertheless, when you look at the escalating homicide rates across the world, most especially those sexually motivated rape/kill cases, you will find most, if not all, the victims did not have a clue as to what was about to happen to them. That is an undeniable fact, too and the police and the serial killers themselves will endorse what I say.

> Society wants to believe it can identify evil people, or bad or harmful people, but it's not practical. There are no stereotypes. We serial killers are your sons, we are your husbands ... we are everywhere. And there will be more of your children dead tomorrow. What's one less person on the face of the Earth, anyways?
>
> THEODORE 'TED' ROBERT BUNDY,
> AGED FORTY-TWO, JUST PRIOR TO HIS
> EXECUTION, 24 JANUARY 1989

Throughout this book, and my previous books, I use simplistic analogies; making no apologies for doing so I referred earlier to the highly camouflaged stick insects and lizards I viewed at the Manila Ocean Park. Indeed, when I was doing an interview about John Cannan with the *Birmingham Mail* (published 12 November 2018), I recently used this example of how serial killers are all but invisible until they cold-bloodily strike their unsuspecting prey, kill them, then discard the once living shells as trash. These insects and lizards have no morals – as far as I can determine. They have no conscience either and this is, to my way of thinking, how sexually motivated serial killers think and act. The other interesting facet to this example is just how easily such little insects and creatures can vanish into their natural environment once the deadly deed has been done. Homicidal psychopaths do this all the time and this is what makes them so difficult to detect amongst us good folk. Then think of the spider spinning its lethal web. Do we not see such careful 'trap setting' amongst so many serial killers such as the former Colonel Russell Williams?

Look at how well the murderous Dr Harold Shipman camouflaged himself; how deadly efficient his mask of normality was and how he lured his two-hundred-plus elderly patients to their deaths. It almost beggars belief that he was able to carry on killing for as long as he did, most especially with his professional peers watching and consulting with him year after year.

Think of Niels Högel, the German nurse who has been sentenced to life imprisonment, convicted of murdering six patients but who has admitted to murdering over a hundred people in his care between 2000 and 2005 by administering lethal doses of medication to them.

So, Ted Bundy was 100 per cent correct when he said:

'Society wants to believe it can identify evil people, or bad or harmful people, but it's not practical. There are no stereotypes. We serial killers are your sons . . . we are your husbands, we are everywhere. And there will be *more of your children dead tomorrow.*'

Can these psychopaths ever be cured? This is a matter of hot debate and probably always will be. For my part the answer has to be a categorical *No* – my reason being that having interviewed and spent decades face-to-face with more serial killers in the real world than most, I do not live on a planet where lead balls bounce, elephants fly and fairies reign supreme. And, as God is my witness, I have tried and tried to find yet a single offender who truly realises who he or she really was; to admit that they were wrong and to show genuine remorse. It can't or will never happen because this is the true nature of beast psychopathy. All the medication in the world will not reform them. Incarceration will not reform them. The only permanent cure offered to these sex killers – most somewhat belatedly having turned to God – is a visit to the Death House, and that is the end of that. You may feel differently – but imagine that you were the parent of one of Peter Kürten's child victims . . . or perhaps your loving daughter had been slaughtered by a Neville Heath, or tortured to death by a Russell Williams . . .

As with all of my books I like to leave my readers on a low note and then a happy note, so here is no exception.

My happy note in ending this book being that I am off to the Philippines as soon as I can.

CONCLUSIONS

You should visit the Philippines sometime, because a spell on the sun-kissed sugar-sand beaches at El Nido, Palawan, is the best tonic ever and it would certainly raise your spirits after reading this book.

Happy days.
Christopher